Illinois Pharmacy Law Review:
An MPJE Study Guide

First Edition

RxPharmacist, LLC

ISBN-13: 978-1974291458
ISBN-10: 1974291456

COPYRIGHT
© 2017 IL Pharmacy Law: An MPJE® Study Guide
First Edition
Published September 2017
Updated: November 2017

Authored by:
Maryam Khazraee, Pharm.D., R.Ph., AE-C
Yen Thieu, Pharm.D., MBAc, BCMAS

Cover by:
Maryam Khazraee, Yen Thieu

Copyright© 2017 by:
RxPharmacist, LLC, Maryam Khazraee

All rights reserved. No part of this publication may be reproduced, distributed, or transmitted in any form or by any means, including photocopying, recording, or other electronic or mechanical methods, without the prior written permission of the publisher, except in the case of brief quotations embodied in critical reviews and certain other noncommercial uses permitted by copyright law. For permission requests, write to the publisher, addressed "Attention: Permissions Coordinator," at help@rxpharmacist.com. All trademarks are trademarks of their respective owners and some marked with a registered trademark symbol to notify, with no intention of infringement of the trademark.

DISCLAIMER: The MPJE® and NABP® marks are federally registered trademarks owned by the National Association of Boards of Pharmacy (NABP®). RxPharmacist LLC, the authors, Maryam Khazraee, Yen Thieu, and third party subsidiaries are not associated with the NABP®, and its products or services have not been reviewed or endorsed by the NABP®.

TERMS OF USE
The work is provided "as is". Rxpharmacist and its licensors make no guarantees or warranties as to the accuracy, adequacy, or completeness of or results to be obtained from using the work, including any information that can be accessed through the work via hyperlink or otherwise, and expressly disclaim any warranty, express or implied, including but not limited to implied warranties of merchantability or fitness for a particularly purpose. Rxpharmacist, LLC and its licensors are not engaged in rendering medical, legal, accounting, or other professional service. If medical or legal advice, or other expert assistance is required, the services of a competent professional should be sought.

Rxpharmacist, LLC and its licensors do not warrant or guarantee that the functions contained in the work will meet your requirements or that its operation will be uninterrupted or error free. Neither rxpharmacist, LLC nor its licensors shall be liable to you or anyone else for any inaccuracy, error or omission, regardless of cause in the work or for any damages resulting therefrom. Rxpharmacist, LLC has no responsibility for the content of any information assessed through the work. Under no circumstances shall rxpharmacist, LLC and/or its licensors be liable for any indirect, incidental, special, punitive, consequential, or similar damages that result from the use of or inability to use the work, even if any of them has been advised of the possibility of such damages. This limitation of liability shall apply to any claim or cause whatsoever whether such claim or cause arises in contact, tort or otherwise.

This guide was created with the help of recent pharmacy student graduates and parts of their work have been reproduced by their permission.

ACKNOWLEDGMENT AND DEDICATIONS

We would like to give a special thanks to our RxPharmacist, LLC Extern, Yen Thieu, for her hard work and dedication to the pharmacy profession for helping us create this guide. Yen is a 2017 pharmacy graduate from Rosalind Franklin University of Medicine and Science in Chicago, IL. She is an aspiring medical writer, and has a passion for medical and scientific communications.

TABLE OF CONTENTS

SECTION 1: UNDERSTANDING THE MPJE 5
SECTION 2: FEDERAL PHARMACY LAW REVIEW 6
SECTION 3: FEDERAL PHARMACY LAW 12
SECTION 4: OVERVIEW OF FEDERAL ACTS 18
SECTION 5: FEDERAL CONTROLLED SUBSTANCES LAWS 22
DEFINITIONS 83
SECTION 6: ILLINOIS STATE BOARD OF PHARMACY 91
SECTION 7: PHARMACY 93
SECTION 8: PHARMACIST 96
SECTION 9: PHARMACY TECHNICIAN 101
SECTION 10: GENERAL PROVISION 105
SECTION 11: PRESCRIPTION ORDER 113
SECTION 12: REFUSAL, REVOCATION, OR SUSPENSION 116
SECTION 13: TYPES OF PHARMACIES 121
SECTION 14: PHARMACY STANDARDS 137
SECTION 15: PHARMACY OPERATIONS 146
SECTION 16: HYPODERMIC SYRINGES AND NEEDLES ACT 149
SECTION 17: ILLINOIS CONTROLLED SUBSTANCES ACT 150
IL Pharmacy Law Practice Exam.. 178
    Answers to IL Pharmacy Law Practice Exam Questions........................ 208
IL Pharmacy Law Bonus Questions 245
    IL Pharmacy Law Bonus Question Explanations 253

SECTION 1: UNDERSTANDING THE MPJE

WHAT IS THE MPJE?
The Multi-Prudence Jurisdiction Examination (MPJE) is a 120-question computer-based exam that uses adaptive testing response questions. For example, if you keep getting questions wrong then the computer will provide you questions that are statistically deemed "easier." It's important to note that of the 120 questions on this exam, only 100 are used to calculate your final score. The remaining 20 questions are pretest questions that will not count into your MPJE score, but you won't be able to tell which ones are pretest questions and which ones are not. The total testing time is two hours with NO breaks during the testing session so it's important to take note of time.

WHAT IS THE PASSING SCORE?
The passing scaled score is 75 with the minimum score being zero and maximum 100. The exam is divided into three major sections:
- Pharmacy Practice- 85%
- Licensure, registration, certification, operational requirements- 15%
- General Regulatory Processes- 2%

Some major points to remember:
- All questions are answered in order so there's no going back
- Lots of situational questions
- Online registration costs $250.00 per examination
- You will need to bring two forms of ID at Pearson Vue
- At least one picture ID with signature (i.e. Driver's License)
- Other can be credit card with signature
- 120 questions, 100 count towards your score
- MUST complete 107 questions for examination to be scored
- If you do fail, you must wait 30 days to retake
- Examination doesn't distinguish between state and federal laws, but answer each question based on state law
- Any misconduct or inkling of misconduct is grounds for failure
- Arrive at least 30 minutes early
- Ensure to read EVERY SINGLE WORD!
    - They will try to trick you so make sure to answer the question they ask, and lookout for unusual words as triggers.
- We recommend reviewing the nabp.net/programs/examination/mpje site and reading over the NAPLEX/MPJE registration bulletin. They provide a more specific overview of the exam, scheduling requirements, and a list of core competencies for you to understand. Don't spend too much time on the core competencies, but more on understanding the laws, as there are many situational type questions.

SECTION 2: FEDERAL PHARMACY LAW REVIEW

Introduction

You may have remembered some of these concepts during your law course in pharmacy school, but it's important to remember our country's regulation policy as much of our industry is highly regulated!

In the United States, all food, drugs, cosmetics, and medical devices, for both humans and animals, are regulated under the authority of the Food and Drug Administration (FDA). The FDA and its laws were created by government bodies in response to promoting and protecting the safety of the public when it comes to food, medicines, and medical devices. I would highly recommend participating in the FDA rotation despite being highly competitive and costly for a budget-minded student, it is well worth the experience! I say this from experience in being lucky enough to participate in the rotation during pharmacy school.

This introduction to federal pharmacy law discusses the FDA's regulatory oversight and that of other agencies, the drug approval and development process, the mechanisms used to regulate manufacturing and marketing, as well as various violation and enforcement actions taken by the FDA to ensure pharmaceutical and corporate industry companies are maintaining compliance.

PHARMACEUTICALS

The main responsibility for the regulation of pharmaceuticals and the pharmaceutical industry is the Food and Drug Administration (FDA), it's headquarters located in Silver Springs, MD. The FDA formed in 1931 and is one of several branches within the US Department of Health and Human Services (HHS). The "sister" agencies to the FDA that also work in HHS are the Centers for Disease Control and Prevention (CDC), National Institute of Health (NIH), and the Healthcare Financing Administration (HCFA). These sites are harder to get rotations during pharmacy school, but a lot of information can be found on their websites. Other agencies that fall under HHS also include the Agency for Healthcare Research and Quality (AHRQ), Centers for Medicare and Medicaid Services (CMS), Substance Abuse and Mental Health Services Administration (SAMHSA), and the Indian Health Service (IHS). Our main focus will be the FDA as they are the agency that solely regulates the drug industry.

The FDA is organized into a number of offices and centers headed by a commissioner. It is a scientifically based law enforcement agency whose mission is to protect the public health and ensure fairness between health-regulated industries (i.e., pharmaceutical, device, biological, and the consumer). The vast amount of tasks done at the FDA is more than you think. It licenses and inspects manufacturing facilities to ensure they follow Good Manufacturing Practices (GMP); tests products on a smaller scale; evaluates claims and prescription drug advertising to ensure there is no false marketing done; monitors research and reviews clinical trial methods; and creates regulations, guidelines, standards, and policies. It does all of this through its Office of Operations, which contains component offices and centers such as the Center for Drug Evaluation and Research (CDER), the Center for Biologics Evaluation and Research (CBER), the Center for Devices and Radiological Health (CDRH), the Center for Food Safety and Applied Nutrition (CFSAN), the Center for Veterinary Medicine (CVM), the Office of Orphan Products Development, the Office of Biotechnology, the Office of Regulatory Affairs, and the National Center for Toxicological Research. It's definitely a lot! The main office where pharmacists work is in CDER. Each of these offices and centers has a defined role to play, but sometimes they overlap on their work. For example, if a pharmaceutical company submits a drug that is delivered to a patient during therapy by a medical device, then the CDER and CDRH may need to coordinate that product's approval. Although CDER is the main center that reviews prescription drugs, any other center or office may become involved with its review depending on the circumstances. One of the most significant resources to industry and consumers is the FDA's web site www.fda.gov. I would highly recommend taking some time in reviewing their site, which also has links to the other offices and centers.

It's important to note that the FDA is not the only agency within the US government that plays a role in pharmaceutical issues. The Federal Trade Commission (FTC) has authority over general business practices in general, such as deceptive and anticompetitive practices (i.e., false advertising). In addition, the FTC regulates the advertising of over-the-counter (OTC) drugs, medical devices, and cosmetics. Also the United States Pharmacopoeia (USP) plays a role in regulating natural supplements, over-the-counter (OTC) drugs, and dietary products. When you think of USP, you may think of those big red "USP-NF" reference standard books during your Dosage Forms and Pharmaceutical Compounding courses. However, they play a big role in offering a voluntary third party auditing and testing system with all dietary supplements and products. Next time you go out to the pharmacy, see if you can spot an USP stamp of approval on an OTC bottle in the aisles. Despite many of these federal and private associations, it's important to note that the FDA plays a main role in drug regulation.

NEW DRUG APPROVAL AND DEVELOPMENT

A drug is a substance that puts an action on the structure or function of the body by chemical action or metabolism, and is intended for use in the diagnosis, cure, mitigation, treatment, or prevention of diseases. A new drug is defined as one that is not recognized as safe and effective use for the indications stated by the manufacturer. "New drug" could also refer to a drug product already in existence, although never approved by the FDA for marketing in the United States. This also spans to new therapeutic indications; a new dosage form; a new route of administration; a new dosing schedule; or any other significant clinical differences than those approved. Make sure to understand that this differs from a new chemical entity. Essentially, any chemical substance intended for use in humans or animals with medicinal purposes "aka pharmaceuticals" is not safe or effective until proper testing and FDA approval are met. It's important to note the "intended for use in diagnosis, cure, etc." part as you will see on non-prescription dietary supplements the latter required statement of, "*These statements have not been evaluated by the FDA. This product is not intended to diagnose, cure, treat, or prevent any disease."

PRECLINICAL INVESTIGATION

Before any manufacturer starts human testing on a new drug, they must provide evidence that the drug can be used safety in humans. This phase is called the preclinical investigation. The basic goal of preclinical investigation is to assess therapeutic effects of the substance on living organisms and to gather enough data to determine the reasonable safety of the new drug in humans through laboratory and animal experimentation. The FDA does not require any prior approval for investigators, manufacturers, or pharmaceutical industry sponsors to begin a preclinical investigation on a drug. However, investigators and sponsors must follow Good Laboratory Practices (GLP) regulations. GLPs govern laboratory facilities, personnel, equipment, and operations. Compliance with GLPs involves procedures and documentation of training, study schedules, processes, and status reports. These documents are submitted to facility management and included in the final study report to the FDA. As far as a timeline, usually preclinical investigation takes 1 to 3 years to complete. If at that time enough data is gathered to reach the goal of a therapeutic effect and reasonable safety, the product sponsor must notify the FDA to pursue further testing on humans. This phase is also very important for the sponsor or investigator to test the drug of any viability. You'll see when reading pharmaceutical news articles of many companies that decide to stop investigation of a drug from the preclinical phase and sometimes up to phase III trials due to safety concerns or lack of therapeutic efficacy.

INVESTIGATION NEW DRUG APPLICATION

The FDA starts getting highly involved in the Investigational New Drug Application (INDA) phase. Because a preclinical investigation is designed to gain data of safety and efficacy of the drug, the INDA phase is the clinical phase where all activity is used to gather evidence on safety and efficacy information about the drug in humans. Clinical trials in humans are heavily scrutinized and regulated by the FDA to protect the health and safety of human test subjects as well as ensuring the strength and ethics of the clinical data. Numerous meetings between both the agency and sponsor occur during this time. The negotiations don't usually take much time, but the investigation phase for the sponsor may take up to 12 years to complete! Only one in five drugs tested may actually show clinical effectiveness and safety to reach the pharmacy shelves.

Once done with preclinical trials, the sponsor submits the INDA to the FDA. The INDA must contain information on the drug proposed itself and information of the study and how it was conducted. All INDAs must have these components: a detailed cover sheet, a table of contents, an introductory statement and basic investigative plan, an investigator's brochure, comprehensive investigation protocols, the drug's actual or proposed chemistry, manufacturing and controls, any pharmacology and toxicology information, any previous human experience with the drug, and any other data the FDA requests from the sponsor. After submission, the sponsor company must wait 30 days to commence clinical trials. Thus, this gives the FDA 30 days to respond to the sponsor. If there is no contact from the FDA after this 30-day period, the sponsor has a right to start the clinical trial testing in humans.

Before the actual start of the clinical trial, there are some ground rules to follow. The sponsor needs to have a clinical study protocol that's reviewed by an Institutional Review Board (IRB). An IRB is required and is a committee of medical and ethical experts designated by an institution, such as a university medical center, where the trial will take place. The purpose of the IRB is to oversee the research to ensure that the rights of human test subjects are protected and rigorous medical and scientific standards are maintained. An IRB must approve the proposed clinical study and monitor the research as it progresses to ensure ethics and rights are protected during the trial. It must develop written procedures of its own regarding its study review process and reporting changes to the IRB board. The IRB must also review and approve informed consent documents before starting the clinical study. Regulations require that participants are informed adequately about the risks, benefits, and treatment alternatives before participating in experimental research. Usually the committee is composed of a diverse number of individuals to review the study in a community, legal, and professional standards point of view. All of the IRB activities must be documented, as they are open to FDA inspection. As soon as the IRB board approves the study, the clinical trial phase starts! It's composed of three phases.

PHASE I
A Phase I study is small, consisting of less than 100 subjects and brief usually lasts less than a year. Usually these subjects are healthy individuals who don't have the disease being studied. Its purpose is to determine toxicology, safety, metabolism, pharmacologic actions, and any early evidence of effectiveness. The results of the Phase I study are used to develop phase II.

PHASE II
Phase II studies are the first controlled clinical studies using several hundred subjects who have the disease being studied. Phase II is to determine the compound's effectiveness against the targeted disease and its safety in humans. Phase II could be divided into two subparts depending on how the sponsor decides the conduct the trial: Phase IIa is a pilot study that is used to determine efficacy, and Phase IIb uses controlled studies on several hundred patients. At the end of the Phase II studies, the sponsor and FDA will usually meet to discuss the data and plans for Phase III.

PHASE III
Phase III studies are considered "pivotal" trials that are designed to collect all of the necessary data to meet the safety and efficacy regulations governed by FDA. Phase III studies usually consist of several thousands of patients in multiple study centers with a large number of investigators who conduct long-term trials over several months or years. Usually it's testing the current "gold standard" against the drug that is being studied. However, this does depend on the disease state being studied. If there is a rare disease state being studied, there only may be twenty patients. Phase III studies also set up the final formulation, marketing claims and product stability, packaging, and storage conditions. Once phase III is complete along with all the safety and efficacy data being analyzed, the sponsor is ready to submit the compound to the FDA for market approval! This process begins with submission of a New Drug Application (NDA).

NEW DRUG APPLICATION
A NDA is a regulatory tool that is designed to give the FDA sufficient information to make an evaluation of a new drug. All NDAs must contain the following: preclinical laboratory and animal data; human pharmacokinetic and bioavailability data; clinical data; methods of manufacturing, processing, and packaging; a description of the drug substance; a list of relevant patents for the drug; its manufacture or claims; and any proposed labeling. In addition, an NDA must provide a summary of the application's contents and a presentation of the risks and benefits of the new drug. Traditionally, NDAs consisted of hundreds of volumes of information, in triplicate, all cross referenced. Since 1999, the FDA has issued final guidance documents that allow sponsors to submit NDAs electronically in a standardized format. These electronic submissions facilitate ease of review and possible approval. If your interested to see how an NDA should look like, you can access this guidance document:

http://www.fda.gov/downloads/Drugs/DevelopmentApprovalProcess/FormsSubmissionRequirements/ElectronicSubmissions/UCM163187.pdf

Once accepted, the FDA then determines the application's completeness. If complete, the agency considers the application filed and begins the review process within 60 days. This starts the mad dash of reviewers such as those in the office of pharmacology or the office of pharmacokinetics who receive piles of documents to read and sift through. Despite much paperwork and review, from the FDA's perspective it's necessary to ensure that the new drug meets the criteria to be "safe and effective." Safety and effectiveness are determined through the Phase III studies based on evidence gained from a controlled clinical study. As there's no absolute safe drug, the FDA needs to review the new drug's efficacy as a measure of its safety. It weighs the risks versus benefits of approving the drug for use in the US marketplace as well as if the drug would help serve a rare disease population, which would place it as an orphan designation- I will go into this later in the book.

The NDA must be clear about the manufacture and marketing of the proposed drug product. The application must define and describe manufacturing processes, validate Current Good Manufacturing Practices (CGMPs), provide evidence of quality, purity, strength, identity, and bioavailability (a pre-inspection of the manufacturing facility is conducted by the FDA). Finally, the FDA reviews all products packaging and labeling for content and clarity. Statements on a product's package label, package insert, media advertising, or professional literature must be reviewed. It's also important to know that "labeling" refers to all of the above and not just the label on the product container.

The FDA is required to review the application within 180 days of filing. At the end of that time, the agency is required to respond with an "action letter." There are three kinds of action letters. An Approval Letter signifies that all substantive requirements for approval are met and that the sponsor company can begin marketing the drug as of the date on the letter.

An Approvable Letter signifies that the application substantially complies with the requirements but has some minor deficiencies that must be addressed before an approval letter is sent. Generally, these deficiencies are minor in nature and the product sponsor must respond within 10 days of receipt. At this point, the sponsor may amend the application and address the agency's concerns, request a hearing with the agency, or withdraw the application entirely.
A Non-Approvable Letter signifies that the FDA has major concerns with the application and will not approve the proposed drug product for marketing as submitted. The available remedies a sponsor can take for this type of action letter are similar to those in the "Approvable Letter."

REFERENCES:
1. NAPLEX/MPJE Registration Bulletin. 2015 National Association of Boards of Pharmacy. Accessed on Nov 1st, 2015. http://www.nabp.net/programs/examination/mpje

2. Strauss S. Food and Drug Administration: An overview. In: Strauss's Federal Drug Laws and Examination Review, 5th edition. Lancaster, PA: Technomic Publishing Co., 1999:323.

3. FDA. 2015 U.S. Food and Drug Administration. http://www.fda.gov/

SECTION 3: FEDERAL PHARMACY LAW

PRESCRIPTION DRUG USER FEE ACT
The new drug application (NDA) review has changed by both the Prescription Drug User Fee Act (PDUFA) and the FDA Modernization Act (FDAMA) in our federal government system. PDUFA allows the FDA to collect fees from sponsor companies who submit applications for review. The fees are used to update facilities, and hire and train reviewers. The fees only apply to NDA drug submissions and biologic drug submissions. It's important to note that the fees do not apply to generic drugs or medical devices. I remember during my FDA rotation, having the opportunity to learn more about medical devices also taught me of how profitable this subsection can be due to no NDA fees and a simple couple of thousands of dollars to get their device through FDA's eyes. To give you an idea, it's an average of a hundreds of thousands of dollars just to submit an NDA at the FDA. This is a way many pharmaceutical companies stress on having a strong regulatory affairs department to ensure acceptance of their drug into market, not just for profitability, but also avoiding the hassles of a delayed approval. In addition, PDUFA requires the FDA to speed up their approval time and is expected by industry due to increased fees to file an NDA. Luckily, the results of the PDUFA legislation were significant; approval rates have increased from approximately 50% to near 80% and the review times have decreased to less than 15 months for most applications.

You'll notice that every couple of years, FDAMA reauthorizes PDUFA. It waives the user fee to small companies who have fewer than 500 employees and are submitting their first application. It allows payment of the fee in stages and permits some percentage of refund if the application is refused. Also, it exempts applications for drugs used in rare conditions (orphan drugs), supplemental applications for pediatric indications, and applications for biological used as precursors for other biologics manufacture. In addition, FDAMA permits a "fast-track" approval of compounds that demonstrate significant benefit to critically ill patients, such as those who suffer from AIDS, hepatitis C, and other specialty disease states.

BIOLOGICS
Biologics are defined as substances derived from or made with the aid of living organisms, which include vaccines, antitoxins, serums, blood, blood products, therapeutic protein drugs derived from natural sources (i.e., anti-thrombin III), or biotechnology (i.e., recombinantly derived proteins). As with the more traditionally derived drug products, biologics follow virtually the same regulatory and clinical testing schema with regard to safety and efficacy. A Biologics License Application (BLA) is used rather than an NDA, although the official FDA Form is designated the 356h and is one and the same. The sponsor merely indicated in check box if the application is for a drug or a biologic. CBER (Center for Biologics Evaluation and Research) reviews these compounds and may work together with CDER depending on the association.

ORPHAN DRUGS
An orphan drug is defined under the Orphan Drug Act of 1993, a drug used to treat a "rare disease" that would not normally be of interest to commercial manufactures in the ordinary course of

business. A rare disease is defined in the law as any disease that affects fewer than 200,000 persons in the United States, or one in which a manufacturer has no reasonable expectation of recovering the cost of its development and availability in the United States. The Act creates a series of financial incentives that manufacturers can take advantage of. For example, the Act permits grant assistance for clinical research, tax credits for research and development, and a 7-year market exclusivity to the first applicant who obtains market approval for a drug designated as an orphan. This means that if a sponsor gains approval for an orphan drug, the FDA will not approve any application by any other sponsor for the same drug for the same disease or condition for 7 years from the date from the first applicant's approval provided certain conditions are met, such as an assurance of sufficient availability of drug to those in need or a revocation of the drug's orphan status. Pharmaceutical companies have also placed high price tags on these orphan drugs.

ABBREVIATED NEW DRUG APPLICATIONS

Abbreviated New Drug Applications (ANDAs) are used when a patent has expired for a product that has been on the US market and a company wishes to market a copy. In the United States, a drug patent is 20 years. After that time, a manufacturer is able to submit an abbreviated application for that product provided that they certify that the product patent in question has already expired, is invalid, or will not be infringed.

The generic copy must meet certain other criteria as well. The drug's active ingredient must already have been approved for the conditions of use proposed in the ANDA, and nothing has changed to call into question the basis for approval of the original drug's NDA. Sponsors of ANDAs are required to prove that their version meets with standards of bioethical and pharmaceutical equivalence.

The FDA publishes a list of all approved drugs called, Approved Drug Products with Therapeutic Equivalence Evaluations, also known as the "Orange Book" because of its orange cover. It lists marketed drug products that are considered by the FDA to be safe and effective and provides information on therapeutic equivalence evaluations for approved multi-source prescription drug products monthly. The Orange Book rates drugs based on their therapeutic equivalence. For a product to be considered therapeutically equivalent, it must be both pharmaceutically equivalent (i.e., the same dose, dosage form, strength), and bioequivalent (i.e., the rate and extent of its absorption is not significantly different than the rate and extent of absorption of the drug with which it is to be interchanged). Realizing that there may be some degree of variability in patients, the FDA allows pharmaceuticals to be considered bioequivalent in either of two methods. The first method studies the rate and extent of absorption of a test drug that may or may not be a generic variation, and a reference or brand name drug under similar experimental conditions and in similar dosing schedules where the test results do not show significant differences. The second approach uses the same method and from which the results determine that there is a difference in the test drug's rate and extent of absorption, except that the difference is considered to be medically insignificant for the proper clinical outcome of that drug.

Bioequivalence of different formulations of the same drug substance involves equivalence with respect to the rate and extent of drug absorption. Two formulations whose rate and extent of absorption differ by 20% or less are generally considered bioequivalent. The use of the 20% rule is based on a medical decision that, for most drugs, a 20% difference in the concentration of the active ingredient in blood will not be clinically significant.

The FDA's Orange Book uses a two-letter coding system that is helpful in determining which drug products are considered therapeutically equivalent. The fist letter, either an A or a B, indicates a drug product's therapeutic equivalence rating. The second letter describes dose forms and can be any one of a number of different letters.

The A codes are described in the Orange Book as drug products that the FDA considers to be therapeutically equivalent to other pharmaceutically equivalent products (i.e., drug products for which):
- There are no known or suspected bioequivalence problems. These are designated AA, AN, AO, AP, or AT, depending on the dose form.
- Actual or potential bioequivalence problems have been resolved with adequate in vivo and/or in vitro evidence supporting bioequivalence. These are designated AB

The B codes are a much less desirable rating when compared to a rating of A. Products that are rated B still may be commercially marketed; but they may not be considered therapeutically equivalent. The Orange Book describes B codes as follows:
- Drug products that FDA at this time, does not consider to be therapeutically equivalent to other pharmaceutically equivalent products, i.e., drug products for which actual or potential bioequivalence problems have not been resolved by adequate evidence of bioequivalence. Often the problem is with specific dosage forms rather than with the active ingredients. These are designated BC, BD, BE, BN, BP, BR, BS, BT, or BX.
- The FDA has adopted an additional subcategory of B codes. The designation, B* is assigned to former A-rated drugs "if FDA receives new information that raises a significant question regarding therapeutic equivalence." Not all drugs are listed in the Orange Book. Drugs obtainable only from a single manufacturing source, drugs listed as Drug Efficacy Study Implementation (DESI) drugs or drugs manufactured before 1938 are not included. Those that do appear are listed by generic name.

PHASE IV AND POST-MARKETING SURVEILLANCE

Pharmaceutical companies that successfully gain marketing approval for their products are not exempt from further regulatory requirements. Many products are approved for market on the basis of a continued submission of clinical research data to the FDA. This data may be required to further validate efficacy or safety, detect new uses or abuses for the product, or determine the effectiveness of labeled indications under conditions of widespread usage. The FDA also may require a Phase IV study for drugs approved under FDAMA's "fast-track" provisions.

Any changes to the approved product's indications, active ingredients, manufacture, or labeling require the manufacturer to submit a supplemental NDA (SNDA) for agency approval. Also, adverse drug reports are required to be reported to the agency. All reports must be reviewed by the manufacturer promptly, and if found to be serious, life-threatening, or unexpected (not listed in the product's labeling), the manufacturer is required to submit an alert report within 15 days working days of receipt of the information. All adverse reaction thought not to be serious or unexpected must be reported quarterly for 3 years after the application is approved, and annually thereafter.

OVER-THE-COUNTER REGULATIONS

The 1951 Durham-Humphrey Amendments of the FDCA specified three criteria to justify prescription-only status. If the compound is habit forming, requires a prescriber's supervision, or has an NDA prescription-only limitation, it requires a prescription. The principles used to establish OTC status (no prescription required) are a wide margin of safety, method of use, benefit-to-risk ratio, and adequacy of labeling for self-medication. For example, injectable drugs may not be used OTC with certain exceptions such as insulin. Over-the-counter market entry is less restrictive than that for prescription drugs and do not require premarket clearance. Pose many fewer safety hazards than prescription drugs because they are designed to alleviate symptoms rather than disease. Easier access far outweighs the risks of side effects, which can be addressed adequately through proper labeling.

OTC products underwent a review in 1972. Although reviewing the 300,000 + OTC drug products in existence at the time would be virtually impossible, the FDA created OTC Advisory Panels to review data based on some 26 therapeutic categories. Over-the-counter drugs are only examined by active ingredient within a therapeutic category. Inactive ingredients are only examined if they are shown to be safe and suitable for the product and not interfering with effectiveness and quality.

This review of active ingredients results in the promulgation of a regulation or a "monograph," which is a "recipe" or set of guidelines applicable to all OTC products within a therapeutic category. Over-the-counter monographs are general and require that OTC products show "general recognition of the safety and effectiveness of the active ingredient." Over-the-counter products do not fall under prescription status if their active ingredients (or combinations) are deemed by the FDA to be "generally recognized as safe and effective" (GRASE). The monograph system is public, with a public comment component included after each phase of the process. Any products for which a final monograph has not been established may remain on the market until one is determined.

There are four phases in the OTC monograph system. In Phase I an expert panel is selected to review data for each active ingredient in each therapeutic category for safety, efficacy, and labeling. Their recommendations are made in the federal register. A public comment period of 30 to 60 days is permitted and supporting or contesting data are accepted for review. Then the panel re-evaluates the data and publishes a "Proposed Monograph" in the federal register, which publicly announces the conditions for which the panel believes that OTC products in a particular therapeutic class are GRASE and not misbranded. A "Tentative Final Monograph" is then developed and published stating the FDA's position on safety and efficacy of a particular ingredient within a therapeutic category and acceptable labeling for indications, warnings, and directions for use. Active ingredients are deemed: Category I (GRASE for claimed therapeutic indications and not misbranded), Category II (not GRASE and/or misbranded), or Category III (insufficient data for determination). After public comment, the final monograph is established and published with the FDA's final criteria for which all drug products in a therapeutic class become GRASE and not misbranded. Following the effective date of the final monograph, all covered drug products that fail to conform to its requirements are considered misbranded and or an unapproved new drug.

The monograph panels are no longer convened, many current products are switched from prescription status. A company who wishes to make this switch and offer a product to the US marketplace can submit an amendment to a monograph to the FDA, who acts as the sole reviewer. They may also file an SNDA provided that they have 3 years of marketing experience as a prescription product, can demonstrate a relatively high use during that period, and can validate that the product has a mild profile of adverse reactions. The last method involves a "Citizens' Petition," which is rarely used.

REGULATING MARKETING

The FDA has jurisdiction over prescription drug advertising and promotion. The basis for these regulations lies within the 1962 Kefauver-Harris Amendments. Essentially, any promotional information, in any form, must be truthful, fairly balanced, and fully disclosed. The FDA views this information as either "advertising" or "labeling." Advertising includes all traditional outlets in which a company places an ad. Labeling includes everything else, including brochures, booklets, lectures, slide kits, letters to physicians, company-sponsored magazine articles, and so on. All information must be truthful and not misleading. All material facts must be disclosed in a manner that is fairly balanced and accurate. If any of these requirements are violated, the product is considered "misbranded" for the indications in which it was approved under its NDA.

The FDA is also sensitive to the promotion of a product for "off-label" use. Off-label use occurs when a product is in some way presented in a manner that does not agree with or is not addressed in its approved labeling. Also, provisions of the Prescription Drug Marketing Act (PDMA) of 1987 apply. The Act prohibits company representatives from directly distributing or reselling prescription drug samples. Companies are required to establish a closed system of record keeping that can track a sample from their control to that of a prescriber in order to prevent diversion. Prescribers are required to receive these samples and record and store them appropriately.

VIOLATIONS AND ENFORCEMENT

The FDA has the power to enforce the regulations for any product as defined under the FDCA. It has the jurisdiction to inspect a manufacturer's premises and records. After a facilities inspection, an agency inspector issues an FDA Form 483s, which describes observable violations. Response to the finding as described on this form must be made promptly. A warning letter may be used when the agency determines that one or more of a company's practices, products, or procedures are in violation of the FDCA. The FDA district has 15 days to issue a warning letter after an inspection. The company has 15 days in which to respond. If the company response is satisfactory to the agency, no other action is warranted. If the response is not, the agency may request a recall of the violated products. The FDA has no authority to force a company to recall a product, but it may force removal of a product through the initiation of a seizure.

Recalls can fall into one of three classes. A Class I recall exists when there is a reasonable possibility that the use of a product will cause either serious adverse effects on health or death. Class II recall exists when the use of a product may cause temporary or medically reversible adverse effects on health or when the probability of serious adverse effects on health is remote. A Class III recall exists when the use of a product is not likely to cause adverse health consequences. Recalls are also categorized as consumer level, in which the product is requested to be recalled for the consumer's homes or control; a retail level, in which the product is to be removed from retail shelves or control; and a wholesale level, in which the product is to be removed from wholesale distribution. Companies who conduct a recall of their products are required to conduct effectiveness checks to determine the effectiveness of recalling the product from the marketplace.

If a company refuses to recall the product, the FDA will seek an injunction against the company. An injunction is recommended to the Department of Justice (DOJ) by the FDA. The DOJ takes the request to federal court, which issues an order that forbids a company from carrying out a particular illegal act, such as marketing a product that the FDA considers a violation of the FDCA. Companies can comply with the order and sign a consent agreement, which specifies changes required by the FDA in order for the company to continue operations, or litigate.

The FDA also may initiate a seizure of violative products. A seizure is ordered by the federal court in the district where the products are located. The seizure order specifies products, their batch numbers, and any records determined by the FDA as violative. United States Marshals carry out this action. The FDA institutes a seizure to prevent a company from selling, distributing, moving, or otherwise tampering with the product.

The FDA also may debar individuals or firms from assisting or submitting an ANDA, or directly providing services to any firm with an existing or pending drug product application. Debarment may last for up to 10 years.

SECTION 4: OVERVIEW OF FEDERAL ACTS

I wouldn't memorize the name or years of the acts necessarily, but would understand the concepts and rules that the acts provided to our current laws in place today.

1890 SHERMAN ANTITRUST ACT
This act outlawed agreements that restricted trade to avoid monopolies, chain-store price hikes, price fixing, and mergers that lessened competition.

1938 FEDERAL FOOD DRUG AND COSMETIC ACT (FDCA)
This was the main law that formed the Food and Drug Administration (FDA) to provide no adulterated or misbranded drugs in interstate commerce, improper advertising, and ingredients being disclosed on the label. Drugs must be proven safe before being marketed out to the public and it gave the FDA power to inspect manufacturers and distributors.

1944 DURHAM-HUMPHREY LABELING AMENDMENTS
This act was an addition to the FDCA as it allowed refills of prescriptions, and established separation between prescription and over-the-counter (OTC) products. At this time, it formed the pregnancy ratings (ABCDX), but note that this has been phased out to create a simpler way for prescribers.

1962 KEFAUVER-HARRIS DRUG EFFICACY AMENDMENTS
This act was another addition to the FDCA to prove that drugs were effective before being marketed out to the public. This act created NDAs and SNDAs with the different phases of research, IRB approval, and INDs to test new drugs in humans. The FDA was allowed a 30-day clinical hold to review materials and if they did not respond, manufacturers and facilities were able to proceed with studies. This act also mandated adverse drug reactions and events through FDA's MedWatch program with clinical studies. Note that this is voluntarily for prescribers and clinicians. All drug labels were required to have brand and generic names, and lastly the act provided the basis for current good manufacturing practices (cGMP).

1970 POISON PREVENTION PACKAGING ACT
This act makes it a requirement for pharmacies to dispense drugs using child-resistant containers unless requested by the patient otherwise. The only exceptions are these drugs: Provera, Prednisone, Amorphous cholestyramine, isosorbide dinitrate, sublingual nitroglycerine, sexy birth controls/ Erythromycin, effervescent aspirin, Effervescent acetaminophen. Plastic containers are not allowed to be reused except for glass containers (hospitals are exempt from this requirement).

1982 FEDERAL FALSE CLAIMS ACT
This act enforced false Medicare and Medicaid billing with fines and criminal charges in addition to reward whistleblowers with up to 25% of government awards if the case went to trial.

1984 HATCH-WAXMAN ACT
This act was also an amendment to the FDCA to establish an abbreviated drug approval process for generic drugs (ANDA) based off of bioequivalence. It also gave additional patent terms similar to

the drug development period, and gave way to the creation of the Orange Book that lists all FDA approved drug products with AB rated drugs being substituted and BX/BC/BE drugs not.

1986 NATIONAL CHILDHOOD VACCINE INJURY ACT
Any adverse reaction or reports with vaccines must be reported to the VAERS form through this act.

1987 PRESCRIPTION DRUG MARKETING ACT
This act prohibits sales, trade, or purchase of drug samples as well as requires states such as IL to license drug wholesalers. It also prohibited counterfeiting any pharmaceutical coupon. Importation of drugs was only allowed by the manufacturer. Thus, patients are not allowed to order or bring foreign drugs into the United States unless for personal use:
1. Product must be for personal use (90-day supply or less)
2. For a serious condition in which the treatment may not be available domestically
3. No commercialization or promotion must be done in the US

Importation of bulk substances is legal only if they are intended for compounding, have an approved drug application, or used in an approved OTC monograph drug label. This act also allowed the use of starter packs and required legend Rx labels.

1990 OMNIBUS BUDGET RECONCILIATION ACT (OBRA 90)
This act requires pharmacists to do prospective drug use reviews and counsel all Medicaid patients for reimbursement. Ensure to know this act!

1992 PRESCRIPTION DRUG USER FEE ACT
This act required manufacturers to pay a user fee for each drug that is marketed, for a facility that manufacturers drugs, and each application for drug approval. The act also specifies a re-authorization period of 5 years and promises that 90% of priority drugs will be reviewed within 6 months and 90% of standard "me too" drugs will be reviewed within 10 months. This act is used to support hiring of drug reviewers to help speed up the review process.

1994 DIETARY SUPPLEMENT HEALTH AND EDUCATION ACT
This act categorizes dietary supplements as food, thus they are not required to be proven safe and effective; however, they must follow cGMP, places cautionary statements on all labeling, allows the FTC to regulate advertisements, and products must be orally formulated only.

1996 HEALTH INSURANCE PORTABILITY AND ACCOUNTABILITY ACT (HIPAA)
This act heavily details patient health information (PHI) in what can be disclosed and what cannot. Pharmacies that bill electronically must limit disclosure of PHI to a "minimal necessary" amount, and not disclose PHI other than for treatment, payment, or regular health operation uses. All personnel must have training, procedures, and safeguards to protect PHI with patients have rights to correct medical records especially in regards to authorizing use of their PHI for marketing purposes.

1997 FDA MODERNIZATION ACT
This act allows fast-track approval for life-saving drugs with surrogate endpoints being acceptable with post-marketing studies as a requirement. It allows manufacturers to provide off-label sales

information if solicited, and allows economic and formulary support from manufacturers. Drugs have a 6-month patent term bonus if manufacturers also submit data on pediatrics.

2000 DRUG ADDICTION TREATMENT ACT
This act allows authorized physicians to treat drug addiction with buprenorphine (Subuxone) in an office-based setting with a limit of 30 patients per physician, and 100 patients after year one. Physicians have a unique provider number starting with "X" with methadone 40 mg tabs/disks also allowed for opioid addiction only. Patients are required to sign a DEA form 363. There is a three-day exception rule that methadone may be given by a physician, or from a hospital setting for surgery or acute medical care outside the program.

2003 MEDICARE PRESCRIPTION DRUG IMPROVEMENT & MODERNIZATION ACT (MEDICARE PART D)
This act provides prescription drug coverage to Medicare patients over the age of 65, disabled, or in End Stage Renal Disease (ESRD) with copays and the infamous donut hole. Prescriptions are covered with the exception of: weight loss, fertility, cosmetic, hair growth, benzodiazepines/barbiturates, over the counter medications, and cold and cough relief medications. Pharmacists are also reimbursed for medication therapy management (MTM) of Medicare patients, and annual training is required for fraud, waste, and abuse.

2005 COMBAT METHAMPHETAMINE ACT
This act was created to fight against methamphetamine use. It restricts pharmacy sales of over the counter (OTC) pseudoephedrine (PSE) to 3.6 grams per person per day, 9 grams of PSE per person per 30-day period, or 7.5 grams of PSE via mail order per person 30-day period. All solid dosage forms of PSE must be sold in blister packs with no more than 2 doses per blister. All PSE must be placed behind the counter or secured in the pharmacy, and purchasers must furnish a picture ID with the retailer maintaining a logbook for four years. Note these requirements and limitations do not apply to prescriptions written for PSE, only OTC; however, some states such as Oregon and Missouri do require a prescription for patients to obtain PSE regardless of amount as it is not sold OTC in this state. Illinois does not have this prescription requirement regulation.

2007 FDA AMENDMENTS ACT
This act focuses on drug safety and creates risk evaluation and mitigation strategies (REMS) for drugs. It also requires all prescription drugs to have side effect statements.

2008 RYAN HAIGHT ONLINE PHARMACY CONSUMER PROTECTION ACT
This act relates to internet prescriptions and prohibits controlled substances from being sold without an in-person medical evaluation. Online pharmacies must also have a DEA registration, have monthly DEA reporting if surpassing sell thresholds, and a statement of compliance.

2012 FOOD AND DRUG ADMINISTRATION SAFETY AND INNOVATION ACT (FDASIA)
This act improved FDA's inspection authority and the drug supply by expediting inspections, creating incentives to promote antibiotic-resistant infections, expands scope of products for a "breakthrough approval" program to ensure that drugs treating serious life-threatening conditions to get fast track benefits.

2013 DRUG QUALITY AND SECURITY ACT/2014 COMPOUNDING QUALITY ACT
This act permits registration of large-scale compounding pharmacies termed "outsourcing facilities" that must have a pharmacist and meet cGMP standards. The pharmacy doesn't need to be licensed with the state. This act also requires products to be labeled "compounded drug" and "not for resale" with the facility open to FDA inspection.

DRUG RECALLS

Drug Recalls involve a manufacturer's voluntary removal or correction of a marketed product in violation of a law with each recall having a recall strategy from the manufacturer.

Class I: There is a reasonable probability that the use or exposure to the product will cause serious adverse health or death.
Class II: The use or exposure to a product may cause temporary or medically reversible adverse health or where the probability of serious adverse health consequences is remote.
Class III: The use or exposure to a product is not likely to cause adverse health consequences.

DIFFERENCE BETWEEN MISBRANDING AND ADULTERATION
MISBRANDING
- Label is false or misleading
- Label is missing name, active ingredients of drug, quantity
- Prescription or OTC label missing required information
- Drug made in a non-registered facility
- Not in compliance with laws or regulations
- Packed without regard to Poison Prevention Packaging Act
- Think "label"

ADULTERATION
- Contains any unapproved, unsafe substance
- Exposed to unsanitary conditions or lack of cGMPS
- Strength, purity, or quality substandard
- Used in substitution of another substance
- Think "drug"

REFERENCES
1. Fundamentals of Regulatory Affairs. Regulatory Affairs Professions Society, 1999:200.

2. Strauss S. Food and Drug Administration: An overview. In: Strauss's Federal Drug Laws and Examination Review, 5th edition. Lancaster, PA: Technomic Publishing Co., 1999.

3. FDA. 2015 U.S. Food and Drug Administration. http://www.fda.gov/

SECTION 5: FEDERAL CONTROLLED SUBSTANCES LAWS

FEDERAL LAWS AND REGULATIONS GOVERNING PHARMACIES, PHARMACISTS AND PRESCRIPTIONS

The Federal Controlled Substances Act (CSA) of 1970 is the basis for all practice-oriented drug law and regulations. It's important to note that this is a closed-loop system that goes from manufacturer through administration, or dispensing to the patient. Each controlled substance dosage is carefully recorded and tightly controlled. A nightmare of any pharmacist is missing controlled substances or wrong counts. I would strongly recommend reading the Pharmacist Manual (most recent update is 2010) for the IL State MPJE.

The CSA was brought about to regulate the manufacturing, distribution, dispensing, and delivery of drugs that have a potential for physical and/or mental abuse. CSA is regulated by the Drug Enforcement Agency (DEA) with a federal registration of all persons in the chain of manufacturing, distribution, and dispensing except the ultimate user- people or their caregivers don't have their very own DEA number to track. The DEA registration number must be renewed every 3 years and specific forms are used to order. All records should be maintained for at least four (4) years. However, federal facilities like veteran administration (VA) hospitals don't fall under the state laws of CSA as it is a federal level of practice. These potentially abusive drugs were termed "controlled substances" and broken down into five schedules. These medications have a "C" on their stock bottles.

The five schedules are based off of medical use and potential for abuse and dependence outlined below. Be sure to know what medications are listed in each of these schedules!

C-I
High potential for abuse drugs have no currently accepted medical use (i.e. Heroin) in the treatment in the United States, and there is also little data on the accepted safety for use of the drug under medical supervision. These drugs may not be prescribed, administration, or dispensed for medical use, but they may be ordered for research and investigational use. This controlled substance class can be ordered using DEA 222/CSOS. Examples: Marijuana, Heroin, LSD, Peyote, Salvia.

C-II
These medications have a high potential of abuse but also have an accepted medical use. It's important to know that no refills or transfer are allowed for this controlled substance class. Patients are able to have multiple fillings of this class as long as they have multiple prescription blanks, the actual date of prescribing, and the earliest date to fill with a 90-day total. So if Sally brings in a prescription for OxyContin, she is allowed to make three fills with three separate prescriptions, but will need to see her prescriber after the 90-day supply is done. Oral prescriptions are allowed only if it's an emergency and written prescription arrives within 7 days. A central fill is not permitted in emergency situations. Facsimile prescriptions are not allowed of CIIs except in these situations:
- Home infusion/IV parenteral therapy if for pain
- Long Term Care Facility (LTCF) residents

- Registered hospice facility

Partial fills are allowed within 72 hours if the pharmacist doesn't have the supply needed to fill the entire prescription, but the prescription must have the amount dispensed noted. If the total amount of the prescription is not completed within 72 hours, then the remainder amount is void and the prescriber should be contacted to get a new supply. In a LTCF, partial fills are allowed with the prescription valid for 60 days from the date it was written; however, the pharmacist must note the date of fill, quantity dispensed and remainder along with a signature. DEA form 222/CSOS is required either typewritten or handwritten with one drug per line. Make sure to take time and accuracy on these forms as any ill markings or misspellings will make the form void. DEA form 222 can also be used by pharmacies to ship drugs back to a reverse distributor or other pharmacy that is in short supply. In this case, the pharmacy acting as a supplier, maintains copy 1 with the reverse distributor disposing the drug using form 41. Examples: Dilaudid, OxyContin, Demerol, Sublimaze, etc.

C-III AND C-IV

These controlled substances also have a potential for abuse, but are not as high as CIIs. Patients are able to get five refills in six months from the date the prescription was written, and one transfer allowed unless the organization has a shared database (CVS to CVS, or Walgreens to Walgreens) they may transfer as many times as needed. Prescriptions in this class may be written, verbal or electronic and partial fills are allowed as long as the total quantity or six-month duration isn't breached. A DEA form 222/CSOS is not required for this controlled substance class. Example for Schedule III: Buprenorphine, Anabolic steroids, Suboxone, Tylenol 3 (Tylenol with codeine), etc. Example for Schedule IV: Benzodiazepines, Lunesta, and Tramadol.

C-V

This is the last class with the lowest risk of abuse. There is no limit for refills with one transfer permitted unless, again, if the chain shares a common database. Most CV drugs don't need a prescription such as cough or antidiarrheal (Immodium) as long as it contains less than 200 mg of codeine or per 100 mLs if a liquid preparation. The catch is dispensing these non-prescriptions need to be done by a pharmacist, and the buyer needs to be at least 18 years old, have a valid ID, and a log book must be kept of each transaction that includes:
- Name and address of buyer, name and quantity purchased along with date, and pharmacist name that dispensed the product

Central fill pharmacies are not allowed to dispense controlled substances at the retail level if someone wants to buy. Partial fills are allowed for CVs as long as total amount or six-month duration is not breached and no DEA 222/CSOS form is needed. Example: Lyrica (requires Rx), Phergan with Codeine, Robitussin AC, etc.

DRUG ENFORCEMENT ADMINISTRATION (DEA) REGISTRATION

As mentioned before, every practitioner involved in the chain needs to have a DEA registration number except those that are federal (VA, US Public Health Service, Bureau of Prisons (BOP), etc.). A DEA registration number for a practitioner begins with the letter A or B. Registration numbers issued to mid-level practitioners begin with the letter M. The first letter of the registration number is followed by the first letter of the registrant's last name (i.e. T for Tanner or M for Munoz), and then a computer-generated sequence of seven numbers (such as MT3614511). So how can pharmacists check if this is a valid DEA number? The computer system generates these numbers based off a formula.

Add the sum of the numbers in the "odd" position to the sum of the numbers in the "even" position multiplied by 2. The second number in the final sum is called the "check digit" and is the last number in the sequence.

For example, take the following MT3614511. The letter M represents the practitioner as a mid-level prescriber. The letter T represents the first letter of the last name Tanner. The numbers are randomly generated and the final check digit is the number 1. The formula is as follows:
- Odd position: $3 + 1 + 5 = 9$
- Even position: $6 + 4 + 1 = 11 \times 2 = 22$
- $22 + 9 = 31$ "1" is the seventh or check digit

Be sure to understand this formula as it will be tested on the MPJE! Even though it is not used in practice much, it is still a valuable tool if a pharmacist suspects fraudulent activities
Pharmacies, not pharmacists, get assigned a DEA registration number by filling out a DEA form 224 if they buy and sell controlled substances. The pharmacy must also comply with distributor and record keeping requirements. This also includes transfer of ownership or change of address, a new DEA registration must be completed before the change happens to note the changes. If the there is a transfer of a pharmacy business to another registrant, then the DEA needs to be notified at least 14 days before the transfer to make the following updates:
- The name, address, and registration number of the registrant transferring the pharmacy
- The name, address, and registration number of the registrant receiving the pharmacy
- Whether the pharmacy will continue at the current location with the current business owner or moved to another location
- The date when the controlled substances will be transferred to the person acquiring the pharmacy

On the day the controlled substances are transferred, a complete inventory must be taken and a copy of the inventory must be included in the records of for both parties involved in the transfer of the pharmacy. If the registrant that is gaining the pharmacy owns another pharmacy licensed in the same state as the one he's acquiring, they will still need to apply for a new DEA number before the date of transfer.

PRACTIONERS
Even though practitioners may acquire a DEA registration, it's important to note that they are still limited in their scope of practice. An order for controlled substances that seems to be a valid prescription, but is not issued in the usual course of professional treatment, or for investigational research, is not a valid prescription within the meaning and intent of the CSA. If a pharmacist suspects fraudulent prescribing but still dispenses the medication is subject to criminal and possibly civil actions. Practitioners are not allowed to get a supply of controlled substances for general dispensing to their patients, and again limited to their scope of practice. For example, dentists can only prescribe for the treatment of the oral cavity area; you shouldn't expect a prescription of

Ambien or Lyrica from them. Mid-level practitioners (MLPs) are registered and authorized by the DEA and the state in which they practice to dispense, administer, and prescribe controlled substances in the course of professional practice. Examples of MLPs are nurse practitioners, nurse midwives, nurse anesthetists, clinical nurse specialists, physician assistants, optometrists, ambulance services, animal shelters, veterinarian euthanasia technicians, nursing homes, and homeopathic physicians. MLPs can also get an individual DEA registration for controlled substance privileges. Also some individual practitioners such as residents, staff physicians, and mid-level practitioners can be an employee of a hospital or facility, and authorize the practitioner to dispense using the hospital's DEA registration number. Usually these institutions also have an internal code that is included in the end of the DEA registration number such as- GB1111119-W19. There's also a current list of internal codes that should be kept in the hospital or institution, and a pharmacist can call to verify the prescriber.

PRESCRIPTION BASICS

Prescriptions must be written in ink, typewritten or print, and information can only be entered by the prescribers or their agent. The only piece of information on the prescription that needs to be in the prescriber's own handwriting is their signature. Prescriptions are allowed to be transmitted orally by telephone or facsimile for Schedules III to V. The name of the person that a pharmacist or pharmacy intern has spoken to must be written down on a pharmacy pad and written into hard copy within 7 days.

In case of an emergency, a pharmacist may dispense a Schedule II medication when receiving the orally transmitted authorization of a prescribing practitioner, provided that the quantity prescribed and dispensed is limited to the amount adequate to treat the patient during the emergency period. The prescribing practitioner then must provide a written prescription for the emergency quantity prescribed to be delivered or postmarked to the dispensing pharmacist within 7 days after authorizing an emergency oral prescription. The prescription must also have written on its face "Authorization for Emergency Dispensing." Upon receipt of the written prescription, the dispensing pharmacist must attach the prescription to the oral one. If the prescribing practitioner fails to deliver a written prescription within 7 days, the pharmacist needs to notify DEA or else will face criminal charges. Pharmacists and prescribers are co-liable for prescriptions written in error or with obvious problems. This is called corresponding responsibility. A prescription for a controlled substance must be issued in good faith and for a legitimate medical purpose by a practitioner in the usual course of his or her professional practice. For example, a pharmacist receives a prescription order of antibiotics for the prescriber's daughter, if the prescriber is a veterinarian, this is obviously out of their scope of practice; however, if the prescriber is a medical family practice practitioner, then it may be allowable to fill the prescription.

A prescription is considered complete when the following information is included on its face:
- Date of issue
- Name and address of practitioner
- Controlled substance registration number
- Name of patient
- Address of patient
- Name, strength, dose, and quantity of controlled substances
- Directions for use and any cautionary statements required
- Number of times to be refilled

- Signature of prescriber

Prescriptions can be filed in a pharmacy in three different ways:
1. Three separate files for:
    - C-II
    - C-III through C-V
    - Non-controlled substances
2. §Two separate files for:
    - C-II
    - C-III through C-V and non-controlled substances
3. §Two separate files for:
    - C-II through C-V
    - Non-controlled substances

Note:
- §A red "C" must be stamped on the face of the prescription at least 1-inch-high in the lower right corner.
    - If a pharmacy utilizes a computer software for prescription that permits identification by prescription number and retrieving of the original documents by prescriber's name, patient's name, the name of the drug dispensed, and the date filled, this requirement is applicable.

The transfer of existing, filled prescriptions is allowed under federal law for prescription drugs in Schedules III through V. The transfer rule only applies with state pharmacy law. Individual states may have more stringent requirements.

METHADONE
Prescriptions for methadone are valid provided that the drug is used as an analgesic. They are not valid through the typical retail pharmacy distribution channels for the purposes of detoxification or maintenance therapy for drug addiction. The only exception is when it was written by a physician for an addicted patient, then you are allowed a single-day quantity for three consecutive days for the purpose of admitting that addicted person to a licensed treatment program.

UNITED STATES POSTAL REGULATIONS
United States postal regulations allow the mailing of any filled prescription containing a narcotic of any quantity or federal schedule to patients. If not, we would not be able to do mail order prescriptions! When mailing controlled substances, two rules must be followed:
1. The inner container must be marked, sealed, and labeled with the name and address of the practitioner, or the name and address of the pharmacy or other person dispensing the prescription and the prescription number.
2. The outside container must be plain with no markings of any kind that would indicate the contents contained within.

PRESCRIPTION LABELING
The prescription label must be on the container and have the following information:
- Pharmacy name, address, and telephone number

- Assigned serial number
- Date of initial dispensing
- Name of patient
- Name of prescriber
- Directions for use and any cautionary statements
- Federal controlled substances warning label or "transfer label" for a Schedule II, III, and IV controlled substance

A controlled substance warning label, also known as the federal transfer label, must on the prescription containers of any drug listed in Schedules II to IV. The label reads as follows:
- "CAUTION: Federal law prohibits the transfer of this drug to any person other than the patient for whom it was prescribed."

Expiration dates listed on a manufacturer's stock container are set based on appropriate stability data that would support some amount of shelf life. Many states though require some form of expiration dating on prescription labels. Most use the Standards as described by the United States Pharmacopoeia (USP). Unless otherwise specified in the individual monograph, the beyond-use date (expiration date) should not be any later than the expiration date on the manufacturer's container, or one year from the date from when the drug is dispensed, whichever is earlier. USP also specifies that the expiration date for insulin products is 24 months from their date of manufacture. Expiration dates on OTC drug products are exempt from expiration dating if they are stable for at least 3 years, have no dosing limitations, and are safe and suitable for frequent and prolonged use (i.e. toothpaste, medicated shampoo).

SAFETY CLOSURES AND CONTAINERS

It's important read the Poison Prevention Packaging Act of 1970 that specifies child-resistant closures must be used on prescription containers unless the prescription is for an exempt drug (i.e., sublingual nitroglycerin, cholestyramine powder, unit dose or effervescent potassium supplements, erythromycin ethylsuccinate preparations, oral contraceptives packaged in mnemonic packages). Patients can authorize easy-to-open packaging and even issue a "blanket waiver" for prescription containers so that all of them are easy-to-open. A physician cannot issue a "blanket waiver" for dispensing in an easy-to-open packaging; the order must be on each prescription.

PHARMACY REQUIREMENTS

Every pharmacy must be registered with the DEA and receive a certificate of registration to distribute or dispense controlled substances. Each pharmacy has its own DEA registration number. These certificates of registration must be renewed every 3 years. Every pharmacy registrant must keep and maintain an accurate record of each controlled substance received. Dated invoices for controlled substances in Schedules III, IV, and V constitute complete records for these drugs. Copy 3 of DEA Form 222 constitutes complete record for the receipt of Schedule II controlled substances. The DEA requires every registrant who changes his or her business address to notify them and receive their approval before moving. Registrants may keep records at a location other than the registered location by notifying the nearest DEA office. Unless this request is denied, registrants may transfer records 14 days after notification. All records must be kept for a period of 4 years.

INVENTORY REQUIREMENTS
When first opening up a new pharmacy store or first having a controlled substance in stock, an initial inventory must be taken even if there is zero stock. The initial inventory must contain the name, address, and DEA number of the registrant; the date and time of the inventory; the signature of the person taking the inventory; as well as the name of the medication, dosage form, dosage, and quantity on hand. Then, once every 2 years, a biennial inventory must be taken of all federally controlled substances (C-II through C-V) after the date on which the original inventory was taken. This biennial inventory can be done on any date within the 2-year period. An exact count of C-II drugs must be done while only an estimation is need for C-III, C-IV or C-V drugs, unless the container holds more than a 1000 units then an exact count must be done.

COMPUTERIZED PRESCRIPTION PROCESSING SYSTEMS
Federal law permits record keeping to be done through a computerized prescription processing system. A pharmacy can use a system for the storage and retrieval of prescription information. It should still be able to supply immediate retrieval of information by either an electronic display or hard copy printout for prescriptions currently being filled. The computerized prescription processing system must still have the following:

- Date of issuance
- Original prescription number
- Name and address of patient
- Physician's name and DEA number
- Name, strength, dosage form, and quantity of control
- Total number of refills authorized by the physician

The system must provide a refill history or hard copy for controlled substances that have been refilled during the past 6 months. Pharmacies who use a computerized prescription processing system must printout a hard copy or receive a hard copy within 72 hours of dispensing. Pharmacists who dispense these prescriptions then must verify that the information on the hard copy is correct and then sign and date the printout. A hard copy printout or other documentation must be stored in a separate file for a period of 4 years.

DRUG ENFORCEMENT ADMINISTRATION (DEA) FORMS
FORM 222
Use this form to order Schedule I and II drugs to stock a pharmacy. Pharmacists who want to borrow or transfer (from registrant to registrant) Schedule II controlled substances from other pharmacies need to use a DEA Form 222. The form is in triplicate and can be signed by the registrant or any person who has written authorization. Each form contains ten lines to write the C-II medication to be ordered. One line on the order form should be used to describe one item ordered, if two lines are used for the same item, they count as only one line. These forms must be submitted to the supplier error free- if there is any error it will be rejected. Therefore, voiding a line on the order form because of an error is not permitted and the entire form should be voided.

When complete, the person ordering the medication must separate the third copy of the form and retain it in the pharmacy. Once receiving the drugs, the person who ordered them, or any other authorized person, must fill out the last two columns of the store's copy with quantity and date. The first copy goes to the supplier and second copy to DEA.

- Copy 1 is brown (supplier)
- Copy 2 is Green (DEA)
- Copy 3 is Blue (Pharmacy)

After a pharmacy places an order, it keeps copy 3 (blue) while copy 1 and 2 are mailed to the supplier to get the drugs requested. The supplier fills the order and keeps copy 1 and 2. Copy 2 (green) is then mailed to the DEA. If the supplier can't fill the order, they can send it to another supplier. However, each form must be signed and dated by a person with power of attorney from the registrant. Once the pharmacy receives the order, it completes copy 3 to ensure the order was received and accurate. These records must be maintained for at least four (4) years.

FORM 106
Loss of controlled substances (federally scheduled II to V) must be reported to the DEA using this form. If the pharmacy is involved in a robbery or significant shortage of controlled substances is caught, after reporting to the local police department, a DEA Form 106 should be filled out in triplicate. Two copies must be sent to the DEA as soon as possible; one copy must be kept on file by the pharmacy. If a pharmacist knowingly fails to report theft within 24 hours of discovery, they could be charged criminal charges and fined.

FORM 41
Use this form for the destruction of controlled substances. The DEA should be contacted for instructions when destroying outdated, damaged, or otherwise unusable controlled substances. Breakage, damage, or spillage of recoverable or destruction of controlled substances must be on DEA form 41, and the drug disposed of through a reverse distributor. However, any spillage or damage of non-recoverable drugs must be documented in inventory records. Two individuals who witnessed the breakage must sign the inventory records.

FORM 224
Use this if filing for a new retail pharmacy, hospital/clinic, practitioner, teaching institution, or mid-level practitioner.

FORM 224a
Use this to renew for facilities listed in form 224.

FORM 224b
Use this as an affidavit for chain renewal operating under a single registration.

FORM 225
Use this if filing a new application for a manufacturer, distributor, analytical laboratory, or importer/exporter.

FORM 363
Use this if filing a new application for narcotic treatment programs such as methadone maintenance program.

FORM 510

Use this if filing a new application for domestic chemical businesses such as precursors for controlled substances.

MISCELLANEOUS

Patient package inserts (PPIs) are required by FDA regulation to be provided to the patient when dispensing certain drugs. Patient package inserts must be given to the patient on the initial dispensing and on refills if so requested. All of the following are drugs that must be dispensed with a PPI:

- Isoproterenol inhalation products
- Oral contraceptives
- Estrogen/progestogen containing drug products
- Intrauterine devices
- Progestational drug products
- Accutane R

SCHEDULE LISTED CHEMICAL PRODUCT (SLCPS)

These are products used in the production of methamphetamine. Drugs commonly used are: ephedrine, pseudoephedrine, and phenlypropanolamine. It's important that sellers must self-certify to the DEA through computer that employees have been trained, and these records of training must be maintained. Sale limits need to be enforced, and products stored behind the counter or in a locked cabinet as well as a written or electronic logbook be maintained at all times.

Drugs listed as "List 1 Chemicals" are drugs involved in the manufacture of a controlled substance such as: Ephedrine, Pseudoephedrine, Ergonovine, Iodine, Sasfrole, Piperidine. Drugs listed as "List 2 Chemicals" are solvents used in the manufacture of a controlled substance such as: Acetone, HCl, K/NA-Permanganate.

REFERENCES

1. Poison Prevention Packaging: A Guide for Healthcare Professionals. Revised 2005. US Consumer Product Safety Commission (CPSC) Accessed on November 25th, 2015 at: https://www.cpsc.gov//PageFiles/113945/384.pdf.

2. Title 21 United States Code (USC) Controlled Substances Act. 2012 Edition. Accessed on November 26th, 2015 at: http://www.deadiversion.usdoj.gov/21cfr/21usc/.

3. Drug Enforcement Administration (DEA). Accessed on November 26th 2015 at: http://www.dea.gov/druginfo/ds.shtml.

Federal Pharmacy Law Exam

Objectives
- This is a 121-question exam that mimics the Federal pharmacy portion of the MPJE exam. We have focused on more questions from federal law as recent graduates have stated the exam focuses heavily on this portion.
- Use these questions as a supplement to test your self-study learning and go back to review questions missed. There will be material covered in the questions not covered in the text above so use the questions as a supplement for further learning.
- Ensure to time yourself at 1 hour and 45 minutes to complete the questions in one sitting.
- Answers can be reviewed after the federal pharmacy law exam section.
- If you do not get above a 75% score, it's prudent to review the laws discussed in the previous chapters and review the IL Statutes online for a deeper review.

GOOD LUCK!

1. Within what period of time of two documented attempts of detoxification does an 18-year-old become eligible for narcotic maintenance treatment?
    A. 1 month
    B. 3 months
    C. 6 months
    D. 12 months
    E. 18 months

2. Which act or amendment granted the FDA the authority to inspect factories?
    A. Pure Food and Drug Act
    B. Food, Drug, and Cosmetic Act
    C. Durham-Humphrey
    D. Food, Drug and Insecticide Administration
    E. FDA

3. Which of the following acts or amendments was the first to regulate the transportation of adulterated or misbranded drugs in interstate commerce?
    A. Pure Food and Drug Act
    B. Food, Drug and Cosmetic Act
    C. Food, Drug and Insecticide Administration
    D. Drug Abuse Control
    E. Drug Importation Act

4. Which of the following must be ordered using a DEA Form 222?
    I. Secobarbital Suppository
    II. Pentobarbital Injection
    III. Amobarbital Capsule

    A. I only
    B. III only
    C. I & II only
    D. II & III only
    E. I, II, & III

5. Which of the following items must be ordered from a wholesaler on DEA order Form 222?
    I. Morphine Sulfate, extended release tablet 100 mg
    II. Meperidine HCL, injection 50 mg/mL
    III. Diazepam tablet 5 mg

    A. I only
    B. III only
    C. I & II only
    D. II & III only
    E. I, II, & III

6. Which of the following products is classified as Schedule III controlled substance?
   I. A product containing 90 mg of codeine per dose
   II. A product containing 15 mg of hydrocodone per dose
   III. A product that contains 3 mg of diphenoxylate and 25 mcg of atropine sulfate per dose

   A. I only
   B. III only
   C. I & II only
   D. II & III only
   E. I, II, & III

7. All of the following would be considered as incidences of misbranding EXCEPT:
   A. The active drug is not identified on the label
   B. The original bottle of 40 contains only 35 tablets
   C. The names of inactive ingredients are not on the label
   D. The level of the drug in the product is 10% V/V but the label states 15% V/V
   E. The pharmacist dispenses a drug without the prescription

8. Partial refilling of which of the following prescriptions of controlled substances may be granted upon request of the patient?
   I. Valium
   II. Concerta
   III. Alfenta

   A. I only
   B. III only
   C. I & II only
   D. II & III only
   E. I, II, & III

9. The formulary of a pharmacy providing services under MMA (Medicare Modernization Act) may be limited to which of the following?
   A. The top 200 drugs
   B. Generic drugs
   C. At least one drug from each of all therapeutic categories developed by the USP
   D. Top 100 drugs
   E. Single-sourced drugs

10. Which portion of the following federal counseling regulations is (are) a requirement for each individual state?
    I. Prospective review
    II. Meta analysis review
    III. Retrospective review

    A. I only
    B. III only

C. I & II only
D. II & III only
E. I, II, & III

11. When a controlled substance inventory is conducted, which of the following must be included?
   I. Drugs returned by a customer
   II. Drugs ordered by a customer but not yet paid for
   III. All controlled substances dispensed over the past month

   A. I only
   B. III only
   C. I & II only
   D. II & III only
   E. I, II, & III

12. An individual is eligible for Medicare Plan D enrollment on May 8th 2017. Which of the following is the exact period he can enroll in the Part D Plan without a penalty?
   A. February 1st to August 31st
   B. May 1st to May 31st
   C. May 1st to August 31st
   D. January 1st to December 1st
   E. May 8th to November 31st

13. Drug products of the same strength and same dosage form may be interchangeable if they are in which of the following classes? (Select ALL that apply)
   A. A
   B. BC
   C. B
   D. BS
   E. AB

14. If the following DEA number is authentic MS242651_ Which of the following is true about the letter S and the last missing digit?
   A. S is the first letter of the practitioner's last name; 1 is the missing digit
   B. S is the practitioner's code; 1 is the missing digit
   C. S is the first letter of the practitioner's last name; 0 is the missing digit
   D. S is the first letter of the practitioner's first name; 1 is the missing digit
   E. S is the first letter of the practitioner's first name; 0 is the missing digit

15. Which one of the following is NOT true about the Pure Food and Drug Act? (Select ALL that apply)
   A. This law was passed because of the mistaken use of diethylene glycol that lead to death
   B. The law prohibits the commerce of foods, drugs and cosmetics to be adulterated or misbranded
   C. This law was passed by the congress in 1938
   D. The law failed to protect the public

E. This law was passed by the congress in 1906

16. Which drug is correctly assigned to its schedule?
    A. Schedule III - 1.5 g of codeine/100 mL
    B. Schedule III - 350 mg of ethylmorphine/100 mL
    C. Schedule IV - 300 mg of ethylmorphine/100 mL
    D. Schedule IV - 150 mg of dihydrocodeine/100 mL
    E. Schedule III - 350 mg of dihydrocodeine/100 mL

17. Health professionals self-prescribing is acceptable:
    I. In most states
    II. Nationwide
    III. It is not acceptable at all

    A. I only
    B. III only
    C. I & II only
    D. II & III only
    E. I, II, & III

18. Examples of drugs that can be exempted from child-resistant packaging requirements are:
    I. No drugs are exempted
    II. Acetaminophen effervescent tablets with 20% of the drug
    III. Aspirin effervescent tablets containing 15% of the drug

    A. I only
    B. III only
    C. I & II only
    D. II & III only
    E. I, II, & III

19. A pharmacy should limit interstate distribution of compounding prescription products to not more than _____% of the total prescriptions filled by the pharmacy.
    A. 2
    B. 5
    C. 10
    D. 15
    E. 20

20. Under which of the following conditions may practitioners of "Traditional Chinese Medicine" sell ephedra containing products?
    A. The level of ephedra is less than 2 mg per dose
    B. Only a 5-day supply of the product is sold
    C. The label does not indicate that the product is a dietary supplement
    D. A prescription is issued for the product
    E. Sales are illegal

21. How should sales of drug products covered by the Combat Methamphetamine Epidemic Act be recorded?
    A. Electronic tracking
    B. Doctor's prescription
    C. Bound log book
    D. Photocopy of purchaser's ID
    E. No record is required

22. The DEA registration form 363 is required from which of the following entities?
    A. Narcotic Treatment Programs
    B. Researchers
    C. Pharmacies
    D. Medical center
    E. Manufacturers

23. What is the main purpose of the Phase 3 clinical trial for a new drug?
    A. To evaluate the drug's safety on animals
    B. To determine adverse effects and dosage
    C. To determine the drug's effectiveness versus the effectiveness of the gold standard
    D. To determine whether the drug can be safely given to humans
    E. To assess the marketability of the drug

24. What is the term for a pharmaceutical agent that has been developed specifically to treat a rare medical condition?
    A. Orphan drug
    B. Targeted drug
    C. Type 3 drug
    D. Type N drug
    E. Subsidized drug

25. What is the correct order for the 3 segments of the NDC code?
    A. Package Segment, Labeler Code, Product Segment
    B. Product Segment, Labeler Code, Package Segment
    C. Labeler Code, Package Segment, Product Segment
    D. Package Segment, Product Segment, Labeler Code
    E. Labeler Code, Product Segment, Package Segment

26. A drug is found to be under-strength, although it is not used to treat a life-threatening disease. What type of recall will be required?
    A. Class I
    B. Class II
    C. Class III
    D. Class IV
    E. No recall is required

27. Failing to repay a student loan issued or guaranteed by the state or the federal government will result in which of the following?
    A. License suspension until proof of a satisfactory repayment has been submitted
    B. A fine equal to 15 percent of the student loan
    C. A fine equal to 15 percent of the defaulted loan
    D. Nothing, the board of pharmacy cannot take legal action
    E. A, B, C

28. For a drug to be considered Pharmaceutically Equivalent, all of the following must be true EXCEPT:
    A. Identical amounts of the same active ingredient
    B. Identical strength or concentration
    C. Same route of administration
    D. Same excipients
    E. Same dosage form

29. Which of the following would NOT be a privacy violation under HIPPA?
    I. Leaving an extensive message regarding a script with the patient's spouse
    II. Allowing a pharmaceutical sales rep to review the script files of only the patients who use the firm's products
    III. Mailing a script reminder to a patient in a sealed envelope

    A. I only
    B. III only
    C. I & II only
    D. II & III only
    E. I, II, & III

30. There is positive evidence that a new drug could create a risk to the human fetus based on investigational studies. However, the potential benefits of the drug may still justify use of the drug in pregnant women despite these possible risks. What pregnancy category would this drug be classified in?
    A. Category A
    B. Category B
    C. Category C
    D. Category D
    E. Category X

31. Heroin would be classified as which type of controlled substance?
    A. I
    B. II
    C. III
    D. IV
    E. V

32. Which of these would be classified as Schedule III controlled substances?
   I. Anabolic Steroids
   II. Marinol
   III. MS Contin

   A. I only
   B. III only
   C. I & II only
   D. II & III only
   E. I, II, & III

33. Schedule III, IV, and V controlled substance prescriptions may be transmitted to a community pharmacy by which of the following means?
   I. Written
   II. Oral
   III. Fax
   IV. Electronic

   A. I, II, III & IV
   B. I, II & III only
   C. I & II only
   D. I, III & IV only
   E. I only

34. A community pharmacist dispenses a partial supply of a C-II controlled substance. Within what period of time must the pharmacist dispense the balance, otherwise the balance may not be dispensed?
   A. 24 hours
   B. 48 hours
   C. 72 hours
   D. 7 days
   E. 14 days

35. A new community pharmacy must register itself with the DEA before it can order and dispense controlled substances. What form does such pharmacy use to initially register with DEA?
   A. DEA Form 41
   B. DEA Form 106
   C. DEA Form 222
   D. DEA Form 224
   E. No form will need to be filed

36. What form does a permitted pharmacy complete in order to destroy damaged, outdated or otherwise unwanted controlled substances?
   A. DEA Form 41
   B. DEA Form 106
   C. DEA Form 222

    D. DEA Form 224
    E. No form will need to be completed

37. Someone broke into your pharmacy but no medications were stolen. What form do you need to file when you discover that no CS drugs have been stolen?
    A. DEA Form 41
    B. DEA Form 106
    C. DEA Form 222
    D. DEA Form 224
    E. No form will need to be filed

38. Which about controlled substance medications is correct? Select all that apply.
    A. Partial refilling of CIII-V RXs is not permitted
    B. Pharmacies placing emergency kits containing CS medications in LTCFs are responsible for the proper control & accountability of such kits within the facility
    C. RXs for CIII-V drugs filled by central fill pharmacies for community pharmacies cannot be refilled
    D. Any community pharmacy that accepts electronic RXs written for CS medications must register as an online pharmacy
    E. Physicians are legally permitted to prescribe methadone (CII) for pain

39. A DEA registrant plans to transfer its business to another registrant. Within what period of time must DEA be notified?
    A. 5 days before the transfer
    B. 7 days before the transfer
    C. 10 days before the transfer
    D. 14 days before the transfer
    E. 30 days before the transfer

40. Which schedule of controlled substance medications must a community pharmacy keep in a locked cabinet?
    A. Schedule I only
    B. Schedule II only
    C. Schedule I & Schedule II drugs only
    D. Schedule II – Schedule V drugs
    E. None of the above, as federal law does not require controlled substances to be kept in locked cabinets

41. How can controlled substances prescription records at a community pharmacy without an electronic order processing system be stored?
    I. 2 Files: One file for all controlled substances & one file for all non-controlled drugs
    II. 3 Files: One file for all Schedule II controlled substances, one file for Schedule III-V controlled substances, & one file for all non-controlled drugs
    III. 2 Files: One file for all Schedule II controlled substances & one file for all other drugs (non-controlled & Schedule III-V)

A. I only
B. II only
C. III only
D. II & III only
E. I, II & III

42. Which of the following about inventory records of controlled substances is incorrect? Select all that apply.
    A. A pharmacy has complied with the CSA if it inventories a newly-scheduled or rescheduled drug within 30 days of the change
    B. Inventories for controlled substances must be completed biennially
    C. Exact counts must be made only in those instances where the container holds 1,000 or more tablets/capsules
    D. Inventory records of CII drugs must be kept separate from the inventory records of CIII-V drugs
    E. Record must be made of whether the inventory was conducted at the beginning or close of business

43. Copy 3 of DEA Form 222 stays in the custody of which entity?
    A. Supplier of the drug
    B. Pharmacy
    C. DEA
    D. Wholesale distributor
    E. Recipient of the drug

44. In states where nurse practitioners may prescribe controlled substances as mid-level practitioners. What letter will that number begin with?
    A. A
    B. B
    C. M
    D. N
    E. P

45. Facsimiles may serve as original prescriptions for Schedule II's for which of the following? Select all that apply.
    A. Any Schedule II substance for a hospice patient
    B. Schedule II narcotic substances compounded by a pharmacy for direct IV administration to a patient undergoing home infusion
    C. Any Schedule II medication for a patient residing in a long-term care facility
    D. Any Schedule II medication for patients of a community pharmacy
    E. Any Schedule II medication for patients of a community pharmacy in emergency situations

46. The Rx label for drugs in Schedule(s)_____ must contain the following warning: "CAUTION: Federal law prohibits the transfer of this drug to any person other than the patient for whom it was prescribed".
    A. I & II only

- B. II only
- C. II & III only
- D. II, III & IV only
- E. II, III, IV, & V only

47. A pharmacist may partially dispense prescriptions for Schedule II controlled substances for an individual residing in a LTCF who has been diagnosed with a terminal illness. How many days are the prescriptions valid for unless terminated earlier by discontinuance of the medication?
    - A. 7
    - B. 30
    - C. 60
    - D. 180
    - E. 365

48. On January 1, 2018, a pharmacist partially dispenses Synalgos-DC® with codeine. What is/was the last date the balance to be filled?
    - A. January 4, 2018
    - B. January 8, 2018
    - C. June 30, 2018
    - D. December 31, 2018
    - E. None of the above because a pharmacist, under federal law, cannot partially dispense drugs in this CSA Schedule

49. Which is correct about the over-the-counter sales of CV meds? Select all that apply.
    - A. Not more than 240 ml. (8 fluid ounces) of any substance containing opium may be distributed at retail to the same purchaser in any given 48-hour period without a valid RX
    - B. All purchasers must provide a valid photo ID, regardless of whether or not the pharmacist knows him/her
    - C. The purchaser must be at least 21 years' old
    - D. A student pharmacist under the direct supervision of a pharmacist is legally authorized to distribute such drugs
    - E. A pharmacy technician may ring up the sale for such drugs after the pharmacist has fulfilled all legal/professional responsibilities

50. How can a community pharmacy transmit controlled-substance prescription information to a central fill pharmacy?
    - I. A pharmacist in the community pharmacy may phone in a prescription for a controlled substance in Schedules II-V, provided that the oral order is given only to a pharmacist at the central fill pharmacy
    - II. A prescription for a controlled substance in Schedules II-V can be transmitted electronically by the community pharmacy to the central fill pharmacy
    - III. A facsimile of a prescription for a controlled substance in Schedules II-V may be provided by the community pharmacy to the central fill pharmacy

    - A. I only
    - B. II only

C. III only
   D. II & III only
   E. I, II & III

51. Dr. Brown is a practitioner & not registered as an opioid treatment program. Which is correct?
    A. Dr. Brown is strictly prohibited from prescribing methadone to her patient for this indication because she is not registered as an OTP
    B. Dr. Brown is permitted to administer up to a day's supply of the drug for this indication for up to 72 hours
    C. Dr. Brown is strictly prohibited from administering the drug to her patient for this indication, for any length of time, because she is not registered as an OTP
    D. A & B only
    E. A & C only

52. A pharmacy registered as a dispenser doesn't need to register as a distributor as long as it does not exceed what percent of controlled substances dispensed by the pharmacy in a calendar year?
    A. 5
    B. 10
    C. 20
    D. 25
    E. 50

53. Abuse of a what class of controlled substance medications may lead to moderate or low physical dependence or high psychological dependence?
    A. Schedule I
    B. Schedule II
    C. Schedule III
    D. Schedule IV
    E. Schedule V

54. For how long is a pharmacy's DEA registration effective?
    A. 6 months
    B. 1 year
    C. 2 years
    D. 3 years
    E. 5 years

55. Which statement about ordering &/or transferring Schedule II medications is correct?
    I. A pharmacy may transfer a bottle of a CII medication to another pharmacy, provided that the pharmacy transferring the drug properly executes a DEA form 222
    II. A pharmacy may purchase a bottle of a CII medication from a wholesale distributor, provided that the distributor properly executes a DEA form 222
    III. A pharmacy may order a bottle of a CII medication electronically, provided that the pharmacy signs an order form using a DEA-issued digital signature

    A. III only

B. I & II only
C. I & III only
D. II only
E. I, II & III

56. Which if the following is required under the Methamphetamine Production Prevention Act of 2005?
    A. Seller must require all purchasers of PSE to sign the sales logbook, either manually or electronically
    B. Seller must maintain each entry in the sales logbook for a minimum of 5 years
    C. All purchasers of PSE must present government issued photographic identification
    D. If the seller uses a bound paper sales logbook, he/she must affix a printed sticker next to the signature line that displays product name, quantity, name of purchaser, date & address, or a unique identification that can be linked to that information
    E. All of the above are required under MAPA

57. The drug products regulated by the federal Combat Methamphetamine Epidemic Act of 2005 are restricted to sale of what quantity (per patient) in one day?
    A. 1.2g
    B. 2.4g
    C. 3.6g
    D. 4.8g
    E. 6.0g

58. Which statement regarding multiple Schedule II prescriptions written on the same day for the same drug & patient is incorrect?
    A. Each RX must be dated on the day the prescription is to be dispensed.
    B. The prescriber must specifically indicate on each RX the earliest date on which each RX may be dispensed.
    C. The total quantity prescribed cannot exceed a 90-day supply.
    D. All of the above
    E. A & C only

59. Which statement about refill transfers of Schedules III through V controlled substances is correct?
    A. Transfers can only be done once if the pharmacies do not share a real-time online database
    B. All refills may be transferred electronically if the pharmacies share a real-time online database
    C. Transferring pharmacist must write "VOID" on the face of the transferred RX
    D. Transfer must occur between two pharmacists
    E. All of the above

60. If a pharmacy opts to print out a daily controlled substances refill record, how long must this record be maintained by the pharmacy?
   A. 6 months
   B. 1 year
   C. 2 years
   D. 3 years
   E. 5 years

61. What information must a controlled substance prescription contain?
   I. Patient name and address
   II. Practitioner's name, address, and DEA number
   III. Drug name and strength
   IV. Directions for use
   V. Date of issue

   A. I, II, III, IV & V
   B. I & II only
   C. I, II & IV only
   D. I, II & V only
   E. I, II, IV & V only

62. Which of the following is true about Risk Evaluation & Mitigation Strategies (REMS)?
   I. REMS are not required for generic products
   II. REMS only be required during the drug pre-approval process
   III. REMS can be required for a single drug or a class of drugs

   A. I only
   B. II only
   C. III only
   D. I & III only
   E. I, II & III

63. How can drug products be switched from prescription status to OTC status?
   I. Manufacturer submits a supplemental NDA
   II. Petition for reclassification is filed
   III. Via the OTC Review Process

   A. I only
   B. II only
   C. III only
   D. II & III only
   E. I, II & III

64. What is the name of the voluntary system for healthcare professionals to report ADRs to FDA?
   A. MEDMARX
   B. STEPS

C. MEDWATCH
D. VAERS
E. CLIA

65. Which of the following recalls is implemented in instances when a product is not likely to cause adverse health consequences?
    A. Class I
    B. Class II
    C. Class III
    D. Class IV
    E. Class V

66. Big Pharma, Inc. wants to change the salt of its existing blockbuster medication from acetate to carbonate. Through which mechanism is Big Pharma likely to proceed in order to gain FDA approval for this change?
    A. Full NDA
    B. 505(b)(2)
    C. ANDA
    D. IND
    E. Any of the above mechanisms are appropriate

67. From what potential violation of the FDCA does the IND provision provide an exemption?
    A. Adulteration
    B. Compounding
    C. Introduction into interstate commerce of an unapproved new drug
    D. Misbranding
    E. Current Good Manufacturing Practices

68. Mrs. Pill is a patient for whom child-resistant medication vial closures are inappropriate. Under the Poison Prevention Packaging Act, who may make a blanket request that all medications be dispensed in non-child resistant closures?
    A. The prescriber only
    B. The patient only
    C. The pharmacist only
    D. Either the prescriber or the patient only
    E. Either the prescriber or the pharmacist only

69. Two products are listed in the Orange Book. One product is rated as AB and the other is rated as AA. What can be concluded based on the Orange book about the equivalence of the two products?
    A. They are therapeutically equivalent
    B. They are bioequivalent
    C. They are rated as bioequivalent
    D. They are not rated as therapeutically equivalent
    E. They are not therapeutically equivalent

70. Which of the following levothyroxine 0.025 mg products are rated as equivalent to one another?
    A. Levothyroxine Sodium (Mylan) & Levothroid (Lloyd)
    B. Unithroid (Stevens J) & Levothroid (Lloyd)
    C. Synthroid (Abbott) & Levothroid (Lloyd)
    D. All of the above
    E. A & B only

71. In the package insert, there is a section that describes any situation in which the drug should not be used because the risk of use clearly outweighs the benefit. What is that section called?
    A. Warnings
    B. Precautions
    C. Prohibitions
    D. Contraindications
    E. Limitations

72. The federal agency that regulates the advertising of OTC drugs is:
    A. The Centers for Medicare and Medicaid Services (CMS)
    B. The Food and Drug administration (FDA)
    C. The Federal Trade Commission (FTC)
    D. The Drug Enforcement Agency (DEA)
    E. Center for Drug Evaluation and Research (CDER)

73. Prescription drug products containing estrogen must be dispensed with what?
    A. Package insert
    B. Patient package insert
    C. Medication guide
    D. REMS
    E. Pamphlet about the importance of routinely taking the drug written by the dispensing pharmacy

74. The term "label" refers to which of the following when it is accompanying an article of drug and is not upon the immediate container of drug?
    A. Written matter only
    B. Written or printed matter only
    C. Printed or graphic matter only
    D. Written or graphic matter only
    E. None of the above

75. Tamper-evident packaging refers to which of the following?
    A. Packaging that contains an indicator or barrier that if missing can reasonably be expected to alert the consumer to the possibility that tampering has occurred
    B. A permanent barrier to the product that only the consumer can remove after purchase
    C. A permanent barrier that the store removes before the consumer purchases
    D. An alarm that notifies the retailer that a product has been tampered with
    E. A statement on the outside of the package that alerts the consumer to the possibility of tampering

76. Which of the following drug(s) is/are exempt from poison prevention packaging? Select all that apply.
    A. Estrogen-containing oral contraceptives in memory-aid packaging
    B. Sublingual nitroglycerin
    C. Combination colestipol products
    D. Anhydrous cholestyramine in any form
    E. Bottles of prednisone in any size & strength

77. Which of the following laws required drug manufacturers to prove to FDA the effectiveness of their products before marketing them?
    A. Durham-Humphrey Amendment of 1951
    B. Kefauver-Harris Drug Amendments of 1962
    C. Drug Price Competition and Patent Term Restoration Act of 1984
    D. Food and Drug Administration Modernization Act of 1997
    E. Food and Drug Administration Amendments Act (FDAAA) of 2007

78. A generic manufacturer wishes to obtain approval of a product believed to be bioequivalent to the FDA-approved innovator product. Through what mechanism will the generic manufacturer most frequently obtain this approval?
    A. Supplemental NDA
    B. Abbreviated NDA
    C. Additional NDA
    D. Bioequivalency NDA
    E. Full NDA

79. Which of the following is a/are requirement(s) of the Compounding Quality Act law?
    A. Compounded medications must be for an identified individual patient on receipt of a valid RX.
    B. Compounding in advance of an RX is allowed, but in "limited quantities," based on historical RX orders.
    C. Drugs removed or withdrawn from the market because they are unsafe or not effective may not be used in compounding.
    D. Generally, a compounded drug may not be "essentially a copy" of an FDA-approved drug, unless the alteration to that copied product produces a significant difference for the patient.
    E. All of the above

80. According to the Health Insurance Portability and Accountability Act (HIPAA), under which situation should the pharmacist generally provide only the "minimum necessary" information about a particular patient? Select all that apply.
    A. When responding to a prescriber's request to discuss the treatment of the patient
    B. When advising the patient about the use of her medications
    C. When communicating with a PBM about potential coverage for a drug a physician has prescribed for the patient
    D. When speaking with a software vendor about a glitch in the patient's electronic medical record

E. When meeting with the pharmacy's attorneys about an RX that was filled incorrectly, causing injury to the patient

81. Which device requires FDA pre-market approval?
    A. Replacement heart valve
    B. Crutch
    C. Liquid bandage
    D. Tongue depressor
    E. Oxygen mask

82. A drug is misbranded if:
    A. Its labeling is false or misleading.
    B. It is manufactured by a drug company not registered with the FDA.
    C. Its manufacturer fails to comply with a REMS requirement.
    D. It is a compounded drug, & the advertising or promotion of it is false or misleading.
    E. All of the above

83. A manufacturer of a nutritional shake decides to add calcium to its product. Which of the following statements can the manufacturer make in the product's labeling and still have it considered a dietary supplement and not a drug?
    A. "Treats osteoporosis"
    B. "You'll feel great"
    C. "Cures the common cold"
    D. "Prevents colorectal cancer"
    E. "Mitigates the incidence of obesity"

84. The *primary* purpose of a Phase 2 clinical trial is to determine:
    A. Safety
    B. Efficacy
    C. Toxicity
    D. Compatibility with other drugs
    E. Cost

85. How many refills may a practitioner authorize on a Schedule II controlled substance prescription?
    A. 0
    B. 1
    C. 2
    D. 5
    E. 12

86. What does federal law say about e-prescribing controlled substances?
    A. Partial fills of e-prescriptions for Schedule II controlled substances are NOT allowed
    B. An office manager can act as a proxy and electronically sign e-prescriptions for a prescriber
    C. E-prescriptions must be maintained electronically for five years
    D. Refills are not allowed for Schedule III controlled substance e-prescriptions
    E. E-prescriptions must be maintained electronically for two years

87. Which is an acceptable Schedule II prescription according to federal law?
    A. A faxed prescription for fentanyl patch 100 mg, one every 3 days, #10 for a patient in hospice
    B. A written prescription for morphine 10 mg, one every 8 hours PRN pain, #60 with 1 refill
    C. A written prescription filled out and signed by a registered nurse for morphine 60 mg, one daily, #30
    D. A phoned in prescription for oxycodone 20 mg, one BID, #60 to be delivered to a homebound patient
    E. A faxed prescription for fentanyl patch 100 mg, one every 3 days, #5

88. What does federal law mandate for multiple prescriptions for Schedule II controlled substances?
    A. There is a limit of 3 prescriptions that can be written on the same day for the same Schedule II controlled substance for a single patient
    B. The date on the prescription should be the same day that they are written and cannot be post-dated
    C. They can total no more than a 90-day supply
    D. They can total no more than a 120-day supply
    E. They must all be filled on the same day they are dropped off at the pharmacy

89. What could you share with a colleague regarding partial fills of Schedule II controlled substances according to federal law?
    A. You are not required to notify the prescriber if you fill the remaining quantity on a partially filled prescription within 7 days
    B. They're allowed only for patients in long-term care facilities
    C. You don't need to document the amount dispensed when you are planning on dispensing the remainder within 72 hours
    D. If you do not dispense the remaining quantity within 72 hours, it will be voided
    E. If you do not dispense the remaining quantity within 24 hours, it will be voided

90. What is a requirement for filling prescriptions for methadone or buprenorphine according to federal law?
    A. A valid prescription for buprenorphine for treating pain requires a valid DEA number only
    B. Naloxone can only be dispensed by a retail pharmacy for the treatment of opioid dependence
    C. Prescribers must obtain a waiver to use buprenorphine for the treatment of pain
    D. Methadone can only be dispensed by a retail pharmacy for the treatment of opioid dependence
    E. When methadone is used for opioid dependence the prescription only needs to include a DEA number

91. Which is a federal rule regarding inventory requirements for Schedule II through V drugs?
    A. You need to get an exact count of the number of units of each Schedule III and IV drug in your facility
    B. A full inventory of Schedule II through V drugs must be performed at least every year
    C. Inventory forms can be kept outside the pharmacy as long as they are readily retrievable

D. A drug changing from Schedule III to II can be inventoried per its new schedule when the next inventory is due
E. A full inventory of Schedule II through V drugs must be performed at least every six months

92. According to FEDERAL law, which is an acceptable form of ID for an adult over 18 years old purchasing a pseudoephedrine product without a prescription?
   A. Social Security card
   B. Birth certificate
   C. U.S. military card
   D. Credit card
   E. ATM Debit card

93. What is a quantity limit imposed by the CMEA?
   A. You cannot sell more than 3.6 g per day of pseudoephedrine HCl to a customer
   B. You cannot sell a customer more than 9 g of pseudoephedrine base per day
   C. You can sell a patient any amount of pseudoephedrine liquid since it is extremely dilute
   D. Non-liquid forms of pseudoephedrine must be sold in blister packs or unit-dose packaging
   E. You cannot sell a customer more than 7.5 g of pseudoephedrine base per day

94. What information can you share with a new employee about DEA Form 222?
   A. It's the form to use when ordering Schedule III controlled substances
   B. If an erasure is made while filling out the form, it will not be accepted by the supplier
   C. Any person employed by the pharmacy can sign Form 222
   D. Your wholesaler must provide the exact package size you specify on Form 222
   E. Your supplier must provide the exact package size you specify on Form 222

95. What should you do in order to comply with DEA 106 procedures?
   A. You must notify the DEA of any theft of controlled substances within one business day of discovery
   B. Your pharmacy is responsible for notifying the DEA of the loss of controlled substances if your receipt from your distributor doesn't match what you received from them
   C. A significant loss is when you lose more than 40% of the total amount of any single controlled substance
   D. A significant loss is when you lose more than 20% of the total amount of any single controlled substance
   E. You need to complete DEA Form 106 right away when you discover missing controlled substances

96. What can you tell a colleague about exclusivity rights?
   A. They give the brand-name drug company property rights to the new drug
   B. Pediatric exclusivity adds an extra 6 months to the life of a patent
   C. Orphan drug exclusivity gives 5-years market exclusivity
   D. Pediatric exclusivity adds an extra 12 months to the life of a patent
   E. They give the brand-name drug manufacturer marketing rights for an unlimited time

97. What does the first manufacturer to successfully bring a generic drug to market gain?
    A. Nothing more than other manufacturers
    B. Significant market share
    C. 30-day generic exclusivity
    D. 180-day generic drug exclusivity
    E. 240-day generic drug exclusivity

98. In order to be approved for marketing, a generic drug must meet ALL of which criteria?
    A. The same rate and extent of absorption
    B. The same strength or concentration, route of administration, and dosage form
    C. The same rate and extent of absorption AND the same strength, route of administration, and dosage form
    D. The same strength, route of administration, and dosage form, AND inactive ingredients
    E. None

99. How much variability in drug levels does FDA allow between brand name products and their generic counterparts?
    A. The same as the variability between different batches of the brand-name drug
    B. 12.5%
    C. 25%
    D. 45%
    E. 23%

100. Which is an accurate description of the Orange Book coding system?
    A. The first letter of the Orange Book code determines the dosage form of the drug
    B. AB2 codes identify drugs that are not FDA-approved
    C. Drug products designated with a "T" code are therapeutically equivalent
    D. BD codes represent drug products that are not therapeutic equivalents
    E. DB codes represent drug products that are not therapeutic equivalents

101. Which is an accurate description of biosimilars?
    A. Biosimilars are true generics to a parent biological product
    B. It is possible for biosimilar products to also be classified as interchangeable
    C. Biosimilar products are listed in FDA's Orange Book
    D. Biosimilar products are listed in FDA's Green Book
    E. Differences in clinically inactive components are not allowable in biosimilar products

102. When can FDA require REMS for a specific drug?
    A. At any time, pre- or post-approval
    B. Only prior to marketing
    C. Only after marketing
    D. Only after marketing based on post-marketing surveillance
    E. If there is a large number of minor side effects

103. Which of the following is an Element to Assure Safe Use (ETASU)?
    A. A Dear Healthcare Provider Letter

B. A REMS advertisement in a major journal
   C. A MedGuide
   D. A Patient Registry
   E. A DrugGuide

104. Which of the following is a part of the long-acting and extended-release opioid REMS?
   A. A mandatory education program for pharmacists
   B. A volunteer education program for prescribers
   C. An implementation system
   D. A volunteer education program for pharmacists
   E. A mandatory education program for prescribers

105. What is required by federal law when logging methamphetamine precursor sales?
   A. You must make sure that the patient name matches their identification
   B. You always have to enter the patient's name and address
   C. You must keep the logbook for at least 7 years
   D. You have to keep a hardcopy logbook
   E. You must keep the logbook for at least 10 years

106. Which is an accurate limit on precursor sales imposed by the CMEA?
   A. You cannot sell more than 3.6 g of pseudoephedrine sulfate to a customer per day
   B. You cannot sell more than 9 g of pseudoephedrine sulfate to a customer in a 90-day period
   C. You cannot sell more than 146 tablets of pseudoephedrine HCL 30 mg in a single day to the same customer
   D. Non-liquid dosage forms of methamphetamine precursors can be sold as loose capsules or tablets
   E. You cannot sell more than 9 g of pseudoephedrine chloride to a customer in a 90-day period

107. Which transaction can be completed based on federal precursor drug sales limits?
   A. 830 mL of pseudoephedrine HCl 30 mg/5 mL syrup per customer per day
   B. 30 tablets of pseudoephedrine HCl 120 mg per customer per day
   C. 155 tablets of pseudoephedrine sulfate 60 mg per customer per day
   D. 90 tablets of pseudoephedrine sulfate 240 mg to a customer in 30 days
   E. 120 tablets of pseudoephedrine sulfate 240 mg to a customer in 30 days

108. What can happen if CMEA rules are violated?
   A. Financial penalties for failing to comply with CMEA requirements can be up to $500
   B. Imprisonment up to 1 year if the violation is committed unknowingly
   C. You can be imprisoned for up to 10 years for knowingly violating CMEA
   D. Your pharmacy may no longer be able to sell precursor drugs
   E. Imprisonment up to 2 years if the violation is committed unknowingly

109. What is important to know about the Drug Quality and Security Act?
   A. Large scale compounding ("outsourcing") is regulated by the FDA
   B. All compounding is regulated by the FDA

C. Only sterile compounding is regulated by the FDA
D. Only non-sterile compounding is regulated by the FDA
E. Small scale compounding ("insourcing") is regulated by the FDA

110. Why can't you fill a prescription for Effexor XR capsules with venlafaxine extended-release tablets?
   A. The tablets are less effective than capsules
   B. The tablets are not as safe as the capsules
   C. The tablets are dosed differently than the capsules
   D. The tablets are not AB-rated to the capsules
   E. The capsules are less effective than tablets

111. What is important to know about the DEA requirements for suspected theft of controlled substances?
   A. You only need to report this if more than five tablets are stolen
   B. You have to report this in writing to the DEA within one business day
   C. DEA Form 106 must be submitted the very same day of discovery
   D. You have to complete a DEA Form 106 EVEN IF the investigation reveals no actual loss or theft
   E. You only need to report this if more than ten tablets are stolen

112. What's important for a pharmacist to know to prevent misbranding and adulteration?
   A. Dispensing a drug stored at room temperature when it's supposed to be refrigerated is considered adulteration
   B. You can re-use returned medications as long as it's been less than 24 hours since you dispensed them
   C. Manufacturers are responsible for providing MedGuides, not pharmacists
   D. Dispensing a light-sensitive drug in a light-resistant container is considered misbranding
   E. Dispensing a scent-sensitive drug in a scent-resistant container is considered misbranding

113. If receiving multiple schedule II prescriptions, what is the maximum day limit for the prescriptions?
   A. 30 days
   B. 60 days
   C. 90 days
   D. 120 days
   E. 160 days

114. The DEA registration form 363 is required from which of the following entities?
   A. Manufacturers
   B. Medical center
   C. Pharmacies
   D. Researchers
   E. Narcotic Treatment Programs

115. Whenever a prescription department of any community pharmacy establishment is closed, who is permitted to enter or remain in the prescription department?
   I. A pharmacy intern
   II. A pharmacy owner
   III. A pharmacist

   A. I only
   B. III only
   C. I, II, and III
   D. II and III
   E. None of the above

116. In IL, the pharmacy technicians are required to be:
   I. Registered
   II. Certified
   III. Licensed

   A. I only
   B. II and III
   C. I and II
   D. I, II, and III
   E. None of the above

117. Sally is upset that her pain medications are not working. She would like to return her controlled substance prescription medication to the pharmacy. What can you do?
   A. Accept the return of unused or unwanted controlled substance medication as long as you are DEA authorized
   B. Give to your pharmacy owner and fill out DEA form 363
   C. Instruct Sally to dispose of her medications with DEA approval
   D. Only return if Sally's medication has a known recall
   E. If you made a dispensing error, you must accept Sally's medication return and refund her money

118. Which of the following references is/are useful for the safe handling of antineoplastic and hazardous drugs?
   I. OSHA Technical Manual—Section VI
   II. NIOSH Alert
   III. MSDSs

   A. I only
   B. I and II only
   C. II and III only
   D. All
   E. None of the above

119. Which of the following is/are TRUE ABOUT preparing allergen extracts as compounded sterile preparations?
   I. All allergen extracts as CSPs shall contain appropriate substances in effective concentrations to prevent the growth of microorganisms.
   II. Before beginning compounding activities, personnel perform a thorough hand-cleansing procedure by removing debris from under fingernails using a nail cleaner under running warm water followed by vigorous hand and arm washing to the elbows for at least 30 seconds with either non-antimicrobial or antimicrobial soap and water.
   III. Compounding personnel don hair covers, facial hair covers, gowns, and face masks.

   A. I only
   B. I and II only
   C. II and III only
   D. All
   E. None of the above

120. Section 503B of the Federal Food, Drug, and Cosmetic Act addresses which of the following?
   A. Traditional Compounders
   B. Outsourcing Facilities
   C. Compounding pharmacies
   D. Compounding nuclear pharmacies
   E. None of the above

121. Which of the following information is/are TRUE ABOUT PPE (Personal Protective Equipment) while reconstituting, preparing or admixing hazardous drugs?
   I. Make sure that gloves are labelled as chemotherapy [ASTM 2005] gloves
   II. Use double gloving for all activities involving hazardous drugs
   III. Use disposable gowns made of polyethylene-non-coated polypropylene

   A. I only
   B. I and II only
   C. II and III only
   D. All
   E. None of the above

Answers to Federal Pharmacy Law Exam

1. **D**
   Please view 42 CFR 8.12 - Federal opioid treatment standards.

2. **B**
   The Federal Food, Drug, and Cosmetic (FDC) Act of 1938 is passed by Congress, containing new provisions:
   - Extending control to cosmetics and therapeutic devices.
   - Requiring new drugs to be shown safe before marketing-starting a new system of drug regulation.
   - Eliminating the Shirley Amendment requirement to prove intent to defraud in drug misbranding cases.
   - Providing that safe tolerances be set for unavoidable poisonous substances.
   - Authorizing standards of identity, quality, and fill-of-container for foods.
   - Authorizing factory inspections.
   - Adding the remedy of court injunctions to the previous penalties of seizures and prosecutions.

3. **A**
   The key to this question is the word "first". The original Pure Food and Drugs Act (by Dr. Wiley) is passed by Congress on June 30, 1906 and signed by President Theodore Roosevelt. It prohibits interstate commerce in misbranded and adulterated foods, drinks and drugs.

4. **D**
   View http://www.deadiversion.usdoj.gov/schedules/. Substances in this schedule have a high potential for abuse which may lead to severe psychological or physical dependence.
   - While secobarbital capsule is C-II, secobarbital suppository is C-III (Remember that multiple DEA Schedules exist based on differences in the route, form, or strength of the substances).
   - Examples of Schedule II narcotics include: hydromorphone (Dilaudid®), methadone (Dolophine®), meperidine (Demerol®), oxycodone (OxyContin®, Percocet®), and fentanyl (Sublimaze®, Duragesic®). Other Schedule II narcotics include: morphine, opium, codeine, and hydrocodone.
   - Examples of Schedule II narcotic stimulants include: amphetamine (Dexedrine®, Adderall®), methamphetamine (Desoxyn®), and methylphenidate (Ritalin®).
   - Other Schedule II substances include: amobarbital, glutethimide, and pentobarbital.

5. **C**
   Morphine and meperidine are schedule II drugs. Diazepam is a schedule IV drug. Only schedule I & II drugs need a DEA form 222 to order.

6. **A**
   Based off the IL laws: http://www.ilga.gov/legislation/ilcs/ilcs5.asp?ActID=1941&ChapterID=53.

For choice I., "Not more than 1.8 grams of codeine per 100 milliliters or not more than 90 milligrams per dosage unit, with an equal or greater quantity of an isoquinoline alkaloid of opium."

For choice II., "Not more than 300 milligrams of hydrocodone per 100 milliliters or not more than 15 milligrams per dosage unit, with a fourfold or greater quantity of an isoquinoline alkaloid of opium." "Not more than 300 milligrams of hydrocodone per 100 milliliters or not more than 15 milligrams per dosage unit, with recognized therapeutic amounts of one or more active ingredients that are not controlled substances." **Note:** Hydrocodone has been reclassified as a C-II drug, a drug that contains any amount of hydrocodone will most likely be considered as C-II.

For Choice III., "Not more than 2.5 milligrams of diphenoxylate and not less than 25 micrograms of atropine sulfate per dosage unit."

7. **D**

Adulteration is reducing the purity of a drug/product by adding a foreign or inferior substance to it or even removing a valuable ingredient. So this could be a difference in strength, quality, or purity from what it was supposed to be or contains harmful or dirty/decomposed substances. Examples include making a drug in a place that results in adulteration, container system (bottle) could cause adulteration (if bottle is opened), strength/quality differs from claim on label, etc.

Misbranding- Presence or absence of information on label of a product which is false, deceptive or misleading. Examples of this would be filling for Crestor but putting Lipitor in the bottle. Lots of examples of this pertains to the label itself (false claims of where product came from or where it was made, size of type is not accordance to standards, wrong name of drug, lack of directions or warnings, medguide wasn't provided when it was supposed to, etc).

A. is considered misbranding
B. is considered misbranding
This is considered misbranding since the bottle is labeled to have 40 but actually contains 35
C. is considered misbranding
D. is considered adulterated. This is considered adulterated as the actual ingredient is inferior to what it is supposed to be
E. is considered misbranding, view **21 U.S. Code § 353**

8. **A**

View Title 21 CFR. PART 1306 — PRESCRIPTIONS. CONTROLLED SUBSTANCES LISTED IN SCHEDULE II. Section 1306.13 Partial filling of prescriptions for exceptions in specific cases.

Prescriptions for schedule II controlled substances cannot be refilled unless noted above in C21 Section 1306.13. A new prescription must be issued. Prescriptions for schedules III and IV controlled substances may be refilled up to five times in six months. Prescriptions for schedule V controlled substances may be refilled as authorized by the practitioner. Concerta and Alfenta are schedule II substances; Valium is a schedule IV substance. List of scheduled medications:
http://www.deadiversion.usdoj.gov/schedules/orangebook/c_cs_alpha.pdf

9. **C**

Part D sponsors that use a classification system that is consistent with the United States Pharmacopeia (USP), will qualify for a safe harbor, meaning that Centers for Medicare and Medicaid (CMS) will approve their formulary classification system.

Medicare drug plans cover both generic and brand-name drugs. Each plan has a list of drugs it covers, called a formulary. This list must always meet Medicare's minimum requirements (for example, plans are required to include at least 2 drug options in each drug category), but it is not required to include all prescription drugs. Medicare may allow plans to change their formularies during the year.

Two examples are: 1. If a new generic version of a covered brand-name drug becomes available, or 2. If new FDA or clinical information shows a drug to be unsafe.

Health plans cannot discontinue or reduce the coverage of a drug you are currently taking. If a formulary change is made that affects you, the plan must let you know at least 60 days before the change takes place. View: https://www.cms.gov/Medicare/Prescription-Drug-Coverage/PrescriptionDrugCovContra/downloads/chapter6.pdf

10. **B**

Drug utilization review (DUR) is an authorized, structured, ongoing review of prescribing, dispensing and use of medication. DUR entails a drug review against criteria that results in changes to drug therapy when these criteria are not met. It involves a comprehensive review of patients' prescription and medication data before, during and after dispensing to ensure appropriate medication decision-making and positive patient outcomes. As a quality assurance measure, DUR programs provide corrective action, prescriber feedback and further evaluations. Types of DUR:
- Prospective - evaluation of a patient's drug therapy before medication is dispensed
- Concurrent - ongoing monitoring of drug therapy during the course of treatment
- Retrospective - review of drug therapy after the patient has received the medication

11. **C**

View Title 21 CFR §1304.11 Inventory requirements- extract below

General requirements. Each inventory shall contain a complete and accurate record of **all controlled substances on hand on the date the inventory is taken**, and shall be maintained in written, typewritten, or printed form at the registered location. An inventory taken by use of an oral recording device must be promptly transcribed. **Controlled substances shall be deemed to be "on hand" if they are in the possession of or under the control of the registrant, including substances returned by a customer, ordered by a customer but not yet invoiced**, stored in a warehouse on behalf of the registrant, and substances in the possession of employees of the registrant and intended for distribution as complimentary samples. Section can be viewed here: https://www.deadiversion.usdoj.gov/21cfr/cfr/1304/1304_11.htm

12. **A**
You can enroll in Medicare Part D coverage during your Initial Enrollment Period (IEP) for Part D, which is the period that you first become eligible for Medicare Part D. For most people, the IEP begins <u>three months before you turn 65 years of age, includes the month you turn 65, and ends three months after</u>. Thus, in this question three months before May is February and three months after is August.

If you enroll in Medicare Part D during your Initial Enrollment Period, your Medicare Part D coverage will begin on the first day of the following month that you apply for the plan. If you enroll in one of the three months prior to turning 65 years of age, your Medicare Part D coverage begins on the first day of the month that you turn 65.

If you do not enroll during your Initial Enrollment Period for Part D, you can enroll into prescription drug coverage during the Annual Election Period (AEP), which occurs from October 15 to December 7 of every year. During this time, you have the chance to make changes to your current Medicare prescription drug coverage for the following year, including:
- Enrolling into a Medicare Prescription Drug Plan.
- Switching from one Medicare Prescription Drug Plan to another Prescription Drug Plan.
- Switching from a Medicare Advantage plan that does not include drug coverage to a Medicare Advantage plan that does, and vice versa.
- Dropping your Medicare prescription drug coverage entirely.

View: https://www.ehealthmedicare.com/medicare-part-d-prescription/enrollment/

13. **A, E**
The FDA considers drug products pharmaceutical equivalents if they contain the same active ingredient(s), are of the same dosage form and route of administration, and are identical in strength or concentration. Bioequivalent products are products with comparable bioavailability (rate and extent of absorption) when studied under similar experimental conditions.

Drug products must demonstrate pharmaceutical equivalence and bioequivalence to be considered A-rated (therapeutic equivalents). The primary reference for therapeutic equivalence is the FDA's Approved Drug Products with Therapeutic Equivalence Evaluations, commonly known as The Orange Book. It's available as a searchable database: http://www.fda.gov/cder/ob/default.htm.

The Orange Book rates each generic with a code. This "code" has two letters and it usually begins with an "A" or a "B" (e.g., **A**B-rated, **B**N-rated, etc). The <u>first</u> letter "A" designates products that have demonstrated therapeutic equivalence. The <u>first</u> letter "B" indicates those that have **not**. The <u>second</u> letter in the Orange Book rating code can give additional information about the product, such as its dosage form. For example, the <u>second</u> letter "A" indicates an oral dosage form, "N" indicates a product for aerosolization, "P" means a parenteral or injectable product, and "T" stands for topical. Products that have been studied and proven to be bioequivalent are AB-rated, which is the most common code you will see. In some states, only products given an "A" rating (e.g., AB-rated, AT-rated, AP-rated, etc) in the Orange Book can be substituted. View this link for more info: http://www.fda.gov/Drugs/InformationOnDrugs/ucm537866.htm

14. **A**
A valid DEA number consists of:
- 2 letters, 6 numbers, & 1 check digit
- The first letter is a code identifying the type of registrant
- The second letter is the first letter of the registrant's last name, or "9" for registrants using a business address instead of name

A sum of the seven digits helps validate the DEA number:
- Add together the first, third and fifth digits
- Add together the second, fourth and sixth digits and multiply the sum by 2
    - Add both of these values together as the check sum
- The rightmost digit of the check sum (the digit in the ones place) is used as the check digit in the DEA number

Common first letter types:
- A – Deprecated (used by some older entities)
- B – Hospital/Clinic
- C – Practitioner
- D – Teaching Institution
- E – Manufacturer
- F – Distributor

15. **A, B, C**
The pure food and drug act was enacted in 1906 (not 1938), thus C is incorrect. Its main purpose was to ban foreign and interstate traffic in adulterated or mislabeled food and drug products, and required that active ingredients be placed on the label of a drug's packaging and that drugs could not fall below purity levels established by the USP or the National Formulary. B is incorrect as it includes "cosmetics" but this act was limited to food and drugs. Choice A is incorrect as the diethylene glycol (or sulfanilamide) deaths led to the passing of the 1938 Food, Drug, and Cosmetic Act as the 1906 act failed to protect the public so it was largely replaced by the 1938 act.

16. **A**
View Title 21 CFR Part 1308 Schedules,
https://www.deadiversion.usdoj.gov/21cfr/cfr/1308/1308_13.htm
C-III controlled substance: "Not more than 1.8 grams of codeine per 100 milliliters or not more than 90 milligrams per dosage unit, with an equal or greater quantity of an isoquinoline alkaloid of opium"

17. **A**
Laws governing physicians differ significantly from state to state. The State of Illinois prohibits self-prescribe or self-dispense controlled substances by a practitioner, including a physician, physician assistance, or advanced practice nurse. Additionally, a practitioner may not prescribe controlled substances to an immediate family member unless there is a bona fide practitioner-patient relationship and appropriate records are maintained. (Section 3100.380 controlled substance rules). However, on a federal level there is no guidance and most

states do not have a defined law regarding self-prescribing.

18. **B**

    View the Poison Prevention Packaging guidance from 2010- https://www.cpsc.gov/s3fs-public/384.pdf
    There are two exceptions to child-resistant packaging from the guidance above-
    1. Effervescent tablets or granules containing not more than 15 percent acetaminophen or aspirin, provided the dry tablet or granules have an oral LD50 of 5 grams or more per kilogram of body weight.
    2. Unflavored acetaminophen or aspirin- containing preparations in powder form (other than those intended for pediatric use) that are packaged in unit doses providing not more than 13 grains of acetaminophen or 15.4 grains of aspirin per unit dose.

19. **B**

    Under the Pharmacy Compounding of Human Drug Products Under Section 503A of the Federal Food, Drug, and Cosmetic Act it limits interstate distribution at a baseline of 5%.
    View:
    http://www.fda.gov/downloads/Drugs/GuidanceComplianceRegulatoryInformation/Guidances/UCM469119.pdf

20. **C**

    According to Section III B of the final rule, the FDA ban applies only to "dietary supplements containing ephedrine alkaloids, including, but not limited to, those from the botanical species *ephedra sinica* Stapf, *ephedra equisetina* Bunge, *ephedra intermedia* var. tibetica Stapf, *ehpedra distachya* L., *sida cordifolia* L. and *pinellia terneta* (Thunb.) Makino or their extracts." However, "conventional food products" that contain ephedrine alkaloids are exempted, as are "OTC (over-the-counter) or prescription drugs that contain ephedrine alkaloids."
    Section IIIB also includes a caveat for the use of ephedra as it applies to "traditional Asian medicine". This final rule does not affect the use of ephedra preparations in traditional Asian medicine. This rule applies only to products regulated as dietary supplements.

21. **C**

    Logbook Provisions
    View: https://www.deadiversion.usdoj.gov/meth/cma2005_general_info.pdf

22. **A**

    - DEA Form 224a – Retail Pharmacy, Hospital/Clinic, Practitioner, Teaching Institution, or Mid-Level Practitioner
    - DEA Form 225a – Manufacturer, Distributor, Researcher, Analytical Laboratory, Importer, Exporter
    - DEA Form 363a – Narcotic Treatment Programs
    - DEA Form 510a – Domestic Chemical

    View: https://www.deadiversion.usdoj.gov/drugreg/

23. **C**
    Phase 1
    Patients: 20 to 100 healthy volunteers or people with the disease/condition.
    Length of Study: Several months
    Purpose: Safety and dosage
    Approximately 70% of drugs move to the next phase

    Phase 2
    Patients: Up to several hundred people with the disease/condition.
    Length of Study: Several months to 2 years
    Purpose: Efficacy and side effects
    Approximately 33% of drugs move to the next phase

    Phase 3
    Patients: 300 to 3,000 volunteers who have the disease or condition
    Length of Study: 1 to 4 years
    Purpose: Efficacy and monitoring of adverse reactions
    Approximately 25-30% of drugs move to the next phase

    Phase 4
    Patients: Several thousand volunteers who have the disease/condition
    Purpose: Safety and efficacy
    Purpose of phase III trials: Efficacy and monitoring of adverse reactions
    View: http://www.fda.gov/ForPatients/Approvals/Drugs/ucm405622.htm

24. **A**
    An orphan drug is defined in the 1984 amendments of the U.S. Orphan Drug Act (ODA) as a drug intended to treat a condition affecting fewer than 200,000 persons in the United States (rare medical condition), or which will not be profitable within 7 years following approval by the FDA
    http://www.fda.gov/downloads/drugs/developmentapprovalprocess/smallbusinessassistance/ucm311928.pdf

25. **E**
    The 3 segments of the NDC identify the labeler, the product, and the commercial package size. The first set of numbers in the NDC identifies the labeler (manufacturer, repackager, or distributor). The second set of numbers is the product code, which identifies the specific strength, dosage form (i.e, capsule, tablet, liquid) and formulation of a drug for a specific manufacturer. Finally, the third set is the package code, which identifies package sizes and types. The labeler code is assigned by the FDA, while the product and package code are assigned by the labeler.
    View: https://www.drugs.com/ndc.html

26. **B**

    Class I - A reasonable probability exists that use of the product will cause or lead to serious adverse health events or death. An example of a product that could fall into this category is a label mix-up on a lifesaving drug.
    Class II - The probability exists that use of the product will cause adverse health events that are temporary or medically reversible. One example is a drug that is understrength but that is not used to treat life-threatening situations.
    Class III - The use of this product will probably not cause an adverse health event. Examples might be a container defect, off taste, or color in a liquid.
    View: http://www.careerstep.com/blog/pharmacy-technician-news/drug-recalls

27. **A**

    More information can be found under 20 ILCS 2105/2105-15
    http://www.ilga.gov/legislation/ilcs/ilcs5.asp?ActID=325&ChapterID=5

28. **D**

    Pharmaceutical Equivalents. Drug products are considered pharmaceutical equivalents if they contain the same active ingredient(s), are of the same dosage form, route of administration and are identical in strength or concentration (e.g., chlordiazepoxide hydrochloride, 5mg capsules). Pharmaceutically equivalent drug products are formulated to contain the same amount of active ingredient in the same dosage form and to meet the same or compendial or other applicable standards (i.e., strength, quality, purity, and identity), but they may differ in characteristics such as shape, scoring configuration, release mechanisms, packaging, **excipients** (including colors, flavors, preservatives), expiration time, and, within certain limits, labeling. View:
    http://www.fda.gov/ohrms/dockets/ac/05/briefing/2005-4137B1_07_Nomenclature.pdf

29. **B**

    The HIPAA guidelines don't tell you how to send your mail or what you have to do. It just must be done in a manner to protect confidentiality and make sure it securely gets to the person it was intended to get to.
    HIPAA violations come in two broad categories: negligent and intentional. Negligent violations can be as simple as faxing documents containing PHI to the wrong number in error, forgetting to log out of the electronic patient record, or in this case identifying a possible security flaw but not doing anything about it. Remember a violation does not have to be reported by someone to count. Just knowing there is a vulnerability of PHI being seen by someone else can get you in trouble. Also if you identify and document your changes in your risk assessment it will show you are proactive about security when you do get audited.
    View: http://mor-of.net/1604_CWirght_SimpleSeal_Envelopes_HIPAA.html

30. **D**

Category	Risk
Category A	The safest drugs to take during pregnancy. No known adverse reactions.
Category B	No risks have been found in humans.
Category C	Not enough research has been done to determine if these drugs are safe.
Category D	Adverse reactions have been found in humans.
Category X	Should never be used by a pregnant woman.

Note that FDA came out with new labeling requirements and the A, B, C, D, and X categories are replaced with the new format (below). Drugs approved after June 2015 will need to follow this format:

Pregnancy (includes Labor and Delivery):
- Pregnancy Exposure Registry
- Risk Summary
- Clinical Considerations
- Data

Lactation (includes Nursing Mothers)
- Risk Summary
- Clinical Considerations
- Data

Females and Males of Reproductive Potential
- Pregnancy Testing
- Contraception
- Infertility

View: https://www.drugs.com/pregnancy-categories.html

31. **A**

Schedule I drugs, substances, or chemicals are defined as drugs with no currently accepted medical use and a high potential for abuse. Some examples of Schedule I drugs are: heroin, lysergic acid diethylamide (LSD), marijuana (cannabis), 3,4-methylenedioxymethamphetamine (ecstasy), methaqualone, and peyote
View: https://www.dea.gov/druginfo/ds.shtml

32. **C**

Schedule III drugs, substances, or chemicals are defined as drugs with a moderate to low potential for physical and psychological dependence. Schedule III drugs abuse potential is less than Schedule I and Schedule II drugs but more than Schedule IV. Some examples of Schedule III drugs are: Products containing less than 90 milligrams of codeine per dosage unit (Tylenol with codeine), Marinol (dronabinol), ketamine, anabolic steroids, testosterone
View: https://www.dea.gov/druginfo/ds.shtml

33. **A**
A prescription for controlled substances in Schedules III, IV and V issued by a practitioner may be communicated either orally, in writing or by facsimile to the pharmacist and may be refilled if so authorized on the prescription. DEA published in the Federal Register an interim final rule that would allow electronic transmissions of prescriptions of controlled substances (CII-CV).
This rule gives prescribers the option of e-prescribing CS, permits pharmacies to receive, dispense & archive electronic RXs, reduces paperwork for DEA registrants, & potentially reduces RX forgeries. DEA believes this rule could reduce the number of RX errors caused by illegible handwriting, as well as the number of misunderstood orally ordered RXs.
http://www.deadiversion.usdoj.gov/ecomm/e_rx/thirdparty.htm

34. **C**
21 USC § 1306.13 Partial filling of prescriptions. (a) The partial filling of a prescription for a controlled substance listed in Schedule II is permissible, if the pharmacist is unable to supply the full quantity called for in a written or emergency oral prescription and he makes a notation of the quantity supplied on the face of the written prescription (or written record of the emergency oral prescription). The remaining portion of the prescription may be filled within 72 hours of the first partial filling; however, if the remaining portion is not or cannot be filled within the 72-hour period, the pharmacist shall so notify the prescribing individual practitioner. No further quantity may be supplied beyond 72 hours without a new prescription
http://www.deadiversion.usdoj.gov/21cfr/cfr/1306/1306_13.htm

35. **D**
DEA Form 224 - Retail Pharmacy, Hospital/Clinic, Practitioner, Teaching Institution, or Mid-Level Practitioner
DEA Form 225 – Manufacturer, Distributor, Researcher, Analytical Laboratory, Importer, Exporter.
DEA Form 363 – Narcotic Treatment Programs
DEA Form 510 – Domestic Chemical
http://www.deadiversion.usdoj.gov/online_forms_apps.html

36. **A**
§1307.21 Procedure for disposing of controlled substances.
http://www.gpo.gov/fdsys/pkg/CFR-2011-title21-vol9/pdf/CFR-2011-title21-vol9-part1307.pdf

37. **E**
http://www.deadiversion.usdoj.gov/pubs/manuals/pharm2/pharm_manual.htm

38. **B & E**
A pharmacist may partially dispense a prescription for schedules III-V controlled substances provided that each partial filling is recorded in the same manner as a refilling, the total quantity dispensed in all partial fillings does not exceed the total quantity prescribed, and no dispensing occurs beyond six months from the date on which the prescription was issued.

LTCFs do not need to register with DEA to house emergency kits containing CS so long as there are safeguards in place to minimize access to the drugs, and only limited amounts are provided. Records of placement of kits in DEA must be maintained & available for inspection.
http://www.deadiversion.usdoj.gov/pubs/manuals/pharm2/pharm_manual.pdf

39. **D**
Transfer of Business: A pharmacy registrant that transfers its business operations to another pharmacy registrant must submit in person or by registered or certified mail, return receipt requested, to the Special Agent in Charge in his/her area, at least <u>14 days</u> in advance of the date of the proposed transfer (unless the Special Agent in Charge waives this time limitation in individual instances), the following information:
    - The name, address, registration number, and authorized business activity of the registrant discontinuing the business (registrant-transferor);
    - The name, address, registration number, and authorized business activity of the person acquiring the business (registrant-transferee);
    - Whether the business activities will be continued at the location registered by the person discontinuing business, or moved to another location (if the latter, the address of the new location should be listed); and

http://www.deadiversion.usdoj.gov/pubs/manuals/pharm2/pharm_manual.pdf

40. **E**

	Schedule II	Schedules III & IV	Schedule V
Registration	Required	Required	Required
Receiving Records	DEA Form 222	Invoices, readily retrievable	Invoices, readily retrievable
Prescriptions	Written prescriptions	Written, oral, or fax	Written, oral, or fax
Refills	No	No more than 5 within 6 months	As authorized when prescription is issued or if renewed by a practitioner
Maintenance of Prescriptions	Separate file	Separate file or readily retrievable	Separate file or readily retrievable
Distribution Between Registrants	DEA Form 222	Invoices	Invoices
Security	Locked cabinet or dispersed among non-controlled pharmaceuticals	Locked cabinet or dispersed among non-controlled pharmaceuticals	Locked cabinet or dispersed among non-controlled pharmaceuticals

| Theft or Significant Loss | Report to DEA and complete DEA Form 106 | Report to DEA and complete DEA Form 106 | Report to DEA and complete DEA Form 106 |

All records must be maintained for 4 years, unless state law requires a longer period.
- Written prescriptions include paper prescriptions and electronic prescriptions that meet DEA's requirements for such prescriptions.
- Emergency prescriptions require a signed follow-up prescription within seven days. Exceptions: A facsimile prescription serves as the original prescription when issued to residents of Long Term Care Facilities, hospice patients, or patients with a diagnosed terminal illness, or for immediate administration
- The record of dispensing can also be a schedule V logbook, if state law allows.

http://www.deadiversion.usdoj.gov/pubs/manuals/pharm2/pharm_manual.pdf

41. **E**

View 20 CFR 1304.04, Maintenance of records and inventories, Section(h):
- "red ink in the lower right corner with the letter "C" ... and **filed either in the prescription file for controlled substances listed in Schedules I and II or in the usual consecutively numbered prescription file for non-controlled substances**. However, if a pharmacy employs a computer application for prescriptions that permits identification by prescription number and retrieval of original documents by prescriber name, patient's name, drug dispensed, and date filled, then the requirement to mark the hard copy prescription with a red "C" is waived.

http://www.deadiversion.usdoj.gov/21cfr/cfr/1304/1304_04.htm

42. **A & C**

The registrant is required to take a biennial inventory (every two years) of all controlled substances on hand. The biennial inventory may be taken on any date which is within two years of the previous inventory date. There is no requirement to submit a copy of the inventory to DEA.

[Pharmacies must make a] count of the substance - if the substance is listed in CII, an exact count or measure of the contents or if the substance is listed in C III-V, an estimated count or measure of the contents, unless the container holds more than 1,000 tablets or capsules in which case, an exact count of the contents is required.

When a drug not previously listed as a controlled substance is scheduled or a drug is rescheduled, the drug must be inventoried as of the effective date of scheduling or change in scheduling.

The CSA also requires that all inventory records be maintained at the registered location in a readily retrievable manner for at least two years for copying and inspection. In addition, the inventory records of schedule II controlled substances must be kept separate from all other controlled substances.

http://www.deadiversion.usdoj.gov/pubs/manuals/pharm2/pharm_manual.pdf

43. **E**

Only Schedule I & II controlled substances are ordered with a DEA Form-222. An Official Order Form is required for each distribution, purchase or transfer of a Schedule II controlled substance.

DEA Form 222 is in triplicate. The pharmacy (or recipient of the CII medications) keeps copy 3, and then sends copies 1 & 2 to the supplier. Once the supplier ships the medication to the pharmacy, it keeps copy 1 and <u>forwards copy 2 to the DEA</u>.

When ordering Schedule II substances, the pharmacist is responsible for filling in the number of packages, the size of the package and the name of the item.

Each Official Order Form must be signed and dated by a person authorized to sign a registration application. When the items are received, the pharmacist must document on the purchaser's copy (copy 3) the actual number of packages received and the date received.

http://ecfr.gpoaccess.gov/cgi/t/text/text-idx?c=ecfr&rgn=div6&view=text&node=21:9.0.1.1.6.2&idno=21

44. **C**

DEA is announcing that, effective immediately, DOD personal service contractors will be issued a new DEA registration number that begins with the letter "G". This new first character will be in addition to the current first characters A, B, F of the DEA registration for practitioners. The G series DEA registration number will be listed in the database provided to NTIS and available on the DEA website validation query system.

Registrant type (first letter of DEA Number):
- A/B/F/G – Hospital/Clinic/Practitioner/Teaching Institution/Pharmacy
- M – Mid-Level Practitioner (NP/PA/OD/ET, etc.)
- P/R – Manufacturer/Distributor/Researcher/Analytical Lab/Importer/Exporter/Reverse Distributor/Narcotic Treatment Program

http://www.deadiversion.usdoj.gov/drugreg/

Mid-level practitioners (MLP) are registered and authorized by the DEA and the state in which they practice to dispense, administer and prescribe controlled substances in the course of professional practice. Examples of MLPs include, but are not limited to, health care providers such as: Nurse practitioners, nurse midwives, nurse anesthetists, clinical nurse specialists, physician assistants, & optometrists

http://www.deadiversion.usdoj.gov/pubs/manuals/pharm2/pharm_manual.pdf

45. **B & C**

View CFR Title 21, Sec. 1306.11 Requirement of prescription.

http://www.accessdata.fda.gov/scripts/cdrh/cfdocs/cfcfr/CFRSearch.cfm?CFRPart=1305&showFR=1

http://www.deadiversion.usdoj.gov/pubs/manuals/pharm2/pharm_manual.pdf

46. **D**

View CFR, Sec. 290.5-

The label of any drug listed as a "controlled substance" in schedule II, III, or IV of the Federal Controlled Substances Act shall, when dispensed to or for a patient, contain the following warning: "Caution: Federal law prohibits the transfer of this drug to any person other than the patient for whom it was prescribed."
http://www.accessdata.fda.gov/scripts/cdrh/cfdocs/cfcfr/CFRSearch.cfm?CFRPart=290&showFR=1

47. **C**
An exception to the partial fill rule (i.e. balance must be filled within 72 hours) has been made for patients in Long Term Care Facilities (LTCF) and patients who have been diagnosed with a terminal illness.
A prescription for a schedule II controlled substance written for a patient in a [LTCF] or for a patient with a medical diagnosis documenting a terminal illness, may be filled in partial quantities to include individual dosage units... Both the pharmacist and the prescribing practitioner have a corresponding responsibility to assure that the controlled substance is for a terminally ill patient.
http://www.deadiversion.usdoj.gov/pubs/manuals/pharm2/pharm_manual.pdf

48. **C**
Synalgos-DC is listed as a Schedule III drug –
http://www.deadiversion.usdoj.gov/schedules/orangebook/e_cs_sched.pdf
The pharmacist may partially dispense a prescription for a Schedule III-V controlled substance if the pharmacist notes the quantity dispensed and initials the back of the prescription order. The partial dispensing may not exceed the total amount authorized in the prescription order. The dispensing of all partially-filled prescriptions and all refills must be within the six-month limit (for CIII & CIV drugs).
http://www.deadiversion.usdoj.gov/pubs/manuals/pharm2/pharm_manual.pdf

49. **A & E**
In states where limited quantities of Schedule V preparations may be sold over-the-counter, the pharmacist is responsible for making sure that such sales comply with state law.
http://www.deadiversion.usdoj.gov/pubs/manuals/pharm2/pharm_manual.pdf

50. **D**
A central fill pharmacy will not be permitted to prepare prescriptions provided directly by the patient or individual practitioner or to mail or otherwise deliver a filled prescription directly to a patient or individual practitioner. Community pharmacies are permitted to transmit prescription information to a central fill pharmacy in two ways.
First, a facsimile of a prescription for a controlled substance in Schedule II-V may be provided by the community pharmacy to the central fill pharmacy. The community pharmacy must maintain the original hard copy of the prescription and the central fill pharmacy must maintain the facsimile of the prescription.
http://www.deadiversion.usdoj.gov/pubs/manuals/pharm2/pharm_manual.pdf

51. **D**
A practitioner who wants to use Schedule II narcotic drugs for maintenance and/or detoxification must obtain separate registration from DEA as a narcotic treatment program pursuant to the Narcotic Addict Treatment Act of 1974. An **exception** to the registration requirement, known as the **"three day rule"** (Title 21, Code of Federal Regulations, Part 1306.07(b)), allows a practitioner who is not separately registered as a narcotic treatment program, to administer (but not prescribe) narcotic drugs to a patient for the purpose of relieving acute withdrawal symptoms while arranging for the patient's referral for treatment, under the following conditions:
Not more than one day's medication may be administered or given to a patient at one time;
This treatment may not be carried out for more than 72 hours and;
This 72-hour period cannot be renewed or extended.
http://www.deadiversion.usdoj.gov/drugreg/faq.htm

52. **A**
A pharmacy registered to dispense controlled substances may distribute such substances (without being registered as a distributor) to another pharmacy or to a registered practitioner for the purpose of general dispensing by the practitioner to patients, provided that the following conditions are met:
The pharmacy or practitioner that will receive the controlled substances is registered under the CSA to dispense controlled substances;
The distribution is recorded by the distributing practitioner and the receipt is recorded by the receiving practitioner
If the pharmacy distributes a schedule II controlled substance, it must document the transfer on an official order form (DEA Form 222) or the electronic equivalent
"Five Percent Rule" - total number of dosage units of all controlled substances distributed by a pharmacy may not exceed five percent of all controlled substances dispensed by the pharmacy during a calendar year. If at any time the controlled substances distributed exceed five percent, the pharmacy is required to register as a distributor.
http://www.deadiversion.usdoj.gov/pubs/manuals/pharm2/pharm_manual.pdf

53. **C**
View 21 USC § 812 (a):
Note that the schedules of controlled substances are based on the potential for abuse, the recognition of a medical use, and the possibility of physical or psychological dependence.
http://www.deadiversion.usdoj.gov/21cfr/21usc/812.htm

54. **D**
Under the CSA, only certain parties are permitted to possess controlled substances legally. These parties must be registered with the DEA, or they must be exempt from registration.
http://www.deadiversion.usdoj.gov/21cfr/21usc/822.htm

Note: A pharmacy registration must be renewed every three years utilizing DEA Form 224a
http://www.deadiversion.usdoj.gov/pubs/manuals/pharm2/pharm_manual.pdf

55. **A**

To order controlled substances in schedules III through V, no special order form is required. However, to order controlled substances in Schedules I or II, a special order form (dea form 222) must be used. Note that in transferring schedule II controlled substances from one registrant to another, it is necessary to use dea form 222. For example, if one pharmacy is temporarily out of a schedule II controlled substance, and another pharmacy agrees to transfer to that pharmacy one bottle of 100 tablets to "help out in a pinch," the receiving pharmacy must send its dea form 222 to the dispersing pharmacy. When the time comes to return the favor, the same process is followed. Be mindful of the 5 percent rule!

View 21 cfr § **1305.21** requirements for electronic orders.
http://www.deadiversion.usdoj.gov/21cfr/cfr/1305/1305_21.htm

56. **D**

The logbook must be maintained by the regulated seller for not fewer than two years after the date on which the entry is made (21 U.S.C. 830(e)(1)(A)(vi)).
http://www.deadiversion.usdoj.gov/fed_regs/rules/2011/fr1201.htm

57. **C**

The Combat Methamphetamine Epidemic Act of 2005 created a new category of products called "scheduled listed chemical product (SLCP)." It includes any product that may be marketed or distributed lawfully in the United States under the Federal Food, Drug, and Cosmetic Act as a nonprescription drug that contains ephedrine, pseudoephedrine, or PPA (includes salts, optical isomers, and salts of optical isomers) (21 U.S.C. § 802(45)).
http://www.deadiversion.usdoj.gov/pubs/manuals/pharm2/pharm_manual.pdf

58. **D**

The DEA does permit the issuance of multiple prescriptions on the same day, all dated on the date of issuance, with instructions to the pharmacist to dispense the medications at a future time.
View 21 CFR § 1306.12 Refilling Prescriptions; Issuance of Multiple Prescriptions
http://www.deadiversion.usdoj.gov/21cfr/cfr/1306/1306_12.htm

59. **E**

View Section 1306.25 Transfer between pharmacies of prescription information for Schedules III, IV, and V controlled substances for refill purposes.
http://www.deadiversion.usdoj.gov/21cfr/cfr/1306/1306_25.htm

60. **C**

Note: Federal law (2 years) vs. IL law (5 years) for recordkeeping of all controlled substance prescriptions, IL law is more stringent. Unless the MPJE specifically asks for federal law, you should always pick the more stringent law, which is 5 years.
***View 21 CFR § 1306.22* Refilling of prescriptions.**
http://www.deadiversion.usdoj.gov/21cfr/cfr/1306/1306_22.htm

61. **A**

A prescription is an order for medication which is dispensed to or for an ultimate user. A prescription is not an order for medication which is dispensed for immediate administration to the ultimate user (for example, an order to dispense a drug to an inpatient for immediate administration in a hospital is not a prescription).

The practitioner is responsible for ensuring that the prescription conforms to all requirements of the law and regulations, both federal and state.
http://www.deadiversion.usdoj.gov/pubs/manuals/pract/section5.htm

62. **C**

REMS are required risk management plans that use risk minimization strategies beyond the professional labeling to ensure that the benefits of certain prescription drugs outweigh their risks. http://www.fda.gov/downloads/AboutFDA/Transparency/Basics/UCM328784.pdf

63. **E**

Ways in which a drug may be switched to OTC from prescription:
- The manufacturer may request the switch by submitting a supplemental application to its approved NDA (i.e. SNDA)
- The manufacturer may petition the FDA
- The drug may be switched through the OTC drug review process. Generally applies to all manufacturers' products at the same time

http://www.fda.gov/Drugs/DevelopmentApprovalProcess/SmallBusinessAssistance/ucm069917.htm

64. **C**

MedWatch, the FDA's safety information and adverse event reporting program, plays a critical role in the agency's post-marketing surveillance--the process of following the safety profile of medical products after they've begun to be used by consumers.
Through MedWatch, a voluntary program, health professionals report adverse reactions, product problems, and use errors related to drugs, biologics, medical devices, dietary supplements, cosmetics, and infant formulas.

65. **C**

FDA classification of recalls.
- A Class I recall applies when there is a reasonable probability that the product will cause serious adverse health consequences or death.
- A Class II recall applies when the product may cause temporary or medically reversible adverse health consequences, but the probability of serious adverse consequences is remote.
- A Class III recall applies when a product is not likely to cause adverse health consequences.

http://www.fda.gov/Safety/Recalls/ucm165546.htm

66. **B**
    View 21 U.S. Code § 355 - New drugs at http://www.law.cornell.edu/uscode/text/21/355
    http://www.fda.gov/downloads/Drugs/Guidances/ucm079345.pdf

67. **C**
    Before a drug can be shown to be safe and effective, it is necessary to study the drug in clinical trials.
    These trials occur throughout the country; thus it is necessary to place the as yet unapproved new drug into interstate commerce so that the drug can be provided to those who will use it for clinical trials.
    If there were no exemption from the FDCA provisions that prevent the introduction into interstate commerce of an unapproved new drug, then clinical trials could not occur. Thus, an exemption has been provided through the IND (Investigational New Drug) provisions of the Act.

68. **B**
    A physician may request that a prescribed medication not be dispensed in child-resistant closures, & this request will be honored as long as it is made for each prescription to which it applies (i.e., no "blanket requests"). However, patients may request that all dispensed drugs not be placed in child-resistant containers.
    http://www.cpsc.gov//PageFiles/113945/384.pdf

69. **C**
    Orange Book – Terminology
    Bioequivalence
    - Products display comparable bioavailability

    Pharmaceutical equivalents (PEs)
    - Products that contain same active ingredients, identical in strength and same dosage form

    Therapeutic equivalents (TEs)
    - PEs that can be expected to have the same clinical effect and safety

    http://www.fda.gov/Drugs/DevelopmentApprovalProcess/ucm079068.htm

70. **A**
    Levothyroxine Sodium. Because there is <u>multiple reference listed drugs</u> of levothyroxine sodium tablets and some reference listed drugs' sponsors have conducted studies to establish their drugs' therapeutic equivalence to other reference listed drugs, FDA has determined that its usual practice of assigning two or three character TE codes may be potentially confusing and inadequate for these drug products.
    See http://www.fda.gov/Drugs/DevelopmentApprovalProcess/ucm079068.htm

71. **D**
    View 21 CFR §201.57
    http://www.accessdata.fda.gov/scripts/cdrh/cfdocs/cfCFR/CFRSearch.cfm?fr=201.57

72. **C**
Accurate and complete information is vital to the safe use of drugs. While drug companies have traditionally promoted their products directly to physicians, more and more they are advertising directly to consumers.
http://www.fda.gov/Drugs/ResourcesForYou/Consumers/ucm143462.htm

73. **B**
View 21 CFR§ 310.515 (a) Requirement for a patient package insert. FDA concludes that the safe and effective use of **drug products containing estrogens** requires that patients be fully informed of the benefits and risks involved in the use of these drugs.
http://www.accessdata.fda.gov/scripts/cdrh/cfdocs/cfcfr/CFRSearch.cfm?fr=310.515

74. **E**
View SEC. 201. [21 U.S.C. 321]
http://www.fda.gov/regulatoryinformation/legislation/federalfooddrugandcosmeticactfdcact/fdcactchaptersiandiishorttitleanddefinitions/ucm086297.htm

75. **A**
View 21 CFR § 211.132 (b)Requirements for tamper-evident package.
http://www.accessdata.fda.gov/scripts/cdrh/cfdocs/cfcfr/CFRSearch.cfm?fr=211.132

76. **A & B**
View 16 CFR 1700.14 - Substances requiring special packaging
http://www.gpo.gov/fdsys/pkg/CFR-2012-title16-vol2/pdf/CFR-2012-title16-vol2-sec1700-14.pdf

77. **B**
Durham-Humphrey Amendment of 1951
Kefauver-Harris Drug Amendments of 1962
http://www.fda.gov/aboutfda/whatwedo/history/milestones/ucm128305.htm

Drug Price Competition and Patent Term Restoration Act of 1984
http://thomas.loc.gov/cgi-bin/bdquery/z?d098:SN01538:@@@D&summ2=m&|TOM:/bss/d098query.html

Food and Drug Administration Modernization Act of 1997
http://www.fda.gov/RegulatoryInformation/Legislation/FederalFoodDrugandCosmeticActFDCAct/SignificantAmendmentstotheFDCAct/FDAMA/FullTextofFDAMAlaw/default.htm
Food and Drug Administration Amendments Act (FDAAA) of 2007
http://www.fda.gov/RegulatoryInformation/Legislation/FederalFoodDrugandCosmeticActFDCAct/SignificantAmendmentstotheFDCAct/FoodandDrugAdministrationAmendmentsActof2007/FullTextofFDAAALaw/default.htm

78. **B**

A new chemical entity that is developed by a sponsor and is approved as a new drug under an NDA is granted a period of exclusive marketing, and during that time no other manufacturer may market the chemical entity. Patent laws protect the new drug's exclusivity for a period of time, and under some circumstances, the FDCA provides additional non-patent exclusivity. After all applicable periods of exclusivity have expired, it is possible for another manufacturer to formulate the chemical entity into a product and market the product as a generic equivalent of the innovator product. The most frequent way of getting to market as a generic equivalent is through an Abbreviated New Drug Application (ANDA). An ANDA relies on the safety and efficacy studies of the innovator product's NDA. Through an ANDA, a sponsor of a generic equivalent is required only to show bioequivalence with the innovator product. If such bioequivalence is shown, then the assumption is made that the bioequivalent product must be as safe and effective as the innovator product.

79. **E**

Applies only to human drugs. Section 503A of the FD&C Act from 1997
http://www.hpm.com/pdf/blog/Summary%20of%20HR3204%20-%20Compounding.pdf

Text of Compounding Quality Act
http://www.fda.gov/Drugs/GuidanceComplianceRegulatoryInformation/PharmacyCompounding/ucm376732.htm

80. **C-E**

View § 164.502 Uses and disclosures of protected health information: general rules.
https://www.law.cornell.edu/cfr/text/45/164.502
http://www.hhs.gov/ocr/privacy/hipaa/understanding/coveredentities/businessassociates.html

81. **A**

View 21 USC § 360c (a) Classes of devices.
http://www.gpo.gov/fdsys/pkg/USCODE-2010-title21/html/USCODE-2010-title21-chap9-subchapV-partA-sec360c.htm

    Sec. 870.3925 **Replacement heart valve.**
        http://www.accessdata.fda.gov/scripts/cdrh/cfdocs/cfcfr/CFRSearch.cfm?fr=870.3925

    Sec. 890.3150 Crutch.
        http://www.accessdata.fda.gov/scripts/cdrh/cfdocs/cfcfr/CFRSearch.cfm?fr=890.3150

    Sec. 880.5090 Liquid bandage.
        http://www.accessdata.fda.gov/scripts/cdrh/cfdocs/cfcfr/CFRSearch.cfm?fr=880.5090

    Sec. 880.6230 Tongue depressor.
        http://www.accessdata.fda.gov/scripts/cdrh/cfdocs/cfcfr/CFRSearch.cfm?fr=880.6230

Sec. 868.5580 Oxygen mask.
http://www.accessdata.fda.gov/scripts/cdrh/cfdocs/cfcfr/CFRSearch.cfm?fr=868.5580

82. **E**
View 21 U.S. Code § 352 - Misbranded drugs and devices
http://www.law.cornell.edu/uscode/text/21/352

83. **B**
The labeling on dietary supplements may make structure/function claims, but may not make therapeutic claims.
View 21 USC § 343(r)(6)
http://www.law.cornell.edu/uscode/text/21/343
http://www.fda.gov/regulatoryinformation/legislation/federalfooddrugandcosmeticactfdcact/fdcactchaptersandiishorttitleanddefinitions/ucm086297.htm

84. **B**
Phase 2 studies begin if Phase 1 studies don't reveal unacceptable toxicity. While the emphasis in Phase 1 is on safety, the emphasis in Phase 2 is on **effectiveness**.
http://www.fda.gov/Drugs/ResourcesForYou/Consumers/ucm143534.htm

85. **A**
View 21 USC § 829
http://www.deadiversion.usdoj.gov/21cfr/21usc/829.htm

86. **E.**
View 75 FR 16236

https://www.deadiversion.usdoj.gov/ecomm/e_rx/faq/faq.htm

87. **A.**
Faxed prescriptions can only be done for patients in hospice or LTCF. No refills can be given for schedule II substances and a registered nurse cannot write for C-II prescriptions. Choice E does not specify what type of patient, and choice D is a phoned prescription for a homebound patient. You need a written prescription for choice D to be true.

https://www.deadiversion.usdoj.gov/pubs/manuals/pharm2/pharm_content.htm

88. **B.**
They can total no more than a 90-day supply.
View: https://www.deadiversion.usdoj.gov/faq/mult_rx_faq.htm

89. **D.**
View: https://www.deadiversion.usdoj.gov/21cfr/cfr/1306/1306_13.htm

90. **A.**

From DEA website, "Practitioners wishing to prescribe and dispense FDA approved schedule II controlled substances (i.e., methadone) for maintenance and detoxification treatment must obtain a separate DEA registration as a Narcotic Treatment Program via a DEA Form 363.

If a practitioner wishes to prescribe or dispense schedules III, IV, or V controlled substances approved by the FDA for **addiction** treatment (i.e., Suboxone® or Subutex® drug products), the practitioner must request a waiver from CSAT which will then notify DEA of all waiver requests. These practitioners are referred to as DATA waived practitioners."

https://www.buppractice.com/node/12256
View: https://www.deadiversion.usdoj.gov/pubs/manuals/pharm2/pharm_content.htm

91. **C.**

"All required records concerning controlled substances must be maintained for at least two years for inspection and copying by duly authorized DEA officials. Records and inventories of schedule II controlled substances must be maintained separately from all other records of the registrant. All records and inventories of schedules III, IV, and V controlled substances must be maintained either separately from all other records or in such a form that the information required is readily retrievable from the ordinary business records."

https://www.deadiversion.usdoj.gov/pubs/manuals/pharm2/pharm_manual.htm

92. **C.**

Buyers must:

Present a photo identification card issued by the State or the Federal Government or a document that is considered acceptable by the seller

Enter into the logbook their information such as name, address, date and time of sale, and signature

93. **D.**

CMEA requires all non-liquid forms (including gel caps) to be in 2-unit blister packs (with exception when blister pack is not technically feasible, the product may be in unit dosage packets or pouches). The daily limit is 3.6 g per day of pseudoephedrine base, or mobile retail vendor (or mail-order) can't sell more than 7.5 g per 30 days. 120 mg of pseudoephedrine HCL is equivalent to 36 tablets, about 4.32 g per day of the salt form.

https://www.deadiversion.usdoj.gov/meth/cma2005.htm

94. **B.**

View https://www.deadiversion.usdoj.gov/faq/dea222.htm

95. **A.**

It is suggested that initial reports be required within one business day and that DEA Form 106 must be filed within 30 days.

https://www.deadiversion.usdoj.gov/fed_regs/rules/2005/fr0812.htm

96. **B.**
    Orphan drug exclusivity adds 7-years not 5-years of market exclusivity.

    https://www.fda.gov/downloads/drugs/developmentapprovalprocess/smallbusinessassistance/ucm447307.pdf

97. **D.**
    View http://www.nejm.org/doi/full/10.1056/NEJMhle1002961#t=article

98. **C.**
    View "What standards must generic medicines meet to receive FDA approval?"-
    https://www.fda.gov/drugs/resourcesforyou/consumers/questionsanswers/ucm100100.htm#a5

99. **A.**
    Any generic drug modeled after a single, brand name drug must perform approximately the same in the body as the brand name drug. There will always be a slight, but not medically important, level of natural variability – just as there is for one batch of brand name drug compared to the next batch of brand name product.

    https://www.fda.gov/drugs/resourcesforyou/consumers/buyingusingmedicinesafely/understandinggenericdrugs/ucm167991.htm

100. **D.**
     The Orange Book Codes supply the FDA's therapeutic equivalence rating for applicable multi-source categories. Codes beginning with 'A' signify the product is deemed therapeutically equivalent to the reference product for the category. Codes beginning with 'B' indicate bio-equivalence has not been confirmed. 'EE' is assigned by RED BOOK Online to products that have been evaluated by the FDA but for which an equivalence rating is not available.

     http://www.micromedexsolutions.com/micromedex2/4.36.0/WebHelp/RED_BOOK/Orange_Book_Codes.htm

101. **B.**
     Biosimilars are listed in the Purple Book.

     https://www.fda.gov/drugs/developmentapprovalprocess/howdrugsaredevelopedandapproved/approvalapplications/therapeuticbiologicapplications/biosimilars/

102. **A.**
     A REMs may be required by the FDA as part of the approval of a new product, or for an approved product when new safety information arises. REMS is a safety strategy to manage

a known or potential serious risk associated with a medicine and to enable patients to have continued access to such medicines by managing their safe use.

https://www.fda.gov/aboutfda/transparency/basics/ucm325201.htm

103. **D.**
Examples of ETASU are:
- Prescribers have specific training/experience or special certifications
- Pharmacies, practitioners or healthcare settings that dispense the drug be certified
- Drug be dispensed only in certain healthcare settings (e.g., infusion settings, hospitals)
- Drug be dispensed with evidence of safe-use conditions such as laboratory test results
- Each patient using the drug be subject to monitoring •Each patient using the drug be enrolled in a registry

https://www.fda.gov/downloads/aboutfda/transparency/basics/ucm328784.pdf

104. **B.**
An education program for prescribers and patients is emphasized but not required.

http://er-la-opioidrems.com/IwgUI/rems/home.action

105. **A.**
Purchaser must sign the logbook and enter his or her name, address, and date and time of sale not the seller.

https://www.deadiversion.usdoj.gov/meth/cma2005.htm

106. **C.**
The daily sales limit of ephedrine base, pseudoephedrine base, or phenylpropanolamine base is 3.6 grams per purchaser, regardless of number of transactions.

Ingredient	Number of Tablets [as base]
25 mg Ephedrine HCl	175
25 mg Ephedrine Sulfate	186
30 mg Pseudoephedrine HCl	146
60 mg Pseudoephedrine HCl	73
120 mg Pseudoephedrine HCl	36
30 mg Pseudoephedrine Sulfate	155
60 mg Pseudoephedrine Sulfate	77
120 mg Pseudoephedrine Sulfate	38

| Phenylpropanolamine | The FDA issued a voluntary recall of this ingredient as being unsafe for human consumption. Veterinary use is by prescription only. |

View: https://www.deadiversion.usdoj.gov/meth/cma2005.html

107. **B.**

View question 106 explanation

108. **D.**

Usually pharmacies lose their right to sell precursor drugs for a period of time in addition to fines.

Here is a real life example: http://www.pharmacytimes.com/news/pharmacy-pays-penalties-for-violating-controlled-substances-laws

109. **A.**

The DQSA was enacted primarily in response to an outbreak of fungal meningitis among patients who received products compounded at the New England Compounding Center. Title I of the DQSA amends Section 503A and clarifies federal authority of compounding and defines "traditional compounders." Title I also creates Section 503B of the FDCA, which addresses outsourcing facilities. The Food and Drug Administration Modernization Act (FDAMA) of 1997 created Section 503A of the FDCA and distinguished manufacturing from compounding activities that could be completed by pharmacies. The DQSA removes advertising and promotion clauses of the original Section 503A that were rendered unconstitutional.

https://www.fda.gov/drugs/guidancecomplianceregulatoryinformation/pharmacycompounding/ucm375804.htm

110. **D.**

Because generic drugs subject to a suitability petition cannot be AB rated, there is a reduced risk of a classic "switch" by pharmacists from Effexor XR to a generic tablet. There is a real risk, however, that managed care organizations may mandate that plan physicians prescribe the generic tablet.

https://www.fda.gov/ohrms/dockets/dailys/03/Sept03/090503/03p-0159-c000001-01-vol1.pdf

111. **B.**

Specifically, the commenter suggested that initial reports be required within one business day and that DEA Form 106 must be filed within 30 days.

https://www.deadiversion.usdoj.gov/fed_regs/rules/2005/fr0812.htm

112. **A.**

As choice A affects the drug contents inside as well as going against the label it is considered adulterated and misbranded.

https://www.fda.gov/cosmetics/guidanceregulation/lawsregulations/ucm074248.htm#Adulterated

113. **C.**
    90-days

114. **E.**
    https://www.deadiversion.usdoj.gov/drugreg/reg_apps/363/363_instruct.htm

115. **B.**
    The pharmacy owner or "registrant" can enter the pharmacy.
    https://www.deadiversion.usdoj.gov/pubs/manuals/pharm2/pharm_manual.htm

116. **D.**
    Pharmacy technicians need to be registered, licensed, and certified to practice in IL.

    https://ptcb.org/who-we-serve/pharmacy-technicians/cphts-state-regulatory-map/il#.WZivg62ZMdU

117. **A.**
    In an effort to reduce drug exposure and abuse, the DEA has allowed the take back of unused, unwanted controlled substances.
    https://ptcb.org/who-we-serve/pharmacy-technicians/cphts-state-regulatory-map/il#.WZivg62ZMdU

118. **B.**
    NIOSH and OSHA provide guidance's to help promote the safe handling of antineoplastics.
    https://www.cdc.gov/niosh/topics/antineoplastic/

119. **D.**
    https://www.aaaai.org/about-aaaai/advocacy/Allergy-Extract-Compounding-Requirements-Updates

120. **B.**
    Outsourcing facilities
    https://www.fda.gov/downloads/Drugs/Guidances/UCM496288.pdf

121. **B.**
    Currently, guidelines are only available for testing "chemotherapy gloves" [ASTM 2005] and information may not be available for other types of hazardous drugs. Wear two pairs of gloves when compounding, administering, and disposing of hazardous drugs.

    https://www.cdc.gov/niosh/docs/wp-solutions/2009-106/pdfs/2009-106.pdf

Illinois State Pharmacy Law Overview

DEFINITIONS

Pharmacy Practice Act 225 ILCS 85/3

"ADDRESS OF RECORD" is the address that the Department recorded in the applicant's or licensee's application file or license file. The Department's licensure maintenance unit maintains the address of record. If there's a change of address, applicant or licensee must notify the Department **within 30 days.**

"BOARD" is the State Board of Pharmacy.

"COMPOUNDING" is the preparation and mixing of components, excluding flavorings. Compounding occurs when (1) there's a prescription drug order or an initiative based on the prescriber-patient-pharmacist relationship in course of profession practice, or (2) it's for the purpose of research, teaching, or chemical analysis and not for sale or dispensing.

Commercially available products may be compounded for dispensing to individual patients only if all of the following conditions are met:
1. The commercial product is not available in a timely manner to meet the patient's needs; and
2. The prescribing healthcare provider has requested the drug to be compounded.

"DISPENSE or DISPENSING" involves interpreting and evaluating a prescription drug order in addition to filling, compounding, packaging, and labeling necessary for delivery the prescription drug order. Recommending, advising, and counseling on the drug contents, therapeutic value, uses, and precaution are also parts of the dispensing process.

Dispense or dispensing does NOT include physical delivery of a drug or device to a patient or patient's representative in a home, institution, or within a pharmacy store while the pharmacist is on duty and the pharmacy is open.

Tip to know: Only a pharmacist or pharmacy technician under the supervision of a pharmacist can input drug information through electronic-data-processing equipment.

"DRUGS" include the following:
1. Articles or any supplement recognized in the official United States. Pharmacopoeia/National Formulary (USP/NF), or any supplement intended for their main use of diagnosis, cure, mitigation, treatment or prevention of disease in human or animals, as approved by the United States Food and Drug Administration (FDA).
2. All other articles that are intended for their main use of diagnosis, cure, mitigation, treatment or prevention of disease in human or animals, as approved by the FDA.
3. Articles other than food that are intended for their main use to affect the structure or any function of the body of human or other animals.

"HOME PHARMACY" is the location where the primary operations of the pharmacy occur.

"MEDICATION THERAPY MANAGEMENT" (MTM) is a distinct service to optimize therapeutic outcomes for individual patients through improved medication use. The pharmacist must communicate the information provided to the patient's prescriber **within 48 hours.**

"NONRESIDENT PHARMACY" is a pharmacy physically located outside of Illinois that dispenses, ships, and delivers any prescription drugs to Illinois residents.

"PATIENT COUNSELING" is the communication between a pharmacist or a student pharmacist under the supervision of a pharmacist, and a patient or the patient's representative about the patient's medication or device. The purpose of patient counseling is to optimize proper use of the medication or device. (See table 1)

Table 1: Patient counseling activities performed by the pharmacist, student pharmacist & pharmacy technician

Tip to know: Individuals who are not licensed may *NOT* make the offer to counsel.

	Patient counseling may include without limitation:	Pharmacist & Student Pharmacist	Pharmacy Technician
1	Obtaining medication history	Yes	Yes
2	Acquiring patient's allergies and health conditions	Yes	Yes
3	Facilitation of patient's understanding of the intended use of the medication	Yes	No
4	Proper directions for use	Yes	No
5	Significant potential adverse events	Yes	No
6	Potential food-drug interactions	Yes	No
7	The need to be compliant with the medication	Yes	No

"PHARMACIST IN CHARGE" (PIC) is responsible for all aspects of the operation related to the practice of pharmacy.

"PRESCRIPTIONS" are any written, oral, facsimile, or electronically transmitted order for drugs or medical devices, issued by a physician, dentist, veterinarian, physician assistance, advanced practice nurse, podiatrist, or optometrist, within the limits of their licenses. A prescription order must contain the following: (See **figure 1**)
 1. Name of the patient.
 2. Date of issue.
 3. Name, strength, and quantity of drug or description of the medical device.
 4. Directions for use.
 5. Prescriber's name, address, and signature.
 6. Prescriber's DEA number and patient's address.

Notes:
- Prescriber's DEA# & patient's address is required for controlled substances only.
- Prescriber's DEA# is not required on inpatient drug orders.
- Prescription may (but is not required to) list the illness, disease, or condition for which the drug or device is being prescribed.

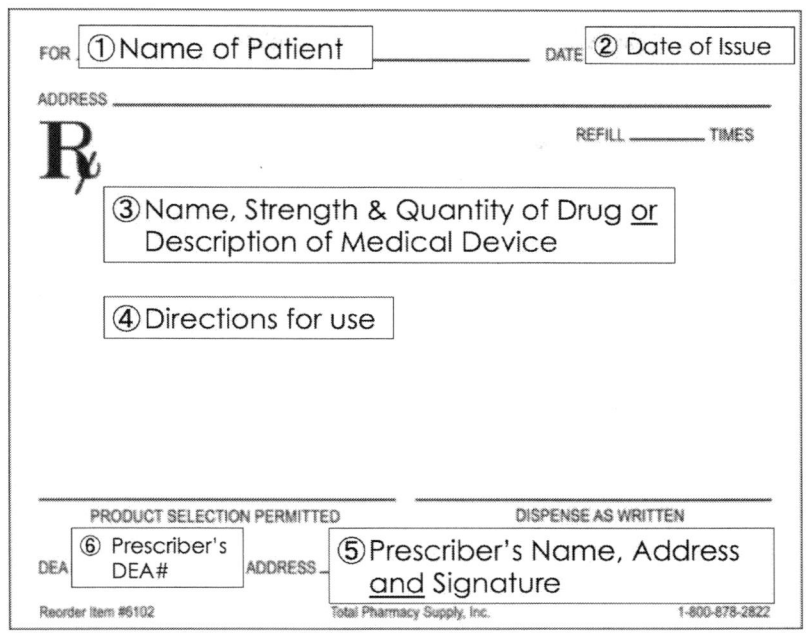

Figure 1: An example of a Prescription (Thieu, Y. and totalpharmacysupply.com, 2017)

"PROTECTED HEALTH INFORMATION" (PHI) is the health information that identifies the individual and that is:
1. Transmitted by electronic media.
2. Maintained in any medium in the Federal Health Insurance Portability and Accountability Act; or
3. Transmitted or maintained in any other form or medium.

EXAMPLE: Name, postal address (street address, city, county, zip code, etc.), birthdate, telephone numbers, social security numbers, and any other unique identifying number or characteristic.

✓Protected health information does not include education records or employment records.

(225 ILCS 85/3: Section scheduled to be repealed on January 1, 2018)

Pharmacy Practice Rules 68 IL ADC Section 1330.10 &1330.670

"BARRIER ISOLATION CHAMBER" is an apparatus designed to provide a Class 5, 6 or 7 environment, as stated in ISO (International Organization for Standardization) 14644-1, for preparation of sterile products using solid walls rather than air movement (laminar air flow) to (1) create a critical zone for preparation handling, (2) a high efficiency particulate air (HEPA) filtration system that allows the air flowing through the unit to remove any initial particles and particles generated within the controlled environment, and (3) a means by which preparations are introduced and people interact with the preparation being prepared within the unit.

"BEYOND USE DATE" (BUD) is the expiration date that is often used in compounded drug products (i.e. vaccines, blood products, etc.).

"BIOLOGICAL SAFETY CABINET" (BSC) is containment unit suitable for the preparation of low to moderate risk agents when there is a need for protection of the preparation, personnel and environment, according to ISO 14644-1.

"COMPOUNDED STERILE PREPARATION" (CSP) is a sterile pharmaceutical that has been prepared by a pharmacist. It must be a preparation prepared for or in anticipation of a specific patient medication order. The preparation may include commercially available dosage forms that may need to be altered to meet a specific patient's need.

"CYTOTOXIC" is a pharmaceutical that has the capability of killing living cells. These agents include agents classified as cancer chemotherapeutic, carcinogenic, mutagenic and antineoplastic.

"DIRECTOR" is the Director of the Division of Professional Regulation with the authority delegated by the Secretary.

"SECRETARY" is the Secretary of the Department of Financial and Professional Regulation. (

"DIVISION" is the Department of Financial and Professional Regulation-Division of Professional Regulation.

"REGISTRANT" includes anyone who's a licensed pharmacist, student pharmacist, registered pharmacy technician, or certified pharmacy technician.

"LAMINAR AIRFLOW HOOD" (LAH) is an apparatus designed to provide a Class 5, 6 or 7 environment, as stated in ISO 14644-1 for preparation of sterile products using air circulation in a defined direction that passes through a HEPA filter to remove the initial particles and particles generated within the controlled environment.

"MEDICATION ORDER" is similar to a prescription order but is the term used in institutional pharmacy for a prescription that is issued by a prescriber for the patient in the facility.

"PARENTERAL" is sterile preparations of drugs for injection through one or more layers of the skin.

"REMOTE CONSULTATION SITE" is the location where the prescriptions are stored and dispensed by a pharmacy technician or student pharmacist under the direct, remote supervision of a pharmacist from the home pharmacy. Note that the home pharmacy fills the prescriptions not the remote consultation site.

"REMOTE MEDICATION ORDER PROCESSING" occurs when a remote pharmacy receives, interprets or clarifies medication orders. The remote pharmacy also does data entry and transferring of medication order information, in addition to performing drug utilization review, interpreting clinical data, performing therapeutic intervention and providing drug information.

"TERMINAL" is a patient whose medical condition indicates his or her life expectancy to be 6 months or less.

"UNIQUE IDENTIFIER" includes electronic signature, handwritten signature or initials, thumb print, or any other electronic identification approved by the Division.

(68 IL ADC Section 1330.10 & 1330.670)

Illinois Controlled Substances Act 720 ILCS 570/102

"ADDICT" includes any person who habitually uses any drug or substance other than alcohol that results in loss of self-control or endangers the public health, safety or welfare.

"ADMINISTER" means the direct application of a controlled substance through injection, inhalation, ingestion, or any other means to the body of a patient or animal.

"AGENT" is any person who acts on behalf of a manufacturer, dispenser, or prescriber. This does not include contract carrier or public warehouseman.

"ANABOLIC STEROIDS" include any drug or hormonal substance related to testosterone (other than estrogen, progestin, and corticosteroid) that promotes muscle growth. Some examples include the following:
- Androstane
- Androstenediol
- Bolasterone
- Boldenone
- Calusterone
- Dehydroepiandrosterone
- Drostanolone
- Fluoxymesterone
- Mesterolone
- Testosterone

"DELIVER" or **"DELIVERY"** is the act of transferring possession of a controlled substance whether or not there is agency relationship.

"DEPRESSANT" includes any drug that (1) causes depression of the central nervous system (CNS), (2) impairs consciousness and awareness, <u>and</u> (3) can be habit-forming or lead to substance abuse. Other than alcohol, it includes the following substances and their analogs, cannabis and their active ingredients, benzodiazepines, barbiturates, and opioid (natural or synthetic). Some other substances are chloral hydrate and similar sedative hypnotics.

"DISTRIBUTE" is physically delivering of a controlled substance other than administering or dispensing

"GOOD FAITH" is the prescribing or dispensing of a controlled substance by a practitioner to treat any person for a pathology or condition. The treatment excludes individual's physical or psychological dependence or addiction to a controlled substance. It is legal if the dispensing of a controlled substance in accordance to a prescriber's order is based on the professional judgment of a pharmacist. The pharmacist shall be guided by accepted professional standards, including the following in making the judgment:
1. Lack of consistency of prescriber-patient relationship (patient has multiple prescribers of the controlled substances).
2. Frequency of prescription for the same drug by one prescriber for large numbers of patients.
3. Quantities beyond those normally prescribed.
4. Unusual dosages (recognizing that there may be clinical circumstances where more or less than usual dose is legitimate).
5. Unusual geographic distances between patient, pharmacist and prescriber.
6. Consistent prescribing of habit-forming drugs.

"MAIL-ORDER PHARMACY" is a pharmacy that's located in a state that delivers, dispenses or distributes a prescribed controlled substance through a mail carrier to IL residents.

"MANUFACTURE" means the production, preparation, propagation, compounding, conversion or processing of a controlled substance other than methamphetamine by directly or indirectly synthesizing, extracting substances from the original natural sources, or a combination of both. Manufacture also includes any packaging or repackaging of the substance or labeling of its container. However, it does <u>NOT</u> include the following:
1. The preparation or compounding of a controlled substance by the ultimate user for his or her own use; <u>or</u>
2. The preparation, compounding, packing, or labeling of a controlled substance by a practitioner to (1) administer or dispense in the course of professional practice; <u>or</u> (2) to research, teach, or analyze and not for sale.

"NARCOTIC DRUG" is produced directly or indirectly by extraction from substances of vegetable origin, chemical synthesis, or combination of both, including the following:
1. Opium and opiate, and their salts, isomers, derivatives, etc.
2. Opium poppy and poppy straw.
3. Coca leaves and their salts, isomers, derivative, etc.
4. Cocaine, its salts, isomers, and isomers' salts.
5. Ecgonine, its salts, isomers, and derivatives.
6. Any preparation of any the above substances.

"OPIATE" is an addiction forming and sustaining liability substance similar to morphine or having the ability to convert into a drug with addiction forming and sustaining liability.

"OPIUM POPPY" is the plant of the species Papver somniferum L., except its seeds.

"POPPY STRAW" includes all parts of the opium poppy after mowing, except its seeds.

"PRACTITIONER" is a physician, dentist, optometrist, podiatrist, veterinarian, scientific investigator, pharmacist, physician assistant, advance practice nurse, registered nurse, and other entities who are permitted by the U.S. or IL to distribute, dispense, conduct research to administer or use in teaching for chemical analysis.

"PRESCRIBER" includes a physician, dentist, optometrist, podiatrist, veterinarian, prescribing psychologist, who issues a prescription, or a physician assistant, advance practice nurse, who issues a prescription for a controlled substance in accordance with a written delegation and collaborative agreement.

"PRESCRIPTION" is a legal written, facsimile, verbal or electronic order of a physician, dentist, optometrist, podiatrist, veterinarian, prescribing psychologist, or a physician assistant, advance practice nurse, in accordance with a written delegation and collaborative agreement.

"STIMULANT" is any drug that (1) causes excitation of the CNS, (2) impairs consciousness, <u>and</u> (3) can lead to substance abuse, including following substances and their analogs amphetamines, methylphenidate and phencyclidine. Other drug is cocaine.

(720 ILCS 570/102)

Illinois Controlled Substances Rules 72 IL ADC Section 3100.10

"ADMINISTRATION" includes the Drug Enforcement Administration (DEA), United States Department of Justice (DOJ), or its successor agency.

"DEA REGISTRATION NUMBER" is the number assigned to controlled substances and controlled drug preparations by the DEA of the DOJ.

"DEPARTMENT OF FINANCIAL AND PROFESSIONAL REGULATION" or (DFPR) is also known as the Department.

"DIRECTOR" is the Director of the Division of the Professional Regulation with the authority delegated by the Secretary of the Department of Financial and Professional Regulation (DFPR).

"DIVISION" is the DFPR-Division of Professional Regulation.

"MID-LEVEL PRACTITIONER" includes (1) a physician assistant (PA) who has been delegated authority to prescribe through written delegation of authority by a physician, (2) an advanced practice nurse (APN) who has been delegated authority to prescribe through a written delegation of authority by a physician or by a podiatrist, or (3) an animal euthanasia agency.

"MID-LEVEL PRACTITIONER CONTROLLED SUBSTANCES LICENSE" is a license to prescribe controlled substances issued to a mid-level practitioner.

(77 IL ADC Section 3100.10)

SECTION 6: ILLINOIS STATE BOARD OF PHARMACY
Pharmacy Practice Act, Chapter 225 ILCS 85/10, Section 1330 IAC et seq.

ILLINOIS STATE BOARD OF PHARMACY
COMPOSITION
Total of 9 members
- 7 licensed pharmacists
- 2 non-pharmacist public members

QUALIFICATION
- Pharmacist members must be licensed and in good standing, a graduate of an accredited college of pharmacy or hold a BS in Pharmacy, with at least 5 years of post-licensure experience in the state of Illinois.
- Non-pharmacist public members are voting members and are not licensed pharmacists in Illinois or any other state.

APPOINTMENT PROCESS
The Board members are appointed by the Governor to 5-year term. If the terms of all members started on March 31, 1999, they would expire on March 31, 2004.

Members of the pharmacy profession and pharmacy organizations may make recommendations to the Governor with no restrictions as to what type or setting of pharmacy practice.

Partial terms over 3 years in length are considered full terms. A member may be reappointed but cannot serve more than 2 full terms in his or her lifetime or 12 consecutive years. The Governor may remove any Board member for the following:
- Misconduct.
- Incapacity; or
- Neglect of duty

✓ The Governor is the sole judge for the removal of Board members.
✓ The Board holds quarterly meetings.
✓ Five members or the majority of the Board members constitute a quorum.

THE DEPARTMENT
The Department is the Department of Financial and Professional Regulation (DFPR). The Secretary of DFPR appoints the following:
- A chief pharmacy coordinator; and
- At least 2 deputy pharmacy coordinators.
  - At least one deputy pharmacy coordinator is assigned to a region composed of Cook County and other counties with their primary office in Chicago.
  - At least one deputy coordinator is assigned to a region composed of balance of counties in IL with their primary office in Springfield.

All of these appointees must be registered pharmacists in good standing in Illinois with at least 5 years' experience in the practice of pharmacy.

The chief pharmacy coordinator is the executive administrator and chief enforcement officer of this Act. The deputy pharmacy coordinators report to the chief pharmacy coordinator. The Secretary employs at least 4 pharmacy investigators who would report to the pharmacy coordinator or a deputy pharmacy coordinator. The Department employs at least one attorney to prosecute violations of this Act and its rules.

(225 ILCS 85/10: *Section scheduled to be repealed on January 1, 2018*)

SECTION 7: PHARMACY

Pharmacy Practice Act, Chapter 225 ILCS 85/15,16 &17, Section 1330 IAC et seq.
Pharmacy Practice Rules (Implementing the Act), 68 IL ADC Sections 1330.400,1330.410, 1330.780 & 1330.790

PHARMACY REQUIREMENTS
It is unlawful for the owner of any pharmacy to operate unless the following occurs:
- It has a licensed pharmacist on duty.
- Security provisions of all drugs and devices are provided during the absence of all licensed pharmacists from the licensed pharmacy; and
- The pharmacy is licensed to conduct the practice of pharmacy. If a facility, company, or organization operates multiple pharmacies from multiple physical addresses, a separate pharmacy license is required for each different physical address.

The Department may allow a pharmacy that is not located at the same location as its home pharmacy, where the pharmacy services are provided during an emergency situation, to be operated as an emergency remote pharmacy.

The Secretary may waive the requirement of a pharmacist to be on duty at all times for State facilities that do not treat human diseases.

The following should be conspicuously displayed in the pharmacy where the individuals engage in the practice of pharmacy:
- The holder of any license or certificate of registration.
- The name of the PIC.
- The pharmacy license.

(225 ILCS 85/15: *Section scheduled to be repealed on January 1, 2018*)

APPLICATION FOR A PHARMACY LICENSE
ESTABLISING, RELOCATING OR CHANGING OWNERSHIP
Any person who wants to establish, relocate or change the ownership of a pharmacy must file an application supplied by the Division along with the required fee, and specify the types of pharmacy services to be provided.

The purchaser of the pharmacy may operate the pharmacy before the issuance of a new pharmacy license only when the purchase and seller have a written power of attorney agreement. **Within 30 days** after the issuance of a pharmacy license, the pharmacy shall be open to the public. Any reduction in hours of operation must be reported to the Division **within 30 days.** The pharmacy cannot relocate unless it has been inspected by the Department. All drugs must be transferred within 24 hours after issuance of the license.

(68 IL ADC Section 1330.400)
When a management company is hired to run a pharmacy, that management company must be the license holder for both the pharmacy and the IL Controlled Substances license, unless the

pharmacy and management company cosigns an agreement that assigns responsibility for controlled substance to the pharmacy.

(68 IL ADC Section 1330.410)

CHANGE OF OWNERSHIP OF A PHARMACY
A new pharmacy application must be filed whenever:
1. 10% or more of the ownership of the business is sold or transferred to a person or entity; or
2. More than half the board of directors or executive officers of a business issued a pharmacy license change.

Any change of ownership of a parent company that owns a pharmacy cannot be considered a change of ownership of the pharmacy.

(68 IL ADC Section1330.780)

CLOSING A PHARMACY
Whenever a pharmacy intends to close, it has to follow the following procedures:
1. Notify the Division in writing **30 days in advance** of the closing date.
2. Notify customers of the closure **at least 15 days in advance** of the closing date and where the customer's records will be maintained.
3. Comply with all DEA requirements for closing a pharmacy.
4. On the day the pharmacy closes:
   - Conduct an inventory of the pharmacy's controlled substances and maintain the inventory record for inspection by the Division **for 5 years.**
   - Return the pharmacy license to the Division's drug compliance investigator or other authorized Division personnel.
   - Notify the Division in writing of where the controlled substances inventory and records will be kept and how the controlled substances were transferred or destroyed. Records involving controlled substances must be kept available for 5 years for inspection by the Division.
   - Notify the Division in writing of the name of the person responsible for and the location where the closing pharmacy's prescription files and patient profiles will be maintained. These records shall be kept for **at least of 5 years** from the date the last original or refill prescription was dispensed.
   - The pharmacy acquiring prescription records from a closing pharmacy must inform the Division prior to the date when the transaction is going to take place.
   - After the closing date, only the PIC, or other designated pharmacist of the discontinuing business can have access to the prescription drugs until those drugs are transferred to the new owner or are properly destroyed.
5. Cover all signage indicating "Drug Store" or "Pharmacy." The signage must be removed in a timely manner. A sign should be posted that the pharmacy is closed.

(68 IL ADC Section1330.790)

WHAT WILL HAPPEN WHEN THE PIC DIES?
Pharmacy license expires 30 days after the PIC dies or leaves the pharmacy, or the PIC's license has been suspended or revoked. When any of such events occurs, the pharmacy owner is required to notify the Department name of the new PIC **within 30 days**. He or she must also report to the Department within 30 days of the date on which the PIC died or ceased to function. The pharmacy needs to name a new PIC in order to continue business operations.

(225 ILCS 85/16: Section scheduled to be repealed on January 1, 2018)

DISPOSITION OF LEGEND DRUGS ON CESSATION OF PHARMACY OPERATIONS
The PIC of a pharmacy with a revoked license or cessation of pharmacy operation, must notify and send the Department a copy of the closing inventory of controlled substances, and include a statement indicating how the pharmacy intends to dispose all legend drugs and prescription files. These must be done **within 30 days** of such revocation or cessation of operation.

The Department must approve the intended manner of disposition of all legends drugs before the PIC can dispose them. The Department will notify the PIC of the approval or disapproval **within 30 days** of the receipt of the statement. If it is disapproval, the Department shall provide reason why. The PIC has **30 days** of the receipt of the disapproval to notify the Department of an alternative manner of disposition.
- If all legend drugs are not disposed within 30 days after the approval is received, or if no alternative method of disposition is submitted to the Department within 30 days after the disapproval, the Director will notify the PIC about the Department's intent to confiscate all legend drugs.

If PIC has died or is physically incompetent to perform the above duties, the owner of the pharmacy is required to fulfill those duties of PIC. The PIC of the pharmacy that acquires prescription files from a pharmacy with the revoked license, or cessation of operation, is responsible to preserve those prescriptions for the remainder of the term required under the Act.

Notes: Invoices of all legend drugs and inventory record are required to be kept for 5 years. Invoices can be maintained on site or at a central location where they are readily retrievable. If invoices are on site, they must be kept for at least one year from the date of the invoice.

(225 ILCS 85/17: Section scheduled to be repealed on January 1, 2018)

SECTION 8: PHARMACIST

Pharmacy Practice Act, Chapter 225 ILCS 85/6, 8, 10, & 12, Section 1330 IAC et seq.
Pharmacy Practice Rules (Implementing the Act), 68 IL ADC Sections 1330.100, 1330.300, 1330.310, 1330.330 & 1330.350

APPROVAL OF PHARMACY PROGRAMS

The Division approves a pharmacy program in a school or college of pharmacy in good standing if it has a curricular offering at least 5 academic years post-secondary, including any pre-professional education requirements, and requiring a minimum of the following subject areas:
1. General Education (a minimum of 30 semester hours).
2. Preclinical Sciences.
3. Professional Studies and Training (in the following areas):
   - Biomedical sciences.
   - Pharmaceutical sciences.
   - Clinical sciences and practice; and
   - Externship and clerkship (a minimum of 400 direct contact hours).

(68 IL ADC Section 1330.300)

GRADUATES OF PROGRAMS OUTSIDE OF THE U.S.

Applicants who graduated from a professional pharmacy program located outside the U.S. or its territories that is not an approved program, must submit proof of the following:
1. Submission of a Foreign Pharmacy Graduate Examination Committee (FPGEC) Certificate.
2. Passage of the preliminary diagnostic examination (Foreign Pharmacy Graduate Equivalency Exam (FPGEE)) designed to determine equivalence of education to the U.S. programs.
3. The minimum acceptable scores of 550 for paper TOEFL and 50 for paper TSE, or 213 for the computer-based TOEFL and TSE combination, or 88 for the Internet-based TOEFL iBT with a minimum score of 26 on the speaking module.
4. Passage of the Test of Spoken English (TSE) examination with a score of 50; and
5. Either:
   a. Completion of a course of clinical instruction totaling 1,200 clinical hours under the supervision of an IL pharmacist. The course must meet the following:
      - Enhance development of effective communication skills by enabling consultation among the applicant, the prescriber and the patient.
      - Promote development of medical data retrieval skills through exposure to patient medical charts, patient medication profiles and other similar sources of patient information.
      - Promote development of the applicant's ability to research and analyze drug information literature; and
      - Promote development of the applicant's ability to interpret laboratory test and physical examination results; or
   b. Have been licensed in a U.S. state or territory for at least 1 year with no disciplinary actions on their license or pending license.

(68 IL ADC Section 1330.310)

PHARMACIST LICENSURE BY EXAMINATION
- To practice as a pharmacist in Illinois, the person must have a currently valid pharmacist license.
- The pharmacist license can be obtained either by examination or by transferring of a pharmacist license from another state.

IL PHARMACIST LICENSE BY EXAMINATION ELIGIBILITY REQUIREMENTS
Each individual seeking licensure to become registered pharmacist can submit an application to the Department and provide evidence showed in **figure 1**:

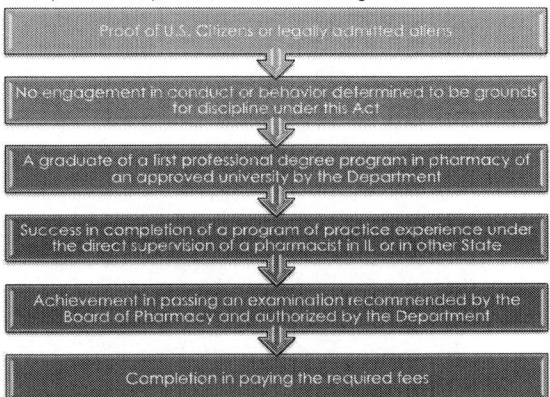

```
┌─────────────────────────────────────────────────────────┐
│   Proof of U.S. Citizens or legally admitted aliens     │
└─────────────────────────────────────────────────────────┘
                            ⬇
┌─────────────────────────────────────────────────────────┐
│ No engagement in conduct or behavior determined to be   │
│       grounds for discipline under this Act             │
└─────────────────────────────────────────────────────────┘
                            ⬇
┌─────────────────────────────────────────────────────────┐
│  A graduate of a first professional degree program in   │
│   pharmacy of an approved university by the Department  │
└─────────────────────────────────────────────────────────┘
                            ⬇
┌─────────────────────────────────────────────────────────┐
│ Success in completion of a program of practice          │
│ experience under the direct supervision of a pharmacist │
│               in IL or in other State                   │
└─────────────────────────────────────────────────────────┘
                            ⬇
┌─────────────────────────────────────────────────────────┐
│  Achievement in passing an examination recommended by   │
│  the Board of Pharmacy and authorized by the Department │
└─────────────────────────────────────────────────────────┘
                            ⬇
┌─────────────────────────────────────────────────────────┐
│         Completion in paying the required fees          │
└─────────────────────────────────────────────────────────┘
```

Figure 1: *Evidence required for IL Pharmacist Licensure Application*

NAPLEX/MPJE EXAMINATION
The Department allows examinations to be given **at least 3 times a year to allow students to sit in the exam**. However, the maximum to take the NAPLEX and MPJE is 5 attempts. If an applicant fails or refuses to take an exam, or fails to pass an exam for licensure **within 3 years** after filing his/her application, the application is denied. Such applicant can submit a new application but has to show evidence of meeting the requirements along with paying required fees. After applicants take the exam, the Department will notify applicants of their results **within 7 weeks** of the NAPLEX/MPJE exam date.

An applicant has one year from the date of notification of successful completion of the exam to apply for a license to the Department. Failure to apply for license within one year would result in the requirement of re-taking and passing the IL MPJE exam.

✓ National Association of Boards of Pharmacy (NABP) develops and provides the exam.

(225 ILCS 85/6: Section scheduled to be repealed on January 1, 2018)
The examination for licensure is divided into two portions:

Theoretical and Applied Pharmaceutical Sciences

- Medicinal Chemistry
- Pharmacology
- Pharmacy
- Pharmceutical Calculations
- Interpretig and Dispensing Prescription Orders
- Compounding Prescription Order
- Monitoring Drug Therapy

Pharmaceutical Jurispurdence portion

- IL law related to pharmacy practice; and
- Federal law related to pharmacy practice

Figure 2: Two Portion of Examination for Pharmacist Licensure

An applicant must score a **minimum of 75 on the Theoretical and Applied Pharmaceutical** Sciences portion and a **minimum of 75 on the combined Pharmaceutical Jurisprudence** portion in order to successfully pass the examination for licensure. Any applicant who fails to pass the NAPLEX and MPJE **5 times** will be required to provide proof of remedial education of the failed portion. An applicant may work as a registered pharmacist for **up to 60 days** prior to the issuance of a certificate of registration upon receipt of a notice from the Division that the examination was successfully completed.

(68 IL ADC Section 1330.330)

PHARMACIST LICENSURE BY ENDORSEMENT; EMERGENCY LICENSURE

If the applicant who are currently licensed in another state and files an application for examination for licensure in IL, the Division will determine whether the requirements in that state are similar to the IL's requirements and notify the applicant the approval or denial **within 30 days** of the application receipt. Applicants still need to pay the fee for licensure.
(68 IL ADC Section 1330.350)

A licensed pharmacist in good standing, could get authorized a temporary license during a natural disaster or other catastrophic event to practice pharmacy in IL. This is also true if a state of emergency is declared in IL.
(225 ILCS 85/8: Section scheduled to be repealed on January 1, 2018)

PHARMACIST LICENSE FOR PREVIOUSLY CONVICTED FIRST-TIME APPLICANT OR LICENSE PERMANENTLY REVOKE OR DENIED

Effective January 1, 2017, the Department's new process allows previously barred first-time applicants for a healthcare worker license (i.e. pharmacist, physician, physician assistant, advance practice nurse, clinical psychologist, etc.) to apply for a license. A pharmacist or other healthcare worker who was permanently revoked or denied due to a forcible felony (i.e. first or second degree murder, robbery, kidnapping a child, armed violence, etc.) may file a Petition for Review that's available on the Department's website if the conviction date has been more than 5 years ago. If the person is found to be a sex offender, have sexually enslaved a minor, or have criminal battery against any patient that is a forcible felony, he or she is not qualified for a review.

EXPIRATION OF LICENSE; RENEWAL

Pharmacists need 30 hours of ACPE accredited pharmacy continuing education (CE) within 24 months. Pharmacists on active duty with the military or in Federal Service may have their license restored without paying any lapsed renewal fees.

(225 ILCS 85/12: *Section scheduled to be repealed on January 1, 2018*)

CONTINUING EDUCATION (CE)

CE REQUIREMENTS:
- Completion of 30 hours of CE during the 24 months before the expiration date of the license.
- CE is not required if it is the first renewal of an original licensure.

APPROVED CE:
- CE credit must be from providers approved by the ACPE and may be completed out of IL.
- Undergraduate coursework completed at a recognized professional pharmacy program can fulfill the CE requirement if (1) completed as college credit or (2) provided on official transcript.
    - One semester = 15 CE hours
    - One quarter hour = 10 CE hours
- The renewal applicant certifies on the renewal application full compliance with CE requirements.
- The same CE hours cannot be used to fulfill the CE requirement for than one renewal period.

WAIVER OF CE REQUIREMENTS

The renewal applicant can request for waiver before the renewal date, by filing with the Division a renewal application, required fee, and a statement requesting for waiver of the CE requirements. If the Division finds good cause through provided evidence, it will waive the CE requirements for the renewal period the applicant applied.

GOOD CAUSE is defined as an inability to fulfill the CE requirements due to the following:
1. Full-time service in the U.S. armed forces; or
2. Extreme hardship is determined by the Board with evidence (documented by a physician) of the following:
    a. An incapacitating illness; or

    b. Physical inability that prevents traveling to the sites of CE program; or
    c. Other similar extenuating circumstance (e.g., illness of family member)

The applicant will receive an interview before the Board if he or she requested it at time filing the request for waiver to the Division. The applicant has at least 20 days' notice of the date, time and place of the interview.

(68 IL ADC Section 1330.100)

DENIAL, SUSPENSION AND REVOKE OF LICENSE & DENIAL OF RENEWAL DUE TO FAILURE OF PAYING STUDENT LOAN

The Department may deny any license or renewal, authorized by the Civil Administrative Code of Illinois to any person who has defaulted on an educational loan or scholarship provided by or guaranteed by the Illinois Student Assistance Commission or any governmental agency of this State. The Department may also suspense or revoke license if the person fails to repay his or her student loan. However, the Department may issue a license or renewal if the aforementioned persons have established a satisfactory repayment record as determined by the Illinois Student Assistance Commission or other appropriate governmental agency of this State." (Proof of a satisfactory repayment record must be submitted.)

(20 ILCS 2105/2105-15)

SECTION 9: PHARMACY TECHNICIAN

Pharmacy Practice Act, Chapter 225 ILCS 85/9, 9.5, 12 &17.1, Section 1330 IAC et seq.
Pharmacy Practice Rules (Implementing the Act), 68 IL ADC Sections 1330.80, 1330.200 & 1330.220

REGISTRATION AS PHARMACY TECHNICIAN

REGISTRATION REQUIREMENT
1. Age 16 or older.
2. Has not engaged in misconduct or bad behavior.
3. Is attending or has graduated from an accredited high school or has a high school equivalency certificate (GED).
4. Has filed an application for registration.

APPLICATION FOR CERTIFICATE OF REGISTRATION AS A PHARMACY TECHNICIAN
An applicant can file an application to the Division, together with the following:
- Copy of his or her high school diploma or its equivalent, or proof of current enrollment in a high school program; and
- The required fee.

A technician certificate of registration must be displayed and visible to the public in the pharmacy where the pharmacy technician is employed. Every registered pharmacy technician shall notify the Division of any change in the address on record **within 30 days** after the change. No person who holds an active Illinois pharmacist license may concurrently hold an active Illinois pharmacy technician registration.

(68 IL ADC Section 1330.200)

PHARMACY TECHNICIAN JOB FUNCTIONS

A registered pharmacy technician under the supervision of a pharmacist can:

- Assisting in the practice of pharmacy
- Assisting in the dispensing process
- Offering counseling by a pharmacist or student pharmacist
- Receiving new verbal prescription orders
- Contacting prescriber concerning prescription order for clarification

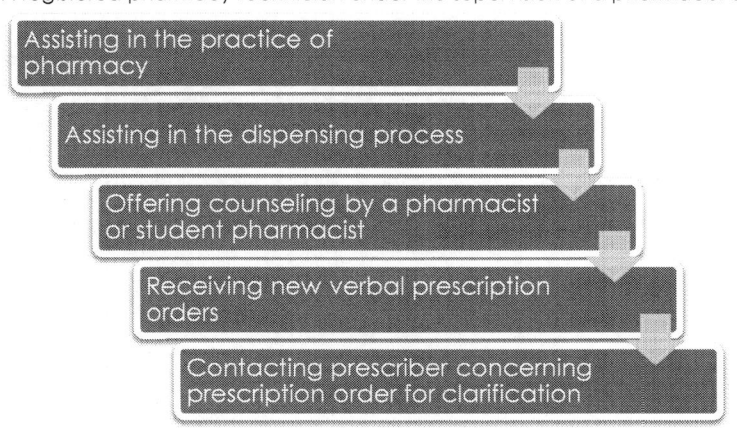

Figure 1: Responsibilities of Registered Pharmacy Technician

WHAT MAY A PHARMACY TECHNICIAN NOT ENGAGE IN THE PRACTICE OF PHARMACY?

A pharmacy technician cannot perform the following job functions:
- Dispensing in the absence of a pharmacist.
- Transferring a prescription to another pharmacy.
- Selling Schedule V controlled substance (exempt narcotics).
- Counseling patients, except for student pharmacist, pharmacy intern, or a pharmacy graduate from another state who works in IL and is waiting to be licensed in IL as a pharmacist.
- Performing drug regimen review or clinical conflict resolution.

STUDENT PHARMACIST AS PHARMACY TECHNICIAN
A student pharmacist is any registered pharmacy technician who enrolled in a professional pharmacy program or has graduated from such program within the last 18 months. He or she must meet all requirements of a pharmacy technician and pay the required fees, but is exempt from certification requirements.

The Department won't renew the pharmacy technician license if you have any of the following:
- Has been registered as a "student pharmacist;" and
- Has dropped out of or been expelled from an ACPE accredited college of pharmacy, failed to complete the 1,200 hours of clinical training within 24 months, or has failed the pharmacist licensure exam 5 times

The Department then will require you to meet the requirements of and become a certified pharmacy technician.

NON-TRADITIONAL PHARMD STUDENTS
Anyone who is enrolled in a non-traditional Pharm.D. program at an ACPE accredited college of pharmacy and is a licensed pharmacist under the laws of another state, is permitted to engage in the practice experience as required by the academic program. These individuals are exempt from the requirement of registering as pharmacy technician while engaging in practice experience program.

An applicant who registers as a pharmacy technician may assist in the practice of pharmacy for **up to 60 days** before the certificate of registration is issued, if application and fees has been submitted. The applicant must keep a copy of the submitted application on the premises where he or she is assisting in the practice of pharmacy.

(225 ILCS 85/9: Section scheduled to be repealed on January 1, 2018)

REGISTRATION AS CERTIFIED PHARMACY TECHNICIAN
CERTIFICATION REQUIREMENT
2 years after first registering as a pharmacy technician, the registrant must meet the following to continue being a certified pharmacy technician:
1. Submitted a written application.
2. Age 18 or older.
3. Is of good moral character, as determined by the Department.

4. Graduated from pharmacy technician training and met requirement in subsection (a) of Section 17.1 of this Act, or obtained documentation from the PIC of the pharmacy they're employed verifying the successful completion of training program.
5. Successfully passed an examination accredited by the National Organization of Certifying Agencies (NOCA), approved by the Board.
6. Paid the required certification fees.

APPLICATION FOR CERTIFICATE OF REGISTRATION AS A CERTIFIED PHARMACY TECHNICIAN
An individual may receive certification as a certified pharmacy technician if he or she has submitted a written application.

(68 IL ADC Section 1330.220)

✓ The following people are exempt from this certification requirement:
- Student pharmacist.
- Foreign graduates who are still completing their clinical hours before the second renewal of registration for pharmacy technician.
- Non-traditional Pharm.D. students.

✓ Pharmacists are not able to register as pharmacy technicians if their license has been denied, revoked, suspended, or restricted for disciplinary purposes.

(225 ILCS 85/9.5: *Section scheduled to be repealed on January 1, 2018*)

Pharmacy technicians must submit their second renewal proof of certification as a certified pharmacy technician, proof of enrollment in professional pharmacy program, or proof of enrollment in clinical training by a graduate from a foreign pharmacy program. This requirement is not applicable to pharmacy technician licensed prior to January 1, 2008. If the individuals fail to provide the necessary proof, they cannot renew their pharmacy technician's registration.

(68 IL ADC Section 1330.80)

PHARMACY TECHNICIAN TRAINING
The pharmacy and its PIC are responsible to train all of its pharmacy technicians or obtain proof of prior training in all of the following topics:
1. The duties and responsibilities of the technicians and pharmacists.
2. Tasks and technical skills, policies, and procedures.
3. Compounding, packaging, labeling, and storage.
4. Pharmaceutical and medical terminology.
5. Record keeping requirements.
6. The ability to perform and apply arithmetic calculations.

All these topics must be done **within 6 months** after initial employment or changing duties and responsibilities of a pharmacy technician.

(225 ILCS 85/17.1: *Section scheduled to be repealed on January 1, 2018*)

CONTINUING EDUCATION

In order to renew a certificate of registration as a certified pharmacy technician, the registrant shall provide:

- Evidence to the Department for completion of a total of 20 hours of continuing pharmacy education during the 24 months before the expiration date of the certificate.
- One hour of continuing pharmacy education in subject of pharmacy law.
- One hour of continuing pharmacy education in subject of patient safety.

(225 ILCS 85/12: *Section scheduled to be repealed on January 1, 2018*)

SECTION 10: GENERAL PROVISION

Pharmacy Practice Act, Chapter 225 ILCS 85/5.5,13, 19.1, 19.5, 20, 35.2 & 41, Section 1330 IAC et seq.
Pharmacy Practice Rules (Implementing the Act), 68 IL ADC Sections 1330.20, 1330.50, 1330.80, 1330.90, 1330.720

EXPIRATION OF LICENSE/CERTIFICATE

Every license (i.e. pharmacy and pharmacist licenses) issued **expires on March 31 of each even-numbered year**, except the certificate of registration as a pharmacy technician that expires **annually on March 31**. The holder of the license or certificate of registration can pay the renewal fee **60 days before the expiration date**.

The registrant is responsible to notify the Division of any change of address, because failure to receive a renewal form is not considered as an excuse for failure to pay the renewal fee. If the person practices on an expired license or certificate, he or she has committed unlicensed practice and is subject to discipline.

(68 IL ADC Section 1330.80)

INACTIVE STATUS

A pharmacist or pharmacy technician can be excused from payment of renewal fees and completion of CE requirements, if he or she notifies the Department in writing to place his or her license on an inactive status. However, to restore their license, they must notify the Department in writing and pay required renewal fees. A pharmacy license cannot be placed on inactive status.

(225 ILCS 85/13: *Section scheduled to be repealed on January 1, 2018*)

RESTORATION OF A PHARMACIST LICENSE

To restore a certificate of registration that has:
- A. Expired for 5 years or less, a pharmacist must (1) pay all lapsed renewal fess <u>and</u> (2) proof of 30 hours of CE.

- B. Been placed on inactive status for 5 years or less, a pharmacist must (1) pay current renewal fee <u>and</u> (2) provide proof of 30 hours of CE.

- C. Been placed on inactive status for > 5 years, a pharmacist must (1) file an application to the Division, (2) pay the fee <u>and</u> (3) provide proof of 30 hours of CE.
    - In addition, the pharmacist must submit either (1) certification of active practice in another state <u>or</u> (2) evidence of military service.
    - If a pharmacist is not able to submit the above proof, he or she must submit a completion of course work or clinical training approved by the Board:
        1. 30 hours of CE; <u>and</u>
        2. Either

a. 600 hours of clinical practice under the supervision of a pharmacist completed within 2 years; or
b. Successful completion of the Pharmacist Assessment for Remediation Evaluation (PARE) exam with an overall score of 80 or higher, and a minimum score of 75 in each of the 3 areas on the PARE exam.

D. The document for restoration is insufficiently provided; the Division will require the registrant to clarify by (1) providing information as necessary and (2) appearing for an interview before the Board.

(68 IL ADC Section 1330.90)

FEES

The following fees are not refundable: (See **table 1**)

	FEES	Pharmacy	Pharmacist	Student Pharmacist	Registered Pharmacy Technician	Certified Pharmacy Technician
1	License/Certificate Application	$100	$75	$40	$40	$40
2	License/Certificate Renewal	$100/year	$75/year	$25/year	$25/year	$25/year
3	Registered Pharmacist Licensure	-	$200	-	-	-
4	§License Restoration	-	$50 plus all lapsed renewal fees	-	-	-
5	Division Review and Verification of Exam Score	-	$20 plus any applicable testing fee	-	-	-
6	Change of PIC	$25	-	-	-	-

Table 1: Fees. §License restoration includes the fee for a pharmacist to restore a license from inactive status and should NOT be greater than $450.

A person who applies for license as a pharmacist must pay the Division or the designated testing service. Examination fee is not refundable if the person fails to appear on the exam's scheduled date and time.

GENERAL FEES include fees for the following:
- Duplicate license, replacement for a lost license, or license with change of name or address is $20. (If there's no duplicate certification issued for name and address changes on Division records, no fee is required.).
- A certification for registrant's record is $20.
- Having the scoring of an examination reviewed and verified is $20.

(68 IL ADC Section 1330.20)

VACCINATIONS/IMMUNIZATIONS

QUALIFICATION
- A pharmacist or student pharmacist under the supervision of a pharmacist may administer vaccinations with a valid prescription or standing order by a physician to the following patients:
  - Patients ≥14 years old, or in accordance with hospital pharmacy and therapeutics committee policies and procedures.
  - Patients ages 10 and older, limited to live and inactivated Influenza and Tdap (tetanus, diphtheria, acellular pertussis) vaccines.
- The pharmacist must successfully complete a training course accredited by the ACPE or similar professional body approved by the Division.
- The pharmacist is required to maintain a current Basic Life Support Certification for Healthcare Providers issued by the American Heart Association, the American Red Cross, the American Safety and Health Institute.
- Each pharmacy or pharmacist that works outside of a pharmacy, is required to have a current copy or electronic version of the CDC reference "Epidemiology and Prevention of Vaccine—Preventable Diseases" available at the location where vaccinations are given.

Note: A standing order can come from any physician; the order doesn't need to be from the patient's primary physician.

PROTOCOLS, POLICIES AND PROCEDURES
- Before giving vaccinations, a pharmacist or student pharmacist under the supervision of a pharmacist must follow the physician's protocols for the administration of vaccines, and treatment of severe adverse events after vaccines was given.
- The pharmacy must maintain written policies and procedures for handling and disposal of all used supplies equipment.
- The pharmacist or student pharmacist under the supervision of a pharmacy must provide the appropriate vaccine information statement (VIS) to the patient or patient's legal guardian before vaccination.
- The pharmacy must report adverse events to the patient's primary care provider and as required by the Vaccine Adverse Events Reporting System (VAERS).

RECORDKEEPING AND REPORTING
All records of vaccinations must be kept for **5 years**. These records include the following:
1. The name, address and patient's date of birth.
2. Date of vaccination.
3. Name, dose, manufacturer, lot number, and beyond use date of the vaccine.
4. Name and address of the patient's primary health care provider.
5. The name or unique identifier of the administering pharmacist.
6. VIS that was provided to the patient.

A pharmacist who administers any vaccine must report to the patient's primary doctor **within 30 days** after vaccination.

(68 IL ADC Section 1330.50)

UNLICENSED PRACTICE; VIOLATION; CIVIL PENALTY
Any person who practices, attempts to practice, or appears to practice pharmacy without being licensed, must pay a civil penalty to the Department in an amount ≤ $5,000 for each offense.
- The Department has the authority and power to investigate any and all unlicensed activities, and assess the civil penalty after a hearing.
- The civil penalty must be paid within 60 days after the effective date of the civil penalty's order imposed.

(225 ILCS 85/5.5: Section scheduled to be repealed on January 1, 2018)

ENFORCEMENT; PENALTIES
If a person who practices as a pharmacist or operate a pharmacy without being licensed, he or she is guilty of a Class A misdemeanor and for each subsequent conviction, is guilty of a Class 4 felony.

INVESTIGATIONS; NOTICE OF HEARING
Before suspending, revoking, or taking disciplinary action, the Department will notify the accused applicant or licensed person **30 days** prior to the date of hearing, any charges made, and the time and date of the hearing. The individual must send their written response to the Board **within 20 days** after the notice is sent. Failure to response may result in license suspended, revoked, placed on probationary status, or other disciplinary action.

(225 ILCS 85/35.2: Section scheduled to be repealed on January 1, 2018)

FILLING AND REFILLING PRESCRIPTION ON FILE IN OTHER PHARMACIES
TRANSFER OF PRESCRIPTION
A prescription may be transferred between pharmacies for the purpose of original fill or refill dispensing if the following are met:
1. The pharmacist transferring the prescription invalidates the prescription on file and records (1) the pharmacy the prescription was transferred to, (2) the date of issuance of the copy and (3) the name of the pharmacist issuing the transferred prescription order; and
2. The pharmacist receiving the transferred prescription directly from the other pharmacist records required information (see **figure 1**).
    - The name, address and original prescription number of the pharmacy from which the prescription was transferred from.
    - All information of a prescription order (i.e. name of the drug, original amount dispensed, date of original issuance of the prescription, and number of valid refills remaining); and
    - The pharmacist informs the patient that the original prescription has been cancelled at the pharmacy from which it has been transferred from.

(68 IL ADC Section1330.720)

Please view figure 1 for an outline of pharmacist responsibilities when transferring prescriptions:

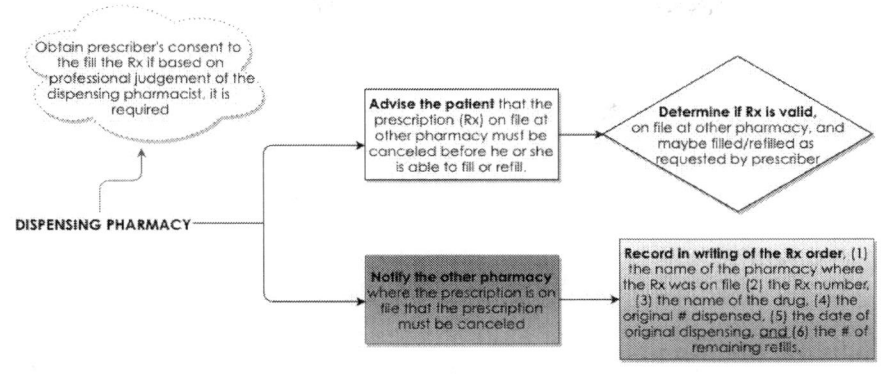

Figure 1: Filling and Refilling Process at the Dispensing Pharmacy

Flowchart contents:
- Obtain prescriber's consent to the fill the Rx if based on professional judgement of the dispensing pharmacist, it is required
- DISPENSING PHARMACY
- Advise the patient that the prescription (Rx) on file at other pharmacy must be canceled before he or she is able to fill or refill.
- Determine if Rx is valid, on file at other pharmacy, and maybe filled/refilled as requested by prescriber
- Notify the other pharmacy where the prescription is on file that the prescription must be canceled
- Record in writing of the Rx order, (1) the name of the pharmacy where the Rx was on file (2) the Rx number, (3) the name of the drug, (4) the original # dispensed, (5) the date of original dispensing, and (6) the # of remaining refills.

(225 ILCS 85/19: Section scheduled to be repealed on January 1, 2018)

PROCEDURES FOR TRANSFEROR PHARMACY

1. After the pharmacist confirms that request is valid, he or she should provide information accurately and completely.
2. The pharmacy records on the face of the prescription the name and pharmacist of the transferee pharmacy, and date of transfer; <u>and</u>
3. The pharmacy cancels the prescription by writing "VOID" on its face.
4. If the prescription is not picked up by the patient, transferee pharmacist should cancel the prescription and notify the original pharmacy.

Federal law permits transferring of controlled substance prescriptions only for purposes of refills. Original prescriptions cannot be transferred. Under IL law, a prescription for Schedule III, IV and V drugs may be transferred only from the original pharmacy and **only one time** for purposes of original fill or refill dispensing, and may not be transferred further. However, a pharmacist who is electronically sharing real-time on-line computerized systems may transfer up to the maximum refills permitted by DEA or federal law and the prescriber's authorization. In IL, the transfer of a prescription between pharmacies that share a common database is no longer considered a transfer. The pharmacy personnel can (1) perform the transaction, <u>and</u> (2) there's no limit on the movement of controlled substance prescription (think CVS or Walgreens as examples). A prescription for Schedule II controlled substances may <u>NOT</u> be transferred.

Note: If the prescription is for a controlled substance, the transferring pharmacist should also record the DEA number of the pharmacy that it's transferred to, and the receiving pharmacist should record the DEA number of the pharmacy the original prescription was transferred.

(68 IL ADC Section 1330.720)

RECORD RETENTION
Every pharmacy shall keep a suitable book, file, or electronic record keeping system for **at least 5 years** to be available for inspection if asked by the Department.
- For the previously unfilled prescription, it has to be maintained in a suitable book, file or recordkeeping system that is readily retrievable. If they were filled prescriptions, the pharmacy may maintain them in an alternative data retention system, such as a direct digital imaging system, but it must be capable of producing a copy of the electronic record if requested by the Department.

(225 ILCS 85/18: Section scheduled to be repealed on January 1, 2018) & (68 IL ADC Section 1330.10)

COMMON ELECTRONIC FILE
If a pharmacy business consists of two or more pharmacies, it may use a common electronic file to maintain required dispensing information.

The dispensing of prescription contained in a common database by a pharmacist licensed in IL or another state does not include transfer, provided the following:
1. All pharmacies involved in the transactions of dispensing the prescription and all pharmacists engaging in dispensing function are licensed, permitted, or registered in IL or another state.
2. A policy and procedures manual for all participating pharmacies and pharmacists is available to the Department upon request.
3. The pharmacists who involved in filling, dispensing, and patient counseling are identified. A pharmacist shall only be accountable for the tasks performed.

(225 ILCS 85/20: Section scheduled to be repealed on January 1, 2018)

DISPENSING OPIOID ANTAGONISTS (NALOXONE)
A licensed pharmacist has the right to dispense naloxone for treatment of opioid overdose. Before dispensing an opioid antagonist, a pharmacist shall complete a training program that includes:
- Completion of the IL State Opioid Antagonist Training program allows certified pharmacist to dispense Naloxone without a prescription.
- The training is an on-demand and web-based program.

OPIOID ANTAGONIST INITIATIVE
Eligible pharmacists who have completed a certificate training-program in opioid overdose prevention and who are CPR certified may dispense Naloxone and educate patients. Pharmacies who have pharmacists with certified Naloxone Antagonist Training, can contact ILPMP at ILPMP.org to request a copy of the Standardized Procedures for Naloxone Opioid Overdose.

(225 ILCS 85/19.1: Section scheduled to be repealed on January 1, 2018)

BIOLOGICAL PRODUCTS
Biological products are products made of virus, therapeutic serum, toxin, antitoxin, vaccine, blood, blood component or derivative, allergenic product, protein (except any chemically synthesized polypeptide), or analogous product, or arsphenamine or derivative of arsphenamine (or any other trivalent organic arsenic compound), applicable to the prevention, treatment, or cure of a disease or condition of human beings.

"INTERCHANGEABLE BIOLOGICAL (BIO-SIMILAR) PRODUCT" is a biological product that:
1. FDA has licensed and determined to meet the standards for interchangeability pursuant to 42 U.S.C. 262(k)(4); or
2. Has determined that it's therapeutically equivalent based on the latest edition of or supplement to the FDA Orange Book.

A pharmacist may substitute a bio-similar product for a prescribed biological product only if all of the following conditions are met:
1. The substituted product has been determined by the FDA to be interchangeable with the prescribed biological product.
2. The prescribing physician doesn't state in writing, verbally, or electronically that substitution is prohibited in a manner consistent with Section 25 of this Act; and
3. The pharmacy informs the patient about the substitution.

Within 5 business day following the dispensing of a biological product, the dispensing pharmacist or pharmacist's designed individual shall make an entry of the specific product provided to the patient, including the name of the product and the manufacturer. The entry's communication shall be conveyed in a way that can be electronically accessed by the prescriber through the following:
1. An interoperable electronic medical records system.
2. An electronic prescribing technology.
3. A pharmacy benefit management system; or
4. A pharmacy record.

If the pharmacist does not utilize the method of electronic communication, he or she can communicate through facsimile, telephone, electronic transmission, or other available means. The pharmacist doesn't have to communicate with the prescriber if (1) there is no FDA-approved bio-similar product for the product prescribed, or (2) refilled prescription is not changed from the product dispensed.

RECORDKEEPING
The pharmacy needs to retain records of biological products dispensed for **5 years**.

(225 ILCS 85/19.5: Section scheduled to be repealed on January 1, 2018)

CURRENT USUAL AND CUSTOMARY RETAIL PRICE DISCLOSURE
WHAT DOES USUAL AND CUSTOMARY PRICE MEAN?
Usual and customary prices are actual prices that pharmacies charge consumers who purchase without insurance for their prescription drugs or medical devices.

If any person who has a prescription for a (brand or generic) drug or medical device, requests for its current usual and customary retail price, the pharmacy must disclose it. This request must be made in person or by phone. The pharmacy may disclose prices of **no more than 10 prescription drugs or medical devices**. The prices that were quoted are valid only on the day of the request. When making the request, the person must provide the name, strength and quantity of the drug.

(225 ILCS 85/41: *Section scheduled to be repealed on January 1, 2018*)

SECTION 11: PRESCRIPTION ORDER

Pharmacy Practice Act, Chapter 225 ILCS 85/22, 22b, 25.5, 25.10, 25.20, 26 Section 1330 IAC et seq.
Pharmacy Practice Rules (Implementing the Act), 68 IL ADC Section1330.60, 1330.770

PRESCRIPTION LABEL

When a prescription is dispensed, the label is affixed to the bottle or package. It must contain the following: (See **figure 1**)

1. Name and address of the pharmacy
2. Name or initials of the person who filled the medication
3. Date medication was filled
4. Name of patient
5. Rx number of prescription
6. Last name of prescriber
7. Directions for use
8. Name of drug, dosage and quantity

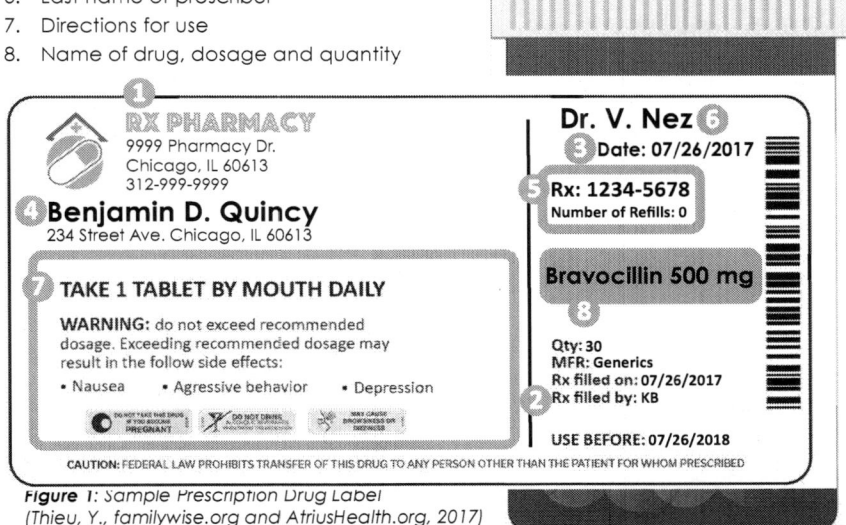

Figure 1: Sample Prescription Drug Label
(Thieu, Y., familywise.org and AtriusHealth.org, 2017)

Tip to know: For the IL MPJE purposes, do know the federal law requirement of "Caution: Federal law prohibits dispensing without a prescription" statement to be on the prescription label (see **figure 1**). For the label on the original manufactured bottle of the prescription drugs, federal law requires it must contain the phrase "Rx Only."

(225 ILCS 85/22: Section scheduled to be repealed on January 1, 2018)

DRUG PRODUCT SUBSTITUTION
GENERIC DRUG

Any generic drug that is determined to be therapeutically equivalent by the FDA is available for substitution. A pharmacist can substitute a brand or alternative generic drug if the selected drug product has the same dosage form and active ingredients with no more than 1% difference from the active ingredient to the substituted drug. An example is switching from Crestor to atorvastatin, or switching from two different manufacturers of generic drugs (i.e. simvastatin to simvastatin from another manufacturer). Unless the physician indicates that the drug "may not substitute" on the prescription, then the pharmacist must dispense the same brand or generic drug as prescribed.

(225 ILCS 85/25: Section scheduled to be repealed on January 1, 2018)

ANTI-EPILEPTIC DRUG PRODUCT SELECTION PROHIBITED (EXCLUDES IN-PATIENT SETTINGS)
To preserve the public peace, health, and safety:
- When a physician indicates on a prescription that an anti-epileptic drug "may not be substituted," the pharmacist must not interchange it without notifying the prescribing physician and the patient.
- The pharmacist must provide a written notice to the patient at the time of the dispensing if he or she substitutes any generic prescription in place of a brand name anti-epileptic drug.

(225 ILCS 85/26: Section scheduled to be repealed on January 1, 2018)

DISPENSING PRESCRIPTION DRUGS
CENTRALIZED PRESCRIPTION FILLING
A pharmacy may fill or refill prescription for another pharmacy, as long as both pharmacies have the same owner or have a written contract specifying (1) the services each pharmacy provided, (2) the responsibilities of each pharmacy, and (3) the manner in which they must comply with Federal and State laws, rules, and regulations.

(225 ILCS 85/25.5: Section scheduled to be repealed on January 1, 2018)

Pharmacies that provide centralized prescription filling has to:
1. Share a common electronic file to allow access to sufficient information necessary to fill or refill a prescription order.
2. Maintain appropriate records to identify the responsible pharmacist in the dispensing process.
3. Maintain a mechanism for tracking the prescription drug order during each step in the process.

(68 IL ADC Section 1330.770)

REMOTE PRESCRIPTION PROCESSING
Remote prescription processing occurs when a pharmacy outsources activities related to the dispensing process to another pharmacy in IL or outside of IL. These activities include anything from receiving, evaluating and transferring prescription, to obtaining refills, performing patient counseling and drug regimen review. However, remote prescription processing **does not include the dispensing of a prescription drug (i.e. giving or mailing the medication to the patient).** Think CVS Caremark centralized filling that fills the medication in a warehouse and then mail to local CVS pharmacies for patients to pick up.

A pharmacy may engage in remote prescription processing under the following conditions:
1. The pharmacies meet all criteria listed under "centralized prescription filling."
2. The pharmacies share a common electronic file.
3. Each pharmacy may maintain its own records or in a common electronic file shared by both pharmacies. The system should be able to produce record at either location of each processing task, the person who performed, and the location where each task was performed.

(225 ILCS 85/25.10: *Section scheduled to be repealed on January 1, 2018*)

ELECTRONIC VISUAL IMAGE PRESCRIPTION

The electronic image can serve as the original prescription without the need of a hard copy if the pharmacy's computer system can capture an electronic visual image of the prescription order that cannot be altered. The computer system must be able to maintain, print and provide all of the prescription information **within 72 hours** of the Department's request.

(225 ILCS 85/25.20: *Section scheduled to be repealed on January 1, 2018*)

INTERNET PHARMACIES

Illinois and all federal regulations adopted Ryan Haight Online Pharmacy Consumer Protection Act of 2008. The purpose of this Act is to regulate rogue online pharmacies and their sale of drugs, particularly to young people.

Online pharmacies cannot dispense controlled substances to anyone without a valid prescription. A prescription is valid only if (1) it's issued for a legitimate medical purpose, and (2) after at least one physician's face-to-face evaluation with the patient.

(68 IL ADC Section 1330.60)

SECTION 12: REFUSAL, REVOCATION, OR SUSPENSION

Pharmacy Practice Act, Chapter 225 ILCS 85/23, 30, 30.1, 31, 33 & 35.5, 35.6 & 35.7, Section 1330 IAC et seq.
Pharmacy Practice Rules (Implementing the Act), 68 IL ADC Sections1330.30, 1330.40, 1330.70 & 1330.110

The Department may refuse, revoke, or suspend a license/registration, or impose **fines that should be $10,000 or less** for each violation for any one or combination of the following causes:

1. Lying about not being convicted of any kind of offense.
2. Violation of the Pharmacy Practice Act.
3. Obtaining licensure by fraudulent means.
4. Demonstration of incompetence or unfitness to practice resulted from a pattern of misconduct.
5. Assisting another person in committing violation of the Pharmacy Practice Act.
6. Failing to respond to written request by the Department within 60 days.
7. Failing to report to the Department within 60 days any disciplinary action in any other state faced by a pharmacist or pharmacy technician.
8. Engaging in unprofessional, dishonorable, or unethical conduct that's likely to deceive, defraud, or harm the public.
9. Directly or indirectly giving or receiving any form of compensation for any professional services that were not actually provided.
10. Selling drug samples.
11. Physical illness, mental illness or any other impairments, including deterioration through aging or loss of motor skill that results in inability to perform with reasonable judgment, skill or safety.
12. Addiction to or excessive use of alcohol, narcotics, or stimulants.
13. Overcharging for professional services.
14. Violation of the Health Care Worker Self-Referral Act.
15. Failing to dispense any drug in "good faith."

Notes:
- If there's a discipline of jurisdiction in one state, discipline follows you wherever you go.
- The person must inform the Division **within 60 days** after he or she is disciplined in another state.
- Health Care Worker Self-Referral Act intents to provide guidance to health care professionals of the type of patient referrals that are acceptable.

The Department may refuse to issue or may suspend the license of those who fail to file tax return, or fail to pay the tax, penalty or interest that is shown in the filed return, until it is paid. The Department will revoke the license of any registrant who has been convicted for a second time of any felony.

Any person who's in need of mental treatment will have their license suspended and may resume practice only if the Board found that he or she has been recovered from mental illness.

(225 ILCS 85/30: Section scheduled to be repealed on January 1, 2018)

PRIOR REVOCATION; HEARING

If a person already owns a pharmacy and receives a revocation or suspension of the pharmacy license, the Department won't allow him or her to open a new pharmacy. The Department will go after any earlier complaint filed against the pharmacy and conduct a hearing, regardless if the new pharmacy has been licensed. If there's enough evidence to revoke the license for pharmacy operation, the application for a license to establish a new pharmacy will be denied.

In the case if the individual, who's applying for a license to establish a new pharmacy, owns a pharmacy with a revoked license, the Department may not issue the license unless the owner presents sufficient evidence indicating rehabilitation.

(225 ILCS 85/31: Section scheduled to be repealed on January 1, 2018)

SUSPENSION WITHOUT HEARING

If the licensed or registered person is found to pose an immediate danger to the public, the Director of the Department may immediately suspend his or her license without a hearing. The Board will have a hearing **within 15 days** of the suspension. The hearing will determine whether the person's license will be revoked, suspended, place on probationary status or reinstated.

(225 ILCS 85/33: Section scheduled to be repealed on January 1, 2018)

UNPROFESSIONAL AND UNETHICAL CONDUCT

THE FOLLOWING ARE CONSIDERED UNPROFESSIONAL AND UNETHICAL CONDUCT:

1. Failing to establish and maintain effective controls against diversion of prescription drugs.
2. Making a false report or record, or failing to file a report or keep record.
3. Knowingly dispensing a prescription drug after the death of the person the prescription was written for.
4. Billing for quantities of drugs that is more than what was delivered or charging patients for a brand drug when a generic is dispensed.
5. Submitting fraudulent billing or reports to a third party payer (insurance company).
6. Failing to exercise sound professional judgment with respect to the accuracy and authenticity of any prescription drug order dispensed.
7. Failing to ensure that patient counseling is offered or refusing to counsel the patient upon the request.
8. Discriminating in any manner against any person based upon his or her race, creed, color, gender, sexual orientation, age or national origin.
9. Failing to keep oneself and the apparel clean or to wear identification bearing name and designation.
10. Directly or indirectly furnishing to a medical practitioner prescription order-blanks that refer to a specific pharmacist or pharmacy in any manner.
11. Actively or passively participating in any arrangement or agreement in which a prescription order-blank is prepared, written, or issued in a manner that refers to a specific pharmacist or pharmacy.

12. Dividing a prescription order unless directed by the prescriber, payer or patient or when the full quantity of that prescription medication is not available at that location.
13. Violating or assisting in the violation in the use of habit-forming controlled substances.

(68 IL ADC Section 1330.30)

VIOLATIONS
These are conduct by a registrant that can result in violations of the following:
1. Engaging in the practice of pharmacy when the person is not authorized to practice pharmacy and does not operate in compliance with the pharmacy practice law.
2. Compounding or selling any drug or chemical recognized in USP/NF for internal or external use, which has different strength, quality, purity, or bioavailability as determined by USP/NF.
3. Compounding or selling any drug or chemical with the strength and purity that are below standards.
4. Purchasing prescriptions drugs from any source that fails to meet the Wholesale Drug Distribution Licensing Act.

Tip to know: If there's a fact pattern, a discipline for the conduct will be likely imposed.

Note: The purpose of the Wholesale Drug Distribution Licensing Act is to implement the Federal Prescription Drug Marketing Act of 1987 (PDMA). The PDMA requires that the person or entity must be licensed by the state in order to engage in the wholesale distribution of human prescription drugs in that state.

(68 IL ADC Section 1330.40)

PROHIBITED TRANSACTION
A pharmacy or pharmacist is prohibited to offer prescribers, health care facility or it owner, or employees who work for a health care institution, any rebate, discount, or commission, in order to receive more pharmacy services, or sales of medication or devices.

(225 ILCS 85/23: *Section scheduled to be repealed on January 1, 2018*)

REPORTING
The PIC must report the termination of a pharmacist or pharmacy technician who has threatened patient's safety, to the chief pharmacy coordinator. And such report shall be in writing and filed to the Department **within 60 days** of the determination to be reported. A form for the pharmacy personnel termination report must be completed and signed and may be emailed to FPR.PharmacyAdverse@Illinois.gov.

(225 ILCS 85/30.1)

SUBPOENA
The Department has the power to require any document or evidence, to take testimony (either oral or written statement), and bring in any witness in IL. The Director and any member of the Board have the power to administer oaths to witnesses at any hearing, in which the Department is authorized to conduct.

(225 ILCS 85/35.5: Section scheduled to be repealed on January 1, 2018)

THE CONCLUSIONS OF THE HEARING
The Board will present to the Director a written report of its findings whether or not the accused person violated the Act. The Board states specific violations and makes a recommendation in aiding the Department's decision on refusal or granting a license. **The findings cannot be used as evidence against the person in a criminal prosecution.**

(225 ILCS 85/35.6: Section scheduled to be repealed on January 1, 2018)

ATTORNEY AS "HEARING OFFICER"
The Director can appoint any attorney to serve as the hearing officer in front of the Board for hearing regarding revocation, suspension, or refusal to issue, or renew a license, or other disciplinary action. At the hearing, at least one member of the Board must be present. The attorney can conduct the hearing, and report his or her findings, conclusions and recommendations to the Board and the Director. The Board has 60 days from receipt of the attorney's report to review, present their findings, conclusions, and recommendations to the Director.

- If the Board fails to do so within 60 days, the defendant can request a direct appeal to the Secretary.
- Within 7 calendar days after the request, the Secretary will issue an order to the Board requesting that the Board present their findings, conclusions, and recommendations of the case within 30 calendar days after the order.
- If the Board fails to do so within that time frame, the Secretary will issue an order based on the attorney's report and record of the proceedings within 30 calendar days thereafter.

In conclusion, there are three circumstances where the Secretary can base its final decision on the attorney's report, (1) a direct appeal is requested, (2) the Board fails to issue its findings, conclusion, and recommendations within 30 calendar days, and (3) the Secretary fails to issue an order within 30 calendar days thereafter.

If the Secretary disagrees with the recommendation of the Board or the attorney, the Secretary may issue its own recommendation.

(225 ILCS 85/35.7: Section scheduled to be repealed on January 1, 2018)

GRANTING VARIANCES

The Director may grant variances from rules under the pharmacy Act if (1) the particular requirement of the rule is not required by the law, (2) no one will be injured if the variance is given, and (3) the rules would be unreasonable burdensome if they were applied.

If the variance is granted, the Director must notify the Board and the reasons for granting the variance the next meeting of the Board.

(68 IL ADC Section 1330.70)

CONFIDENTIALITY

All information collected by the Department for the purpose of investigation of a licensee or applicant is confidential, unless there's a formal complaint filed by the Department, then this will be a public record.

(68 IL ADC Section 1330.110)

SECTION 13: TYPES OF PHARMACIES

Pharmacy Practice Act, Chapter 225 ILCS 85/16a, 16b, 22b & 25.15, Section 1330 IAC et seq.
Pharmacy Practice Rules (Implementing the Act), 68 IL ADC Sections1330.500 – 1330.560

- Non-controlled substance prescriptions expire **1 year** from the date it was originally issued, regardless of the number of refills remaining or as needed (PRN) refill.
- Whenever a pharmacy intends on changing or adding to the type of pharmacy services it offers, it must notify the Division **at least 30 days** prior to the change or addition.

COMMUNITY PHARMACY SERVICES

Pharmacies engage in general or specialty community pharmacy practice, and offer pharmacy service to the general public must comply with the following:
(A community pharmacy that, in addition to offering pharmacy services to the general public, provides institutional services shall also comply with Section 1330.520)

I. **STAFFING OF THE PHARMACY**
There are no minimum requirements for hours of operation for a community pharmacy.
  A. A sign must be conspicuously displayed of (1) the pharmacy's schedule of services whenever the hours of the pharmacy are different from those of the establishment where the pharmacy is located, <u>and</u> (2) message regarding the unavailability of a pharmacist to provide pharmacy services when the pharmacy is open.
  B. No prescription can be dispensed when a pharmacist is not physically present and on duty.

II. **RECORDKEEPING REQUIREMENTS FOR DISPENSING PRESCRIPTION DRUGS**
  A. For every prescription dispensed, the prescription record must contain the (1) name, (2) initials <u>or</u> (3) other unique identifier of the pharmacist who dispenses the prescription drugs. If the pharmacy technician dispenses the prescription, then the name, initial or the unique identifier of both the pharmacist and the pharmacy technician must be included on the prescription record.

Note: For the controlled substance prescriptions, at the time of filling, initials or unique identifier are not sufficient, the pharmacist must sign and date on the face of the prescription.

  B. A written prescription copy, or prescription label is for information purposes only and cannot be used as a valid prescription order. The pharmacist must contact the prescriber to obtain a new prescription order. A prescription copy must be marked "For Information Purposes Only" when it's given to a costumer.

  C. When refilling a prescription, the prescription must be maintained and readily retrievable. Each refill must indicate the number of the prescription and entered on a prescription, or other uniformly maintained form of record the information as listed under "Refill Prescription" in **table 1**.
    - If the pharmacist does not indicate in a uniformly maintained record, he or she is considered to have dispensed a refill for the full-face amount of the prescription.

- All refill data must be maintained in the pharmacy store for **5 years.** If requested by the Division upon on-site inspection, a hard copy printout must be provided **within 48 hours.**

Tip to know:
- If a refill prescription is partially filled, it's NOT considered as full refills.
- A pharmacist is allowed to combine or consolidate refills without calling the physician in order to provide the patients greater quantity, up to the total quantity authorized on the original prescription, plus any refills.
    - Example: Lisinopril 10 mg with quantity of 30, SIG: once daily. Refills: 3
        - The pharmacist can combine or consolidate refills by dispensing a 90-day supply, which would give the patient a quantity of 90 instead of 30 without calling the doctor. This improves the patient's adherence and compliance.
    - If the prescription is for a controlled substance, although it's legal to combine the refills without calling the prescriber, the pharmacist must use his or her professional judgment to call the doctor before combining if there's a pattern of controlled substance abuse. The combine effect is limited to a 90-day supply.

D. Any information (i.e. original prescriptions, refill prescriptions) required to be kept may be recorded, and stored in a computerized information system that meets the standards of performance stated in the regulations of the Drug Enforcement Administration (DEA) and must include the capability to:
- Retrieve the original prescription order information for those prescriptions that can be refilled.
- Retrieve the current prescription orders, including information about name of drug, date of refill, quantity dispensed, name and identification code of the manufacturer when there's a prescription of generic drug or a generic interchange, name or initials of the dispensing pharmacist and technician for each refill, and the total number of refills dispensed to date.
- Supply hard copy documentation of each day's refill information to confirm that it been entered and verified for correctness by the pharmacist. For each prescription refilled, this printout must include information as listed under "Hard Copy Printout of Refill Data" in **table 1**.

	Refill Prescription Information	Refill Prescription	Hard Copy Printout of Refill Data
1	The name & dosage form of the drug	✔	✔
2	The date of each refilling	✔	✔
3	The quantity dispensed	✔	✔
4	The name or initials of the pharmacist in each refilling and the pharmacy technician, if applicable	✔	✔
5	The total number of refills remaining for the prescription	✔	-
6	The patient's name	-	✔
7	The prescriber's name	-	✔
8	The prescription number for the prescription	-	✔

Table 1: Refill Prescription Information Required on a Refill Prescription & Hard Copy Printout of Refill Data

E. Instead of printing out hard copy documentation of each day's refill information, the pharmacy can use a log book or separate file. This book or file must be maintained at the pharmacy store for **5 years** after the date of dispensing the refill.

A pharmacy must be licensed with the Division and have on file with the Division these verified statements below before it can be established or moved to a new location:
1. The pharmacy is or will be engaged in the practice of pharmacy; and
2. The pharmacy will maintain and have sufficient prescription drugs and materials to protect the public it serves **within 30 days** after opening of the pharmacy.

UNDER WHAT CIRCUMSTANCES ARE PHARMACIES NOT REQUIRED TO DELIVER PRECRIBED DRUGS AND DISTRIBUTE FDA-APPROVED NONPRESCRIPTION DRUG RESTRICTED TO PHARMACY DISTRIBUTION ONLY?
Under the following circumstances:
- When based on the pharmacist's professional judgment, she or he determines if the drug should be dispensed due clinical reasons.
- National or State emergencies or guidelines affecting availability, usage or supplies of drugs.
- Lack of specialized equipment or expertise needed to safely produce, store or dispense drugs, such as certain drug compounding or storage for nuclear medicine.
- Potentially fraudulent prescriptions.
- Unavailability of drug; or
- The drug is not typically carried in similar practice settings in IL.

WHAT ALTERNATIVES SHOULD A PHARMACY PROVIDE THE PATIENT IF THE PRESCRIBED DRUG, OR NONPRESCRIPTION DRUG IS NOT AVAILABLE OR THE PRECSRIPTION CANNOT BE FILLED DUE TO A CLINICAL REASON?
These alternatives include the following:
- Contact the prescriber to address clinical concerns identified, such as drug-disease contraindication, drug-drug interaction, etc.
- Return unfilled prescriptions to the patient if patient requested; or
- Communicate the original prescription information to a pharmacy of the patient's choice to fill the prescription in a timely manner.

If pharmacies do not receive a payment for dispensing the drug, they are not required to dispense the drug. All pharmacies are required to maintain the following current resource materials, either in hard copy or electronic format:
1. Copies of the Act and this Part.
2. The Illinois Controlled Substances Act and 77 Ill. Adm. Code 3100.
3. 21 CFR (Food and Drugs; 2014); and
4. The Illinois Hypodermic Syringes and Needles Act [720 ILCS 635].

(68 IL ADC Section1330.500)

WHAT IS THE PHARMACIST'S ROLE IN DRUG DIVERSION OR ABUSE PREVENTION?
A pharmacist has a corresponding responsibility in preventing drug diversion or abuse. Therefore, it is important that he or she must able to recognize the following red flags for a potential drug diversion or abuse:
- Prescriptions for the same controlled substance regardless of patient's weight or age.
- Customers present in groups.
- Patient's physician is located in unusual distance from your pharmacy.
- Pay with cash for the controlled substances.
- Prescriptions of opiate, benzodiazepine and muscle relaxant (i.e. hydrocodone, alprazolam and carisoprodol).
    - This combination of drugs is known was trio or trinity.
    - Hydrocodone can be replaced by an oxycodone, the combination of oxycodone, alprazolam and carisoprodol is known as "holy trinity."
    - Addicts use these combinations of drug "cocktail" to intensify the effect.
- A prescription written by a physician who's not associated with pain management
- Multiple prescription early refills.
- Multiple prescribers for the same medication (possible doctor or medication shopping).
- Possible federal or state action against the prescriber.
- Patient has unusual behavior and/or uses street slang for the controlled substance.

RULES AND REGULATIONS FOR INTERNET & MAIL-ORDER PHARMACIES
The Department shall grant a non-resident special pharmacy registration if the following is met:
1. The pharmacy is licensed in the state where the dispensing facility is located and the drugs are dispensed from.
2. There's the disclosure of the location, names, and titles of all principal corporate officers and all pharmacist who are dispensing drugs to residents of IL.
3. The pharmacy is compliant with all directions and requests by the law for information from the Board of Pharmacy of each state where the pharmacy is licensed. The pharmacy must respond directly to all communications from the Board or Department concerning any circumstances arising from the dispensing of drugs to IL residents.
4. The pharmacy maintains its record of drugs dispensed to IL residents.
5. The pharmacy cooperates with the Board or Department in providing information to the board of pharmacy in its licensed state concerning matters related to dispensing drug to IL residents; and
6. During the pharmacy's regular hours of operation, but **not less than 6 days per week**, for a **minimum of 40 hours per week**, a toll-free telephone service is provided to facilitate communication between IL patients and a pharmacist who has access to the patients' records. The toll-free number must be on each drug container label.

(225 ILCS 85/16a: *Section scheduled to be repealed on January 1, 2018*)

PRESCRIPTION PICK-UP AND DROP-OFF
There are no restrictions in IL to prevent prescriptions from being delivered to a patient's home, employment location, hospital, or medical care facility.

(225 ILCS 85/16b: *Section scheduled to be repealed on January 1, 2018*)

DISCIPLINARY ACTIONS
Permitting any of the following will result in disciplinary actions:
- Intentionally destroying unfilled prescriptions.
- Refusing to return unfilled prescriptions.
- Violating a patient's privacy.
- Discriminating against patients or their agents in a manner prohibited by State or federal laws.
- Intimidating or harassing a patient; or
- Failing to comply with the requirements of this Section.

(68 IL ADC Section1330.500)

TELE-PHARMACY
Tele-pharmacy occurs when a pharmacist provides care through the use of telecommunications or other technologies to patients who are remote within the U.S. (i.e. remote dispensing and remote counseling. See **figure 1**)

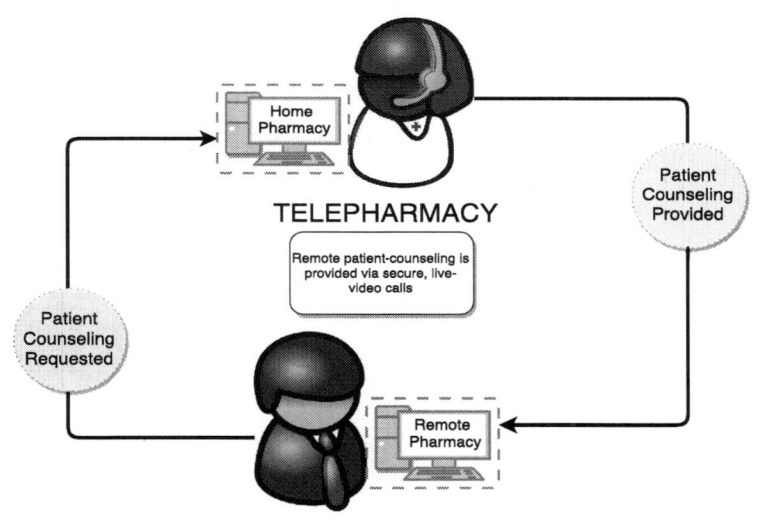

Figure 1: Remote Counseling Using Telecommunication (Thieu, Y., Draw.io., and PixaBay.com, 2017)

Each site where tele-pharmacies occur must have a separate pharmacy license. Home pharmacies that are located outside of IL must be licensed in IL as a nonresident pharmacy. Nonresident pharmacies are required to follow IL laws and rules when filling prescriptions for IL residents. The dispensing pharmacist employed by the nonresident (home) pharmacy is not required to be licensed in IL but must have an active pharmacist license in the state where the nonresident pharmacy is located. Only the PIC of the remote site must be licensed in IL.

There are three types of tele-pharmacy practice, (1) remote dispensing site, (2) remote consultation site, and (3) remote automated pharmacy site. Each remote site must display a sign that is easily viewable by the customer and states the following:
1. The type of tele-pharmacy practice.
2. The facility is a tele-pharmacy supervised by a pharmacist located at (address); and
3. The pharmacist is required to talk to you, over an audio/visual link, each time you pick up a prescription.

WHAT ARE THE REQUIREMENTS FOR A PHARMACY TO PRACTICE TELE-PHARMACY?
A pharmacy must meet all of the following conditions to practice tele-pharmacy:
1. All contents of an automated pharmacy system must be stored in a secure location and may be recorded electronically.
2. The Department must inspect and approve before an automated pharmacy system may be used together with the practice of tele-pharmacy.
3. The PIC shall be responsible for the following:
   - The practice of tele-pharmacy at a remote pharmacy, including the supervision of any automated medication system.
   - Make sure that the home pharmacy has enough staff on duty.
   - Ensure that a certified pharmacy technician at the remote pharmacy has accurately and correctly prepared prescriptions for dispensing.
   - Be responsible for the supervision and training of certified pharmacy technicians at the remote pharmacies; and
   - Ensure that patient counseling is performed by a pharmacist or student pharmacist.

Tip to know: A certified pharmacy technician is different from a registered pharmacy technician, because he or she was a registered pharmacy technician that became certified after graduating from pharmacy technician program or passing the certification exam (refer to "registration as certified pharmacy technician" under 225 ILCS 85/9.5 for more information about pharmacy technician certification requirements).

(225 ILCS 85/25.15: Section scheduled to be repealed on January 1, 2018)

I. REMOTE DISPENSING SITE

This is the pharmacy location where the prescription drugs supply is maintained, and is staffed by a certified pharmacy technician, not a pharmacist. Prescriptions are filled and dispensed by a certified pharmacy technician with at least one year of experience or student pharmacist under the direct, remote supervision of a pharmacist from the home pharmacy. A pharmacist at the home pharmacy has an audio and video connection to the remote dispensing site, and is required to verify the prescription order and prescription drugs in the vial before dispensing it.

Written prescriptions at the remote dispensing site must be scanned into the computer system to ensure that both the remote dispensing and home pharmacy sites can view the initial dispensing, each refill and the original prescription. All written prescriptions must be delivered to the home pharmacy for filing **within 72 hours**. Records have to be maintained in a separate file at the home pharmacy.

The remote site uses its home pharmacy and pharmacy management system for the following:
1. All records are maintained at the home pharmacy.
2. Prescriptions dispensed at the remote site are kept separately from those dispensed at the home pharmacy.
3. Daily reports must be separated for the home and remote sites.

Counseling must be done by a pharmacist via video and audio links before the drug or medical device is delivered at the remote pharmacy. The pharmacist must counsel the patient on all new prescriptions and refills. A PIC or his or her designated pharmacist must complete monthly inspections of the remote site. Inspection criteria shall be included in the policies and procedures for the site. The inspection report must be available on site for pharmacy investigator inspection. The communication link has to be checked daily. If it is malfunction, the remote site pharmacy must be closed, unless a pharmacist is physically present at the remote site. Each pharmacist at the home pharmacy may electronically supervise **no more than 3 remote sites** that are simultaneously open.

II. REMOTE CONSULTATION SITES

These sites have no prescription inventory and are staffed by pharmacy technicians. Only filled prescriptions that are filled at the home pharmacy, with final patient labeling attached are at these sites. The home pharmacy fills, dispenses, and delivers the prescriptions to the remote consultation site, where the drugs are given to the patient. Similar to remote dispensing sites, written prescriptions must be delivered to the home pharmacy **within 72 hours**. Recordkeeping must be conducted by the pharmacist (time/date) when dispensing and counseling occurred.

III. REMOTE AUTOMATED PHARMACY SYSTEM (RAPS)

AUTOMATED PHARMACY SYSTEMS

Only a pharmacist or designated personnel has access to an automated pharmacy system for dispensing.

REMOTE DISPENSING

If an automated pharmacy system is located separate from a remote site, a registered pharmacist from the home pharmacy is required to continuously oversee all of its operations, but is not required to be physically present at the remote site. Drugs may be dispensed only after the pharmacist has approved the filled medications.

STOCKING OR RESTOCKING REMOVABLE CARTRIDGES OR CONTAINERS

If an automated pharmacy system uses removable cartridges or containers to store a drug, before stocking or restocking medications, the pharmacy must verify that all cartridges or containers transported from the wholesale drug distributor were in secure and tamper evident container. A record of each transaction with the automated pharmacy system must be maintained for **5 years**.

(225 ILCS 85/22b: *Section scheduled to be repealed on January 1, 2018*)

RAPS

These are automated dispensing machines that dispense drugs directly to a patient. The site maintains a prescription drug inventory that is secured in an automated pharmacy system, and electronically connected to and controlled by the home pharmacy. A pharmacist must approve all the prescription orders before they are released from the RAPS. Dispensing and counseling are performed via video/audio link by a pharmacist from the home pharmacy.

Similar to the above two sites, the PIC of the home pharmacy, or a designated registrant, must conduct monthly inspections of the RAPS on its policies and procedures and have the report available when requested.

The RAPS must be licensed with the Division as an automated pharmacy system and will be subject to random inspection by pharmacy investigators. If there's a random inspection, a pharmacist with access to the system must be available at the site **within 1 hour**. Written prescriptions may be received at a RAPS and must be scanned to be viewed by a pharmacist.

A kiosk is a device maintaining individual patient prescription drugs that were verified and labeled at the home pharmacy. A home pharmacy can only use the kiosk with prior approval of a patient.

A pharmacy can use an automated pharmacy system to deliver prescriptions to a patient when the device does the following:
1. Is secured against a wall or floor.
2. Provides a method to identify the patient and delivers the prescription only to that patient or the patient's authorized agent.
3. Has adequate security systems and procedures to prevent unauthorized access, to comply with federal and State regulations, and to maintain patient confidentiality.
4. Records the time and date that the patient removed the prescription from the system.

(68 IL ADC Section1330.510)

All pharmacists performing services in support of a remote dispensing site, remote consultation site, kiosk, or remote automated pharmacy system (RAPS) must display a copy or electronic image of their licenses at the remote site where they provide services.

The remote site cannot be open when the home pharmacy is closed, unless a pharmacist employed by the home pharmacy is present at the remote site or is remotely providing supervision and consultation as required.

(68 IL ADC Section1330.510)

OFFSITE INSTITUTIONAL PHARMACY SERVICES

These pharmacies are not located in the facilities they serve. Their primary purpose is to provide services to patients or residents of facilities licensed under the Nursing Home Care Act, the Hospital Licensing Act, or the University of Illinois Hospital Act.

Note: Facilities that are licensed under the following:

- The Nursing Home Care Act, are long-term care facilities that serve young to elderly residents (i.e. nursing home).
- The Hospital Licensing Act, include any institution or building (public or private) that primarily focuses on maintenance and operation for the diagnosis and treatment or care of patients (i.e. hospital).
- The University of Illinois Hospital Act, include any hospital, clinic or outpatient department that's owned or leased by the University, which is The Board of Trustee of the University of Illinois.

RECORDKEEPING REQUIREMENTS FOR DISPENSING PRESCRIPTION ORDERS
Every prescription dispensed must be documented with the name, initials or other unique identifiers of the pharmacist (and pharmacy technician if applicable) that dispenses the prescription.

Each pharmacy must maintain records for **5 years**. This system may require 2 or more documents that, when read together, will provide all the required information. Records must include the following:
1. Name of resident.
2. Date of order.
3. Name, strength and dosage form of drug, or description of the medical device ordered;
4. Quantity dispensed (a separate record should be maintained when the quantity billed differs from the quantity dispensed, i.e., unit dose transfer systems).
5. Directions for use.
6. Quantity billed.
7. Prescriber's name.
8. Prescriber's signature and/or DEA number when required for controlled substances; <u>and</u>
9. The drug name and identification code or the manufacturer in case of a generically ordered medication or a generic interchange.

Similar to a community pharmacy, any information required to be kept that is stored in a computer system must be readily retrievable and able to supply hard copy printout of pharmacist's verification, dating and signing the dispensing. A log book or separate file can be use instead of the computer system.

WHAT HAPPENS WHEN THE LONG-TERM CARE FACILITY CHANGES PHARMACY PROVIDERS?
The new pharmacy provider must obtain the orders from the long-term care facility, and verify the authenticity and accuracy of the orders with the prescriber.

STAFFING OF THE PHARMACY
When the pharmacy is closed, the public and any employees who are not registered are not allowed to have access to the filling and dispensing area.

LABELING REQUIREMENTS
Medications for future use, including parenteral solutions with drug or diluent added and non-parenteral repackaged, must contain the information as shown in **table 2.**

	Labeling Requirements of Medication for Future Use	Parenteral Solutions	Non-Parenteral Repackaged
1	Name, Concentration & Volume of the Base Parenteral Solution	✓	-
2	Name & Strength of Drugs Added	✓	-
3	§Beyond Use Date & Date of Admixture	✓	✓
4	§Reference Code to Identify Source & Lot Number	✓	✓
5	Brand and/or Generic Name	-	✓
6	Strength	-	✓

Table 2: Labeling Requirements of Medications for Future Use (Parenteral Solutions & Non-Parenteral Repackaged).

Note:
- Unless specified in the individual monograph, the beyond used date must not be later than the beyond use date on the manufacturer's container <u>or</u> one year from the date the drugs is repackaged, whichever is earlier.
- §For non-parenteral repackaged, date of admixture is not applicable.
- §For parenteral solutions, reference code to identify source & lot number <u>of the drug or diluent added</u> should be on the label.

Medications prepared for immediate use, including all medications prepared by the pharmacy for immediate dispensing to a specific resident or patient in the facility and to specific resident, or patient in the facility via unit dose, must be dispensed in a container identified with information as shown in **table 3**.

	Labeling Requirements of Medication Prepared for Immediate Use	Specific Resident or Patient	Specific Resident or Patient via Unit Dose
1	Name of the resident	✓	✓
2	Resident's room and bed number	✓	✓
3	Dispensing date	✓	-
4	Date of order	-	✓
5	Name, strength and dosage form of drug <u>or</u> description of the medical device ordered	✓	✓
6	Quantity dispensed	✓	-
7	Directions for use	✓	✓
8	Prescriber's name	✓	✓
9	Beyond use date if less than 60 days from date of dispensing	✓	-

Table 3: Labeling Requirements of Medication Prepared for Immediate Use.

MEDICATION DISPENSING IN THE ABSENCE OF A PHARMACIST
During the hours when the institutional pharmacy is not open, medications available for immediate use must be met in the following manner:

I. AFTER-HOUR CABINETS
It is a locked cabinet located outside of the pharmacy area containing a minimal supply of the most frequently required medication. The cabinet must be sufficiently secure to only allow access to authorized personnel. After-hour cabinets can only be used when the pharmacy is close. When medication is removed from the cabinet, the written physician's orders must be placed in the cabinet. A log must be maintained within the cabinet and the person who removes medication must indicate on the log (1) his or her signature, (2) the name of the medication removed, (3) the

strength (if applicable), (4) the quantity removed and (5) the time of removal. An automated dispensing and storage system may be used as an after hours cabinet.

Tip to know: After-hour cabinets are NOT the same as automated dispensing systems, because an automated dispensing system can be accessed when the pharmacy is open. For example, think of Pyxis MedStation™ machines in a hospital setting where nurses constantly retrieve medications.

II. EMERGENCY KITS

These kits contain drugs that may be required in patients with immediate therapeutic needs. Emergency kits may be used to avoid delaying in treatment when there's no other source available in sufficient time to prevent risk of harm to patients.

Emergency kits are sealed in a way that indicates when the kit has been opened. A label is affixed to the outside of the emergency kit indicating the beyond use date of the emergency kit. The beyond use date of the emergency kit is based on the earliest beyond use date of any drug in the kit. After an emergency kit has been used or the seal has been broken or the kit is expired, it must be secured and returned to the pharmacy to be checked and restocked by the last authorized user only when the pharmacy opens. An automated dispensing and storage system may be used as an emergency kit.

WHAT HAPPENS IF THE AFTER-HOUR CABINETS AND EMERGENCY KITS ARE NOT AVAILABLE?
An authorized nurse can obtain from the pharmacy a sufficient quantity for immediate need of a patient. The authorized nurse must place a copy of the physician's order authorizing the removal of the medication and the drug's container from which it was removed in the pharmacy where it can be conspicuously seen. This way the pharmacist can find and check promptly. A form must be available in the pharmacy to record (1) the signature of the authorized nurse who removed the medication, (2) the name, (3) strength (if applicable) and (4) quantity of medication removed.

(68 IL ADC Section 1330.520)

ONSITE INSTITUTIONAL PHARMACY SERVICES

Pharmacies located in facilities licensed under the following must comply with this section:
- Nursing Home Care Act
- Hospital Licensing Act
- University of Illinois Hospital Act
- Are operated by the Department of Human Services or the Department of Corrections; and
- provide pharmacy services to residents, patients, employees, prescribers and students of these facilities.

RECORDKEEPING REQUIREMENTS

Every medication order filled or refilled must contain the name, initials or other unique identifier of the pharmacist (and pharmacy technician if applicable) that fills or refills the medication order. This record must indicate the following information:
1. The name and dosage form of the drug.
2. The date of filling or refilling; and
3. The quantity dispensed.

For all products, the label affixed to the drug container must have the initials of the pharmacist who approves the dispensing. If the pharmacy uses a drug distribution system which reissues the same label, a separate record must be maintained that identifies the pharmacist who approved the dispensing.

The PIC has to maintain the following records for **at least 5 years**:
1. Records of medication orders and medication administration to patients.
2. Procurement records for controlled substances.
3. Records of packaging, bulk compounding or manufacturing; and
4. Records of actions taken pursuant to drug recalls.

LABELING REQUIREMENTS

All medications repackaged by the pharmacy for future use inside the institution, and not intended for immediate dispensing to a specific patient must be labeled as shown in **table 4** and be identified as follows:
- Single dose or multi-dose drugs, except sterile solutions to which a drug has been added,
- Sterile solutions to which drugs have been added.

	Labeling Requirements of Medication Repackaged for Future Use	Single or Multi Dose Drugs	Sterile Solutions with Drugs Added
1	Brand and/or generic name	✔	-
2	Strength (if applicable)	✔	-
3	§Beyond use date & time of the admixture	✔	✔
4	§Reference code to identify source and lot number	✔	✔
5	Name, concentration & volume of the base sterile solution	-	✔
6	Name & strength of drug added	-	✔

Table 4: Labeling Requirements of Medications Repackaged for Future Use Inside the Institution.

Note:
- §For single or multi dose drugs, <u>only</u> beyond used date should be on the label.
- §For sterile solutions with drugs added, reference code to identify source and lot number of drugs added should be on the label.

All medication prepared by the pharmacy for immediate dispensing to a specific patient or resident in the institution or facility must be labeled as shown in **table 5** and be identified as follows:
- Single or multi dose drugs, except parenteral solutions to which a drug has been added.
- Sterile solutions to which drugs have been added.

	Labeling Requirements of Medication for Immediate Dispensing to a Specific Patient/Resident	Single or Multi Dose Drugs	Sterile Solutions With Drugs Added
1	Brand and/or generic name	✔	-
2	Strength (if applicable)	✔	-
3	Name, concentration & volume of the base sterile solution	-	✔
4	Name & strength of drugs added	-	✔
5	Beyond use date & time of the admixture	-	✔

Table 5: Labeling Requirements of Medications for Immediate Dispensing to a Specific Patient/Resident in the Institution.

All medications dispensed to a specific patient in the institution must be dispensed in a container identified with (1) the name of the patient <u>and</u> (2) the patient's location. A unit-dose and medication cart system may be identified with the name of the patient and the patient's location on the outside of the bin of the medication carts when they are filled by the pharmacy (the same applies in "Labels on Investigational New Drugs" if unit-dose and medication cart system are being utilized).

Labels on all medications dispensed by the pharmacy for immediate dispensing to a patient being discharged, emergency room patient and/or employee, must contain information as shown in **figure 2**.

Investigational new drugs, authorized by the FDA, must be dispensed in accordance to a valid prescription order of the principal physician-investigator or his authorized clinician. All investigational drugs must be stored in and dispensed from the pharmacy. The labels must identify information as shown in **figure 2**.

Labels on Drugs for Immediate Dispensing to a Patient Being Discharged, Emergency Room Patient and/or Employee

- Name & dosage form of the drug
- Date filled
- Quantity dispensed
- Directions for use

Labels on Investigational New Drugs

- Name of drug & strength (if applicable)
- Beyond use date
- Reference code to identify source & lot number
- A label indication "For Investigational Use Only"
- Name & location of the patient

Figure 2: *Labeling Requirements of Medications for Immediate Dispensing to a Patient Being Discharged, Emergency Room Patient and/or Employee and of Investigation New Drugs.*

Tip to know: Labeling requirements will appear as "pharmacy practice" questions in the MPJE. Therefore, they may be weighted more heavily than other questions.

Note: Drugs dispensed from the emergency room must meet labeling requirements pertaining to the community pharmacy prescription label.

A pharmacist providing a copy of a prescription to the patient for the purpose of transfer or any other purpose shall cancel the face of the original prescription and record the date the copy is issued, to whom issued, and the pharmacist's signature on the face of the original prescription. Copies of prescriptions shall be marked "For Information Purposes Only" and require prescriber authorization to fill.

STAFFING OF THE PHARMACY

Information regarding after-hour cabinet and emergency kits is similar to what's in the "staffing of the pharmacy" at the offsite institutional pharmacy services.

Drugs may be dispensed from the emergency room only by a practitioner licensed to prescribe and dispense, and only to patients treated in the institution. This must occur only during hours that the outpatient institutional pharmacy services are unavailable. The quantity dispensed is limited to **72-hour supply or less**, except for antimicrobial drugs and unit of use packages (e.g., inhalers, ophthalmic, otics, etc.).

(68 IL ADC Section1330.530)

NUCLEAR PHARMACY SERVICES
These pharmacies provide and/or sell radiopharmaceuticals.

WHAT SHOULD HAPPEN BEFORE A PHARMACY CAN PRACTICE AS A NUCLEAR PHARMACY?
1. The pharmacy must provide a copy of its Illinois Radioactive Material License issued by the Illinois Emergency Management Agency in accordance with the Radiation Protection Act.
2. The Division has to conduct an on-site inspection of the facility.

HOW SHOULD THE NUCLEAR PHARMACY FACILITY BE SET UP?
1. Space is appropriate for services to be provided, but at least 300 square feet; and
2. A radioactive storage and product decay facility separate from the "hot" laboratory, compounding, dispensing, quality assurance and office areas.

WHAT EQUIPMENT MUST A NUCLEAR PHARMACY HAVE?
1. Laminar flow hood.
2. Fume hood – minimum of 30 inches in height, which shall be vented through a filter with a direct outlet to the outside.
3. Dose calibrator.
4. Refrigerator.
5. Class A prescription balance or a balance of greater sensitivity.
6. Single-channel or multi-channel gamma scintillation counter.
7. Microscope.
8. Low level, thin-window portable radiation survey meter.
9. Drawing station – lead glass and lead lined.
10. Syringe shields; and
11. Energy Compensated Geiger Mueller (GM) Probe or ion chamber.

Each nuclear pharmacy must have the following reference texts available:
1. The current edition or revision of the USP – Dispensing Information.
2. The current edition or revision of the USP/NF.
3. State and federal regulations governing the use of applicable radioactive material; and
4. U.S. Public Health Service Radiological Health Handbook.

LABELING REQUIREMENTS
In addition to the labeling requirements of pharmaceuticals, the immediate outer container and the immediate container of a radioactive drug, diagnostic agent or device to be dispensed must also be labeled to include information as shown in **table 6**.

	Labeling Requirements of Radioactive Drug, Diagnostic Agent or Device to be Dispensed	Immediate Outer Container	Immediate Container
1	The standard radiation symbol	✔	✔
2	The words "Caution-Radioactive Material"	✔	✔
3	Name of the radionuclide	✔	✔
4	Name of the chemical form	✔	✔
5	Amount of radioactive material (milliCuries or microCuries) in the container contents at the time of calibration	✔	-
6	Volume of container content (mL) if in liquid form	✔	-
7	Requested calibration time for the amount of radioactivity contained	✔	-
8	Prescription number	✔	✔
9	Name or initials of the nuclear pharmacist filled the prescription	✔	-
10	Name and address of the pharmacy	-	✔

Table 6: Labeling Requirements on the Immediate Outer Container & Immediate Container of Radioactive

NUCLEAR PHARMACIST REQUIREMENTS

The PIC and all other pharmacists employed in the nuclear pharmacy must provide the following evidence to the Division:
1. Licensure as a pharmacist in IL; <u>and</u>
2. That he/she is named as an authorized user, or works under the supervision of a pharmacist, on a commercial nuclear pharmacy license issued by the Illinois Emergency Management Agency (IEMA), or when a nuclear pharmacist who works under a broad medical license at a university or research hospital has been approved as a user by that institution's radiation safety committee in accordance with conditions of the license issued by IEMA.

(68 IL ADC Section1330.540)

NONRESIDENT PHARMACIES

The Division requires all nonresident pharmacies to be registered. This also includes home pharmacies that are located outside of IL even though its remote pharmacies are in IL. The PIC and pharmacists employed at those pharmacies are not required to be licensed in IL. Nonresident special pharmacy registration shall be granted by the Division upon the disclosure and certification by a pharmacy.

(68 IL ADC Section1330.550)

REMOTE PRESCRIPTION/MEDICATION ORDER PROCESSING

Any pharmacy may provide remote prescription/medication order processing services to any other pharmacy (view section 25.10 of this act), and must follow these requirements:
1. Any nonresident pharmacy remote prescription/medication order processing services must first be registered in its resident state and in IL.
2. There must be a secure, HIPAA compliant, electronic communication system that includes computer, telephone and facsimile connections.
3. The communication system must be able to give remote access of all relevant patient information to allow the pharmacist of the remote pharmacy to perform remote medication order processing, including all lab results and patients' medication profile as appropriate.

4. If the secure electronic communication system malfunctions, the remote processing pharmacy must stop its operations.

RECORDKEEPING REQUIREMENTS
The remote prescription/medication order processing pharmacy must maintain a policy and procedure manual related to the pharmacy's operations. The manual must include the following:
1. Be accessible to the staff at the remote prescription/medication order processing pharmacy and the dispensing pharmacy.
2. Be available for inspection by the Division.
3. Outline the responsibilities of staff at the remote prescription/medication order processing pharmacy and the dispensing pharmacy.
4. Include a current list of the name, address, telephone number and license number of each pharmacist involved in remote prescription/medication order processing.
5. Include policies and procedures for the following general key themes:
    - Ensure HIPAA compliance.
    - Maintaining records to identify patients and pharmacists.
    - Participating in a continuous quality improvement program.
    - Reviewing the written policies and procedures annually.

Every pharmacist providing remote prescription/medication order processing services must record on the order in the computer system, or on another uniformly maintained and readily retrievable record the following information:
1. The name, initials or other unique identifier of the pharmacist who verifies the medication order or prescription.
2. The name of the patient or resident.
3. The name, dose, dosage form, route of administration and dosing frequency of the drug.
4. The date and time of verification.
5. The name of the prescribing/ordering practitioner.
6. Any other information that is required by the dispensing pharmacy for use in its own records.

The PIC must maintain the following records for at least 5 years:
1. Records of medication orders processed.
2. Records of the electronic communication system maintenance.

The remote prescription/medication order processing pharmacy must keep a record containing the names and license numbers of all pharmacies to which they are providing services and the working hours of the pharmacy.

In a non-retail setting, all pharmacists providing remote prescription/medication order processing at a remote pharmacy must be licensed in IL. However, when pharmacists from a community pharmacy licensed in IL but located out-of-state, provide remote prescription/medication order processing for a community pharmacy licensed in IL, only the PIC of the remote pharmacy must be licensed in Illinois. Only licensed pharmacists at the pharmacy providing remote pharmacy services can conduct the drug utilization evaluation or review and validation of any order processed within the remote pharmacy.
(68 IL ADC Section1330.560)

SECTION 14: PHARMACY STANDARDS
Pharmacy Practice Rules (Implementing the Act), 68 IL ADC Sections 1330.600 – 1330.680

SECURITY REQUIREMENTS
The pharmacy must be walled off, locked or secured with electronic equipment to prevent any access from a non-licensed person (i.e. employees and public) when a registrant is not present in the pharmacy.

Note: A pharmacy technician is a licensed personnel, therefore, he or she is allowed to be in the pharmacy even though the pharmacist is not present.

(68 IL ADC Section 1330.600)

PHARMACY STRUCTURAL/EQUIPMENT STANDARDS
All pharmacies must comply with the following provisions:
1. Notification must be submitted to the Division that the pharmacy will be remodeled.
2. Other than on-site institutional pharmacies, all dispensing and drug storage areas of the pharmacy must be next to each other.
3. The pharmacy and all storerooms must have enough light and be properly ventilated.
4. Refrigerators are used exclusively for storage of prescription drugs. Proper storage of drugs based on their storage temperature.
5. The pharmacy area is not used for storage of merchandise that interferes with the practice of pharmacy.
6. Suitable current reference sources, either in book or electronic data form (available in the pharmacy or on-line), which must include Facts and Comparisons (http://www.factsandcomparisons.com) or other suitable references determined by the Division to be pertinent to the practice carried on in the licensed pharmacy.
7. A telephone must be accessible in the pharmacy area.
8. These requirements are in addition to any other requirements found in this Part.
9. At a minimum, the equipment and references listed in Section 1330.640 must be maintained at all dispensing pharmacies.

(68 IL ADC Section 1330.610)

ELECTRONIC EQUIPMENT REQUIREMENTS FOR REMOTE PHARMACIES
All remote pharmacies operating in IL share services with home pharmacies. The new regulations require the following:
1. The pharmacy must have a computer, scanner, fax capability and printer.
2. All prescriptions have to be scanned and sequentially numbered, and the prescription labels must be produced on site and viewed at the home pharmacy.
3. Scanned prescriptions must be viewable on at computers from both the remote pharmacy and home pharmacy.

4. All patient demographic and prescription information must be viewable at both the remote and home pharmacy in real time.
5. Prescriptions dispensed at the remote pharmacy site must be distinguishable from those dispensed at the home pharmacy.
6. If electronic data processing equipment is used, the original prescription must be kept on file to allow access to the prescription when a computer malfunctions.

(68 IL ADC Section1330.620)

SANITARY STANDARDS
All pharmacies and equipment in the pharmacy must be kept in clean and good condition.

(68 IL ADC Section1330.630)

PHARMACEUTICAL COMPOUNDING STANDARDS
The minimum standards and technical equipment considered adequate for compounding drugs must include the following:
1. A storage area to separate for materials used in compounding.
2. Scales for the compounding done in the pharmacy.
3. An area of the pharmacy used for compounding activities.
4. A heating apparatus.
5. A logbook or record keeping system to track each compounded prescription and the components used.
6. A book or reference containing formulas with directions for compounding. The books and references can be in electronic format and/or available via the Internet.
7. The pharmacy operations manual to contain the policies and procedures pertinent to the level of complexity and the size of the compounding operations. Electronic versions are acceptable.
8. Consumable materials as appropriate to the pharmacy services, such as filter paper, powder papers, empty capsules, ointment jars, bottles, vials, safety closures, powder boxes, labels and distilled water.
9. The pharmacy may compound drug products to be used by practitioners in their office for administration to patients.
10. Sales of compounded drugs to other pharmacies or to clinics, hospitals or manufacturers are not allowed. However, sales provided by pharmacies contracted to provide centralized prescription filling services, are exceptional.

(68 IL ADC Section1330.640)

PHARMACY COMPUTER REGULATIONS
Only a pharmacist, or a pharmacy technician under the pharmacist's supervision, can input drug information into the electronic data processing equipment. The pharmacist must verify the

accuracy of the order information after the pharmacy technician entered it. The identity of the supervising pharmacist and the technician must be maintained in the prescription record.

Electronic data processing equipment or media, when used to store or process prescription information, must meet the following requirements:
1. Must guarantee the confidentiality of the information contained in the database.
2. Must require that the transmission of electronic prescriptions from prescriber to pharmacist cannot manipulate the prescription by any other party.

(68 IL ADC Section1330.650)

PIC

A pharmacy cannot obtain a license without a pharmacist being designated on the pharmacy license as PIC.

A pharmacy must have one PIC who is routinely and actively involved in the operation of the pharmacy, and can be PIC for more than one pharmacy. However, the PIC must work on average at least 8 hours per week at each location. If he or she is absent more than 90 days, a new PIC must be designated.

The responsibilities of the PIC include the following:
1. Supervision of all employees' activities related to the practice of pharmacy.
2. Establishment and supervision of the method for storage and safekeeping of pharmaceuticals, including security maintenance used when the pharmacy is closed and
3. Establishment and supervision of the recordkeeping system for the purchase, sale, delivery, possession, storage and safekeeping of drugs.

(68 IL ADC Section1330.660)

COMPOUNDED STERILE PREPARATION STANDARDS

There are standards for pharmacies that perform the practice of preparation, labeling and distribution of compounded sterile preparations. These activities include the following:
1. Sterile preparation of parenteral therapy and parenteral nutrition.
2. Sterile preparations of cytotoxic or antineoplastic agents; and
3. Other sterile preparations to be used topically or internally by humans or animals.

PHYSICAL REQUIREMENTS OF PHARMACIES PREPARING STERILE (PARENTERAL) PRODUCTS

The pharmacy must have a designated area to prepare sterile products. The area should be designed to minimize outside traffic and airflow disturbances from activity within the facility. It must have sufficient size to accommodate a laminar airflow hood (LAF), barrier isolation chamber (BSC), and to provide for the proper storage of drugs and supplies under appropriate conditions of temperature, light, moisture, sanitation, ventilation and security. It must be ventilated in a way so that it doesn't interfere with the proper operation of the sterile products preparation apparatus.

The licensed pharmacy preparing compounded sterile products must have the following:
1. LAF workstation
    - LAF must be certified annually in accordance with ISO 14644-1.
    - In the event the preparation apparatus is moved from its site of certification, recertification should occur it can be use.
    - Pre-filters must be replaced or cleaned monthly. Documentation of this should be maintained.
2. Sink with hot and cold running water that is convenient to the compounding area;
3. National Institute for Occupational Safety and Health (NIOSH) approved disposal containers for used needles, syringes, etc., and, if applicable, cytotoxic waste from the preparation of chemotherapy agents.
4. Biohazard cabinetry for environment control when cytotoxic compounded sterile preparations are prepared.
5. Refrigerator and/or freezer with a thermometer; and
6. Temperature controlled containers for off site deliveries.

The following current resource materials and texts are to be maintained in the pharmacy:
1. American Hospital Formulary Service.
2. Copies of the IL Pharmacy Practice Act and Rules, the Illinois Controlled Substances Act and 77 Ill. Adm. Code 3100, 21 CFR and the Illinois Hypodermic Syringes and Needles Act [720 ILCS 635].
3. One compatibility reference such as the following:
    - Trissel's Handbook on Injectable Drugs.
    - King's Guide to Parenteral Admixtures; or
    - Any other Division approved publication.
4. A reference on extended (more than 24 hours) stability data given to finished preparations.

STAFFING
A pharmacist must be accessible at all times at the facility to respond to patients' and health professionals' questions and needs during working hours. A 24-hour telephone number should be included on all labeling of compounded medication and medication infusion devices if used off site.

DRUG DISTRIBUTION AND CONTROL
Patient profile or medication record system in the pharmacy must be maintained in addition to the prescription file and must contain the following:
1. Patient's full name.
2. Date of birth or age.
3. Gender.
4. Compounded sterile preparations dispensed.
5. Date dispensed, if off site.
6. Drug content and quantity.
7. Patient directions, if preparation being administered off site.
8. Identifying number.

9. Identification of dispensing pharmacist and, if applicable, pharmacy technician;
10. Other drugs or supplements the patient is receiving, if provided by the patient or his or her agent.
11. Known drug sensitivities and allergies to drugs and foods.
12. Diagnosis; and
13. Lot numbers of components or individual medicine if the compounded sterile preparation is **not used within 48 hours after preparation.**

LABELING

Each compounded sterile preparation dispensed to patients shall be labeled with the following information: (See **figure 1**)
1. Name, address and telephone number of the licensed pharmacy, if not used within facility.
2. Administration date and identifying number if used on site, date dispensed, and identifying number if used off site.
3. Patient's full name and room number, if applicable.
4. Name of each drug, strength and amount.
5. Directions for use and/or infusion rate if used off site.
6. Prescriber's full name if used off site.
7. Required controlled substances transfer warnings, when applicable.
8. Beyond use date and time.
9. Identity of pharmacist compounding and dispensing, or other authorized individual; and
10. Auxiliary labels storage requirements, if applicable.

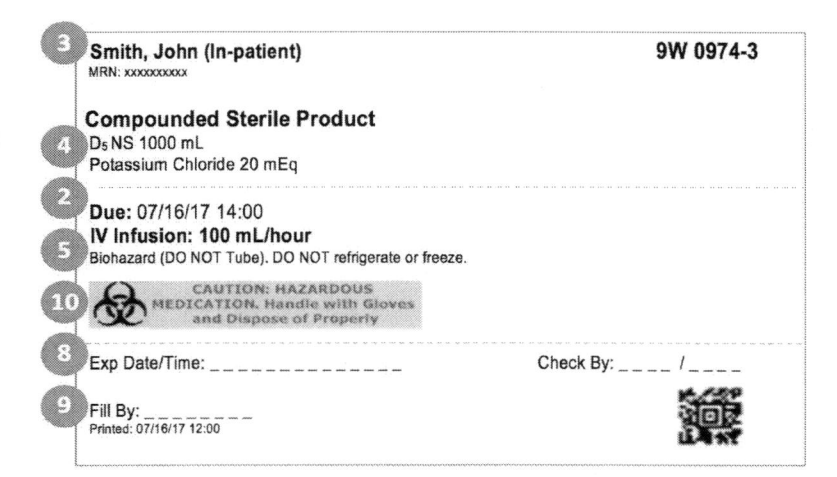

```
③ Smith, John (In-patient)                           9W 0974-3
   MRN: xxxxxxxxxx

   Compounded Sterile Product
④  D5 NS 1000 mL
   Potassium Chloride 20 mEq

② Due: 07/16/17 14:00
   IV Infusion: 100 mL/hour
⑤ Biohazard (DO NOT Tube). DO NOT refrigerate or freeze.

        CAUTION: HAZARDOUS
⑩      MEDICATION. Handle with Gloves
         and Dispose of Properly

⑧ Exp Date/Time: _ _ _ _ _ _ _ _ _ _ _ _ _    Check By: _ _ _ _ / _ _ _ _

⑨ Fill By: _ _ _ _ _ _ _ _
   Printed: 07/16/17 12:00
```

Figure 1: Label Sample of an Inpatient Compounded Sterile Product. (Thieu, Y. and Jerry Fahrni.com 2017)

RECORDKEEPING

The PIC shall ensure records are maintained for **5 years** and are readily retrievable and in a format that provides enforcement agents an accurate and comprehensive method of monitoring distribution via an audit trail. The records must include the following information:

1. Patient profile.
2. Medication record system.
3. Purchase records; and
4. Lot numbers of the components used in compounding sterile prescriptions/orders traceable to a specific patient, if not included on patient profile and if the preparation is not utilized within 48 hours after preparation.

DELIVERY SERVICE
The PIC must assure that any compounded sterile product shipped or delivered to a patient must be in temperature controlled (as defined by USP Standards) delivery containers.

CYTOTOXIC DRUGS
The following requirements are necessary for pharmacies that prepare cytotoxic drugs:
1. Safety and containment techniques for compounding cytotoxic drugs must be used.
2. Disposal of cytotoxic waste must comply with all applicable local, State and federal requirements.
3. Prepared doses of cytotoxic drugs must be dispensed, labeled with proper precautions inside and outside, and shipped in a way that minimizes the risk of accidental rupture of the primary container.
4. The pharmacy must have as a reference Safe Handling of Hazardous Drugs Video Training Program and Workbook American Society of Health-System Pharmacists (ASHP).

EMERGENCY MEDICATIONS
Pharmacies that dispense compounded sterile products to patients in facilities off site, or in the patient's residence must stock supplies and medications appropriate for treatment of allergic or other common adverse effects, to be dispensed upon the order of the prescriber.

(68 IL ADC Section1330.670)

AUTOMATED DISPENSING AND STORAGE SYSTEMS
These are any mechanical system that can perform pharmacy operations related to storage, packaging or dispensing of medications. It also collects, controls, and maintains all transaction information. Automated dispensing and storage systems are not be used in nuclear pharmacies.

Only IL licensed personnel can administer medications or those who work under the supervision of those individuals can have access to the automated dispensing and storage system (i.e. physicians, nurses, pharmacy technician, etc.). If the system is used in a pharmacy, then the pharmacist must be responsible for dispensing the drug.

DOCUMENTATION
Documentation for type of equipment, serial numbers, content, policies and procedures, and locations, must be maintained on-site in the pharmacy for review by the Division. Documentation includes the following:

1. Name and address of the pharmacy or facility where the automated dispensing and storage system operates.
2. Manufacturer's name and model.
3. Quality assurance policy and procedures to determine continued appropriate use and performance of the automated device; and
4. Policies and procedures for system operation, safety, security, accuracy, patient confidentiality, access, controlled substances, data retention or archival, definitions, downtime procedures, emergency or first dose procedures, inspection, installation requirements, maintenance, medication security, quality assurance, medication inventory, staff education and training, system set-up and malfunction.

The system shall only be used when medication orders have been reviewed by a pharmacist. This does not apply when used as an after-hours cabinet or emergency kit.

SECURITY AND PROCEDURE

Records and/or electronic data kept by automated dispensing and storage systems must meet the following requirements:
1. All events involving access to the contents of the automated dispensing and storage systems must be recorded electronically;
2. Records must be maintained by the pharmacy and must be readily available to the Division, which include the following:
    - Identity of system accessed.
    - Identification of the individual accessing the system.
    - Type of transaction.
    - Name, strength, dosage form and quantity of the drug accessed.
    - Name of the patient for whom the drug was ordered.
    - Identification of the registrants stocking or restocking and the pharmacist checking for the accuracy of the medications to be stocked or restocked in the automated dispensing and storage system; and
    - Such additional information as the PIC may consider necessary.

STOCKING OR RESTOCKING MEDICATIONS

Only authorized persons (i.e. pharmacy technician) can perform stock or restocking. All medications stored in the systems must be packaged as a unit of use for single patient (e.g., unit dose tab/cap, tube of ointment, inhaler, etc.) and labeled properly as indicated in the labeling requirements for sterile solutions with added drug or diluent, or sterile solutions that are not in their original manufacturer's packaging, and non-parenterals repackaged for future use. Exceptions apply to "unit of use" label requirements, in which (1) injectable medication should be stored in their original multi-dose vial (i.e. insulin, heparin) when the medication may be withdrawn into a syringe or other delivery device for single patient use, or (2) over-the-counter (OTC) products store in their original multi-dose container (e.g., antacids, analgesics) when the medication may be withdrawn and placed into an appropriate container for single patient use.

REQUIREMENTS FOR OUTER LABELS OF STERILE SOLUTIONS WITH ADDED DRUG OR DILUENT & NON-PARENTERAL REPACKAGED FOR FUTURE USE

Sterile solutions with a drug or diluent that has been added or are not in their original manufacturer's packaging and non-parenteral repackaged for future used should contain the required information on the outer label (See table 2).

Exceptions to the "unit of use" requirements are as follows:
1. Injectable medications stored in their original multi-dose vial (e.g., insulin, heparin) when the medication may be withdrawn into a syringe or other delivery device for single patient use; or
2. Over-the-counter (OTC) products stored in their original multi-dose container (e.g., antacids, analgesics) when the medication may be withdrawn and placed into an appropriate container for single patient use.

WHAT INFORMATION IS BEING DOCUMENTED WHEN MEDICATIONS ARE REMOVED FROM THE SYSTEM FOR ON-SITE PATIENT ADMINISTRATION?

The following information is documented:
1. Name of the patient or resident.
2. Patient's or resident's unique and permanent identifier, such as admissions number or medical records number.
3. Date and time medication was removed from the system.
4. Name, initials or other unique identifier of the person removing the drug; and
5. Name, strength and dosage form of the drug or description of the medical device removed.

The documentation can be in paper, via electronic media or other mechanisms.

SECURING AND ACCOUNTING REQUIREMENTS

The automated dispensing and storage systems should account for medications removed and subsequently returned to the systems (e.g., return bin). Medication or devices once removed must not be reused or reissued except for the following:
1. Medical devices that can be properly sanitized prior to reuse or reissue; and
2. Medications that are dispensed and stored under conditions defined and supervised by the pharmacist and are unopened in sealed, intact containers.

QUALITY ASSURANCE REQUIREMENTS

The quality assurance documentation for the use and performance of the automated dispensing and storage systems must include the following:
1. Safety monitors (e.g., wrong medications removed and administered to patient).
2. Accuracy monitors (e.g., filling errors, wrong medications removed); and
3. Security monitors (e.g., unauthorized access, system security breaches, and controlled substance audits).

Errors in the use or performance of the automated dispensing and storage systems resulting in patient hospitalization or death must be reported to the Division by the PIC **within 30 days** after the incident.

POLICIES AND PROCEDURES

Policies and procedures for the use of automated dispensing and storage systems must include pharmacist review of the prescription or medication order prior to the system profiling, and/or removal of any medication from the system for immediate patient administration. This does NOT apply to the following situations:

1. The system is being used as an after-hours cabinet in the absence of a pharmacist.
2. The system is being used in place of an emergency kit.
3. The system is being used to provide access to medication required to treat the immediate needs of a patient. When a pharmacist is on duty and available, he or she must check the orders promptly (for example, floor stock system, emergency department, surgery, ambulatory care or same day surgery, observation unit, etc.).

Policies and procedures for the use of the automated dispensing and storage systems include the following:

1. List of medications to be stored in each system; and
2. List of medications qualifying for emergency or first dose removal without pharmacist prior review of the prescription or medication order.

The PIC must have access to all records or documentation for **5 years.**

DUTIES AND RESPONSIBILITIES OF THE PIC

1. Assuring the automated dispensing and storage system is in good working condition, and accurately provides the correct strength, dosage form and quantity of the drug prescribed while maintaining appropriate recordkeeping and security safeguards;
2. Establishment of a quality assurance program prior to implementation of an automated dispensing and storage system and the supervision of an ongoing quality assurance program that monitors appropriate use and performance of the system as written in the pharmacy policies and procedures;
3. Providing the Division with written notice **30 days** prior to the installation of the system (or at the time of removal). The notice must include the following:
    - The name and address of the pharmacy.
    - The address of the location of the automated dispensing and storage system, if different from the address of the pharmacy.
    - The automated dispensing and storage system's manufacturer and model;
    - The PIC; and
    - A written description of how the facility intends to use the automated storage and dispensing system.
4. Determining and monitoring access (e.g., security levels) to the system. Access must be written in policies and procedures of the pharmacy that comply with State and federal regulations.

Additional responsibilities include the following:

1. Authorizing access to, discontinuing access to, or changing access to the system.
2. Ensuring that access to the medications complies with State and federal regulations. and
3. Ensuring that the system is stocked/restocked accurately as written in pharmacy policies and procedures.

(68 IL ADC Section1330.680)

SECTION 15: PHARMACY OPERATIONS

Pharmacy Practice Rules (Implementing the Act), 68 IL ADC Sections 1330.700 – 1330.800

PATIENT COUNSELING

An offer to counsel should be made on all new and refill prescriptions. The pharmacist can use alternative forms of patient information if oral counseling is not practicable for the patient. The alternative forms of patient information must let the patient know that he or she can contact the pharmacist for consultation at the pharmacy or by telephone service. A pharmacist at an institutional pharmacy should provide patient counseling when drugs are dispensed by the pharmacy upon a patient's discharge from the institution.

WHAT HAPPENS IF THE PATIENT REFUSES TO ACCEPT PATIENT COUNSELING?
The refusal should be documented. The absence of any record of a refusal to accept the offer to counsel is considered that the offer was accepted and that counseling was provided.

(68 IL ADC Section 1330.700)

REPORTING THEFT OR LOSS OF CONTROLLED SUBSTANCES

A pharmacy is required by federal regulation to file with the U.S. Drug Enforcement Agency a Report of Theft or Loss of Controlled Substances (Form 106). A copy should concurrently be sent to the Division, Attention of the Drug Compliance Unit, along with the printed name of the person who signed the form. Failure to do so may result in discipline of the pharmacy or the PIC. Recordkeeping for this is **2 years.**

(68 IL ADC Section 1330.710)

DRUG PREPACKAGING

Drug prepackaging means any drug being removed from the original manufacturer container, and placed in a dispensing container to be dispensed to a future patient.

Prepackaged drugs must have a label that contains (1) the name and strength of the drug, (2) the name of manufacturer or distributor, (3) beyond use date (BUD), and (4) lot number. Maximum BUD allowed for prepackaged drugs must be the manufacturer's BUD or 12 months, whichever is less. The required label is not needed if pharmacies store drugs with an automated counting device. They can maintain separate records of lot numbers and beyond use dates as long as those records are fully traceable and readily retrievable for an inspection.

Automatic counting cassettes must have a label affixed to the cassette containing the same label information listed on the above.

(68 IL ADC Section 1330.730)

MULTI-MED DISPENSING STANDARDS FOR COMMUNITY PHARMACIES

Instead of dispensing two or more prescribed drug products in separate containers, a pharmacist may provide a customized patient medication package (patient med pack) with the consent of the patient, the patient's caregiver, or a prescriber. The patient med pack indicates the day and time when the contents in each container are to be taken.

The patient med-pack must include information about the following:
1. Name of the patient.
2. A serial number for the patient med pack itself and a separate identifying serial number for each of the prescription orders for each of the drug products contained in the med pack.
3. The name, strength, physical description or identification, and total quantity of each drug product contained in the med pack.
4. The directions for use and cautionary statements, if any, contained in the prescription order for each drug product contained in the med pack.
5. Any storage instructions.
6. Name of the prescriber of each drug product.
7. The date of preparation of the patient med pack; and
8. The name, address and telephone number of the pharmacist and any other registrant involved in dispensing.

Once a med pack has been delivered to an institution or a patient, the drugs in the med pack can be returned only when a medication must be added or removed, or when drug therapy is discontinued. Med packs returned to the pharmacy can only be re-dispensed for the same patient. Medications removed from the med pack cannot be reused and must be disposed of properly. Any revised med pack has to have a new serial number. When a pharmacist utilizes drugs dispensed from another pharmacy in creating an initial med pack, that pharmacist has to bear full responsibility for the drugs as if dispensed from that pharmacy.

(68 IL ADC Section1330.740)

RETURN OF DRUGS

Once the patient carries the dispensed drug outside of the pharmacy store, the drug cannot be accepted for return or exchange. If there are returns, the pharmacist ensures the following:
1. The drugs were stored in compliance with Sections 1330.610 and 1330.630.
2. The drugs are not contaminated or beyond their use date.
3. The returns are properly documented; and
4. Obtaining payment twice for the same drug is prohibited.

This does not apply to drugs returned for purposes of destruction. In this case, the returned drugs must be stored separately from the pharmacy's active stock. For the wrong medication that was dispensed, the returned drugs cannot be reused or returned to active stock.

(68 IL ADC Section1330.750)

ELECTRONIC TRANSMISSION OF PRESCRIPTION

This includes any prescription order that is electronically transmitted by telephone, computer, facsimile machine, or any other electronic device, to the pharmacy of the patient's choice. Electronic transmission prescriptions include both data and image prescriptions.

Electronic transmission of prescriptions is allowed if the following conditions are met:
1. The prescription can be transmitted directly from the prescriber to the pharmacy of the patient's choice. The prescription information or content of the prescription cannot be altered during transmission.
2. The prescriptions comply with all applicable statutes and rules regarding the form, content, record keeping and processing of a prescription drug.
3. The electronically transmitted prescription include the following:
    - The transmitting prescriber's fax number, if applicable;
    - The time and date of the transmission;
    - The identity of the person sending the prescription;
    - The address and contact information of the person transmitting the prescription.
4. The electronic device in the pharmacy that receives the electronically transmitted prescription is located within the pharmacy area.
5. The fax of an electronically transmitted prescription is legible.
6. The fax of the electronically transmitted prescription is stored in the pharmacy and may serve as the record of the prescription as long as it's readily retrievable.
7. Adequate security and systems safeguards are required to prevent and detect unauthorized access, modification or manipulation of electronically transmitted prescriptions.
8. A pharmacy or pharmacist should not enter an agreement with a practitioner or healthcare facility if the electronic transmission of prescriptions can adversely affect a patient's freedom to select the pharmacy of his or her choice.
9. Electronically transmitted prescriptions for controlled substances may be dispensed only as provided by federal law. Prescriber can issue an electronic prescription for C-II, III, IV, or V.

(68 IL ADC Section1330.760)

PHARMACY SELF-INSPECTION

Every pharmacy should conduct an annual self-inspection using forms provided by the Division. The annual self-inspection should be conducted during the same month, annually, as determined by the pharmacy. Documentation of the self-inspection needs to be maintained at the pharmacy for **5 years**.

(68 IL ADC Section1330.800)

SECTION 16: HYPODERMIC SYRINGES AND NEEDLES ACT
Chapter 720 ILCS 635/1-6

POSSESSION OF HYPODERMIC SYRINGES AND NEEDLES
The purpose of this Act is to prevent the use of hypodermic syringes and needles for drug abuse. Only persons and entities identified in this Act can possess syringes and needles (i.e. physician, dentist, pharmacist, chiropodist or veterinarian, registered professional nurse, wholesale drug supplier, etc.). A person who is at least 18 years of age may purchase from a pharmacy, and have in his or her possession up to 20 hypodermic syringes or needles.

Note: A pharmacist may dispense syringes and needles to patients who have a prescription. However, a prescription is not always required.

(720 ILCS 635/1)

SALE OF HYPODERMIC SYRINGES AND NEEDLES
The following are the requirements for sale of a syringes or needles without a prescription:
- A person 18 years or older may purchase up to 20 sterile hypodermic syringes daily without a prescription from a pharmacist in the pharmacy department of the pharmacy.
- Syringes or needles sold must be stored at a pharmacy in a manner that limits access to the syringes or needles to pharmacists at the pharmacy or persons designated by the pharmacists.
- There are no recordkeeping requirements.
- Illinois Department of Public Health must provide materials for proper disposal of needles and syringes to the pharmacies that choose to sell them.

Note: If dispensing needles and syringes pursuant to a prescription, the prescription, record keeping, refill, and labeling requirements applicable to prescriptions for non-controlled substances must be followed. The new law applies only when dispensing without a prescription.

Hypodermic syringes or hypodermic needles can be used for treatment of livestock or poultry by the owner, or a person engaged in chemical, clinical, pharmaceutical or other scientific research.

(720 ILCS 635/2 & 2.5)

PENALTY
A person who violates this Act is guilty of a Class A misdemeanor for the first such offense; and a Class 4 felony for a second or any succeeding offense.

(720 ILCS 635/3)

SECTION 17: ILLINOIS CONTROLLED SUBSTANCES ACT
Chapter 720 ILCS 570/100-313, Section 3100 IAC et seq.
Controlled Substances Act, 77 IL ADC Sections 3100.10-3100.530

REGULATION OF CONTROLLED SUBSTANCES
Controlled substances are regulated by both federal and IL laws. If there's an overlap of the federal and IL laws, the IL law has to be more stringent to be valid. The federal and IL laws for controlled substances regulate the manufacturing, distribution, dispensing, and delivery of controlled substances.

Note: In answering questions on the IL MPJE, if the federal and IL laws are found to be different, the questions should be answered with the more stringent law, which usually is the IL state law.

(720 ILCS 570/100)

DEPARTMENT DUTIES RELATED TO SCHEDULES
The Department can add, delete, or reschedule all controlled substances in the Schedules. In making the determination of whether to add, delete, or reschedule, the Department has to consider the following:
1. The actual or relative potential for abuse.
2. The scientific evidence of its pharmacological effect, if known.
3. The state of current scientific knowledge regarding the substance.
4. The history and current pattern of abuse.
5. The scope, durations, and significance of abuse.
6. The risk to the public health.
7. The potential of the substance to produce psychological or physiological dependence.
8. Whether the substance is an immediate precursor of a substance already controlled.
9. The immediate harmful effect in terms of potentially fatal dosage; <u>and</u>
10. The long-range effects in terms of permanent health impairment.

If any substance is scheduled, rescheduled, or deleted as a controlled substance under Federal law, the Department can object that decision **within 30 days** from the date of the notice is given to the Department.

(720 ILCS 570/201)

Note: Multiple DEA Schedules exist based on differences in route, form, or strength of the controlled substances. As we have learned in school, controlled substance products that are short acting and quickly absorbed increase tendency for abused use. Hence, these products will be scheduled accordingly. For examples:
- C-II pentobarbital and secobarbital will be in oral and injectable route of administration (short-acting).

- C-III combination barbiturates (pentobarbital, secobarbital) will be in suppository dosage form (short acting).
- C-IV phenobarbital is long acting.

SCHEDULING

The State of Illinois largely follows federal law. Under the federal law, a controlled substance is scheduled by the DEA into one of five schedules based on its medical utility, abuse potential, and addictive propensities.

Tip to know:
- For controlled substances, you should be familiar with their brand and generic names. A comprehensive list of controlled substances can be found at: https://www.deadiversion.usdoj.gov/schedules/
- For non-controlled substances, you should be familiar with the most commonly prescribed drugs and their brand and generic names.
- If a drug is available both prescription and OTC, you should know its prescription strength and OTC strength.

FINDINGS REQUIRED FOR INCLUSION IN SCHEDULE I (C-I)

The Department may issue a rule scheduling a substance in Schedule I for the following reasons:
1. The substance has a high potential for abuse.
2. The substance has no currently accepted medical use in the U.S. or lack accepted safety for use under medical supervision.

Some examples of C-I substances are as follows:
- Acetylmethadol
- Benzethidine
- Betamethadol
- Clonitazene
- Dextromoramide
- Diampromide
- Diethylthiambutene
- Heroin
- Nicocodeine
- Normorphine

Anything that contains any quantity of these substances or their salts, isomers, and salts of isomers is considered C-I substance.

(720 ILCS 570/203 & 204)

FINDINGS REQUIRED FOR INCLUSION IN SCHEDULE II (C-II)

The Department may issue a rule scheduling a substance in Schedule II for the following reasons:
1. The substance has high potential for abuse.

2. The substance has a currently accepted medical use in the U.S. or currently accepted medical use with restrictions.
3. Abuse of the substance may lead to severe psychological or physiological dependence.

Some examples of C-II substances are as follows:
- Narcotics, opium, codeine, hydrocodone (Zohydro ER®), hydromorphone (Dilaudid®), morphine (MS Contin®), oxycodone (Oxycontin®, Percodan®), dextromethorphan, topical cocaine, methadone (Dolophine®), meperidine (Demerol®), and fentanyl (Sublimaze®, Duragesic®, Actiq®).
- Stimulants, amphetamine (Dexedrine®, Adderall®), methamphetamine (Desoxyn®), methylphenidate (Ritalin®), dexmethylphenidate (Focalin®), and lisdexamfetamine (Vyvanse®).
- Depressants, amobarbital (Amytal®), glutethimide, pentobarbital (Nembutal®), and secobarbital (Seconal®).

Note: Effective October 6, 2014, all hydrocodone combination products (HCPs) will be classified as C-II controlled substances required by the DEA. Some examples are hydrocodone/APAP (Vicodin®, Norco®, Lortab®), hydrocodone/ibuprofen (Vicoprofen®). Any HCP prescription written before October 6, 2014 should be treated, filled, or refilled as a C-II drug, including partially dispensing.

(720 ILCS 570/205 & 206)

DEXTROMETHORPHAN
Possession of a drug product that contains dextromethorphan in violation of the Controlled Substances Act is a Class 4 felony. The sale, delivery, distribution, or possession with the intention of selling, delivering, or distributing a drug product that contains dextromethorphan in violation of this Act is a Class 2 felony.

(720 ILCS 570/218)

FINDINGS REQUIRED FOR INCLUSION IN SCHEDULE III (C-III)
The Department may issue a rule scheduling a substance in Schedule III as follows:
1. The substance has potential for abuse less so than Schedule I and II.
2. The substance has currently accepted medical use in the U.S.
3. Abuse of the substance may lead to low or moderate physiological or high psychological dependence.

Some examples of C-III substances are as follows:
- 1.8 g or less of codeine per 100 mL or 90 mg or less per dosage unit, with an equal or greater quantity of an isoquinoline alkaloid of opium.
- 1.8 g or less of codeine per 100 mL or 90 mg or less per dosage unit, with one or more active, non-narcotic ingredients in recognized therapeutic amounts
  - Examples: Acetaminophen with codeine (Tylenol #3®, Tylenol #4®) and aspirin w/ codeine (Empirin #3®, Empirin #4®).

- 1.8 g or less of dihydrocodeine per 100 mL or 90 mg or less per dosage unit, with one or more active, non-narcotic ingredients in recognized therapeutic amounts.
    - Example: ASA/caffeine/dihydrocodeine (Synalgos-DC®) and APAP/Caffeine/Dihydrocodeine (Panlor-DC®, Panlor-SS®, Zerlor®, Trezix®).
- 300 mg or less of ethylmorphine per 100 mL or 15 mg or less per dosage unit, with one or more active, non-narcotic ingredients in recognized therapeutic amounts.
- 500 mg or less of opium per 100 mL or per 100 g or 25 mg or less per dosage unit, with one or more active, non-narcotic ingredients in recognized therapeutic amounts.
- 50 mg or less of morphine per 100 mL or per 100 g, with one or more active, non-narcotic ingredients in recognized therapeutic amounts.
- Anabolic steroids
    - Examples: testosterone (Testoderm®), stanozolol (Windstrol®).
- Barbituric acid/barbiturates & combination products
    - Examples: butalbital (Butisol®), thiopental (Pentothal®), butobarbital (Soneryl®), pentobarbital and secobarbital in suppository dosage form, aprobarbital (Alurate®), butalbital with APAP (Fioricet®, Esgic®), butalbital/ASA/caffeine (Fiorinal®).
- Ketamine (Ketlar®)
- Buprenorphine/naloxone (Suboxone®)
- Lysergic acid

Note: C-III controlled substances mainly consist of analgesic agents.

(720 ILCS 570/207 & 208)

FINDINGS REQUIRED FOR INCLUSION IN SCHEDULE IV (C-IV)
The Department may issue a rule scheduling a substance in Schedule IV for the following:
1. The substance has lower potential for abuse relative to schedule III drugs, and higher than schedule V drugs.
2. The substance has currently accepted medical use in the U.S.
3. Abuse of the substance may lead to limited psychological or physiological dependence.

Some examples of C-IV substances are as follows:
- Alprazolam (Xanax®)
- Barbital
- Carisoprodol (Soma®, Vanadom®)
- Clonazepam (Klonopin®)
- Diazepam (Valium®)
- Lorazepam (Ativan®)
- Meprobamate (Equanil®, Miltown®)
- Modafinil (Provigil®)
- Fospropofol (Lusedra®)
- Phenobarbital
- Zaleplon (Sonata®)
- Zolpidem (Ambien®)
- Tenazepam (Restoril®)

- Tramadol (Ultram®)

Note: C-IV controlled substances mainly consist of anxiolytics and sedatives agents.

(720 ILCS 570/209 & 210)

FINDINGS REQUIRED FOR INCLUSION IN SCHEDULE V (C-V)
The Department may issue a rule scheduling a substance in Schedule V for the following:
1. The substance has low potential for abuse relative to schedule V drugs.
2. The substance has currently accepted medical use in the U.S.
3. Abuse of the substance may lead to limited psychological or physiological dependence
4. They consist primarily of preparations containing limited quantities of certain narcotic and stimulant drugs.

Some examples of C-V substances are as follows:
- 200 mg or less of codeine or any of its salts, per 100 mL or per 100 g
    - Codeine with APAP elixir
- 10 mg or less of dihydrocodeine or any of its salts, per 100 mL or 100 g
- 100 mg or less of ethylmorphine or any of its salts, per 100 mL or per 100 g
- 2.5 mcg or less of diphenoxylate and 25 micrograms (mcg) or more of atropine sulfate per dosage unit
    - Example: diphenoxylate with atropine (Lomotil®)
- 100 mg of opium or less per 100 mL or per 100 g
- 0.5 mg or less of difenoxin (DEA Drug Code No. 9618) and 25 mcg or more of atropine sulfate per dosage unit
- Guaifenesin with codeine (Robitussin AC®)
- Promethazine with codeine (Phenergan® with codeine)
- Lacosamide (Vimpat®)
- Pregabalin (Lyrica®)

Notes:
- C-V controlled substances mainly consist of cold, cough, and anti-diarrheal agents.

(720 ILCS 570/211 & 212)

EXEMPT NARCOTICS – NONPRESCRIPTION SCHEDULE V CONTROLLED SUBSTANCES
Some Schedule V controlled substances can be dispensed without a prescription, which are known as "exempt narcotics." Both Illinois and Federal laws permit pharmacies to sell these Schedule V substances without a prescription.
- Under IL law, the sale of exempt narcotics is regulated more strictly compared to Federal law. For the IL MPJE purpose, you must go with the more stringent IL law. We will go more into details under the requirements for dispensing Schedule V drugs.
- It is important to remember that rules for dispensing and selling of exempt narcotics (nonprescription C-V controlled substances) and methamphetamine precursors (ephedrine and PSE) without a prescription are different. (See sales rules below for methamphetamine

precursors & sales rules for exempt narcotics under Requirements for Dispensing Schedule V Controlled Substances that will be discussed later)

The Department revises and republishes the Schedules twice a year for two years from the effective date of this Act and thereafter annually. If the Department does not republish the Schedules, the last published Schedules remains in full effect.

(720 ILCS 570/213)

EPHEDRINE – METHAMPHETAMINE PRECURSOR

Any drug product that contains ephedrine, its salts or isomers, cannot be marketed, advertised, or labeled for indications of stimulation, mental alertness, weight loss, or appetite control.

Similar to violation of practicing pharmacy without being licensed, a violation of this requirement is a Class A misdemeanor. A second or subsequent violation is a Class 4 felony.

This violation does not apply to dietary supplements, herbs, or other natural products which:
1. Are not otherwise prohibited by law; and
2. May contain naturally occurring ephedrine, pseudoephedrine, or their salts, isomers, or salts of isomers, or a combination of these substances such that:
    a. Are contained in a matrix of organic material; and
    b. Do not exceed 15% of the total weight of the natural product.

Notes: In May 2004, the FDA banned OTC supplements that contain ephedra (a naturally-occurring herb) and ephedrine. This ban does not pertain to teas or traditional Chinese herbal remedies prescribed by a tradition Chinese physician (i.e. Sunflower Botannicals Mormon tea).

(720 ILCS 570/216)

WHAT YOU SHOULD KNOW ABOUT METHAMPHETAMINE PRECURSORS:
Ephedrine and pseudoephedrine (PSE) are precursors of methamphetamine. Although they are not scheduled under Federal law, they are scheduled as C-V in Illinois. A prescription is not required to purchase ephedrine and PSE. Single or combination ephedrine and PSE products in all dosage forms are C-V controlled substances. For reporting of theft or loss of significant amount of PSE, pharmacists are not required to report to the DEA with DEA form 106, because it is not scheduled as a controlled substance under the federal law.

LIMITS OF SALES
The rules for purchasing and dispensing of ephedrine and PSE are different from those of exempt narcotics (see "Requirements for Dispensing Schedule V" for more information about nonprescription C-V controlled substances sales limits).
- Sales of ephedrine and PSE are limited to 7.5 g or less within 30-day period.
- Maximum of one convenience package can be purchase within 24-hour period.

- o   A convenience package is defined as 360 mg or less of ephedrine and PSE in liquid or liquid-filled capsule form.
- Maximum of two packages of products containing ephedrine or PSE, including convenience packages, can be purchased per transaction.

REQUIREMENTS FOR SALES
- Ephedrine and PSE may only be administered, dispensed, distributed by a pharmacist, practitioner, a pharmacy, a retail distributor (i.e. drug store, grocery stores=, merchandise store, etc.), authorized by DEA to distribute bulk quantities of List I chemicals.
- Pharmacy technician may sell ephedrine and PSE behind the pharmacy counter, including obtaining an ID and patient's signature. (**Note:** In contrast, only pharmacists can sell exempt narcotics.)
- The customer must be at least 18 years of age and provide a valid idea (i.e. driver license or other government issued ID).
- The product must be contained in blister packs, each contains 2 or less dosage units or if it's in unit dose packet, it should only contain 3,000 mg or less of ephedrine or PSE or its salts or isomers.
- The products may only be distributed by a pharmacist or pharmacy technician in a pharmacy.
- Non-pharmacy retailers may only sell convenience packages.
- In pharmacies, ephedrine and PSE products must be kept behind the pharmacy counter. At the retail distributor, they must be kept behind the store counter or in locked case.

RECORDKEEPING
The pharmacist must maintain a log-book or an electronic record of the following information for **at least 2 years:**
1. Name and address of the purchaser
2. Date and time of the transaction
3. Product name and brand of ephedrine or PSE
4. Quantity distributed

(720 ILCS 648/20, 25, and 30)

REGISTRATION REQUIRED FOR MANUFACTURING, DISTRIBUTION, & DISPENSING
The Department of Financial and Professional Regulation (DFPR) issues the registration. Activities related to controlled substances are divided into 11 categories. In order to perform any of these groups of activities, a person must register with the Federal Drug Enforcement Administration (DEA). The following groups of activities are required to be registered with Federal DEA
1. Manufacturing
2. Distributing
3. Dispensing (including prescribing, administering and filling) C-II through C-V controlled substances
4. Narcotic treatment program C-II through C-V controlled substances

5. Detoxification compounding (compounding by mixing, preparing, packaging, or changing dosage form of C-II through C-V narcotic for us in maintenance or detoxification by a narcotic treatment program)
6. Engaging in chemical analysis
7. Research controlled substances C-II through C-V controlled substances; other than narcotic treatment program
8. Research with C-I controlled substances
9. Importer
10. Exporter of C-I through C-IV controlled substances
11. Purchasing, storing or administering euthanasic (pain killing) drugs to the extent allowed by his or her registration

Tip to know: The most important categories or groups of activities are the ones relevant to pharmacy, including (1) manufacturing, (2) distributing, (3) dispensing, (4) narcotic treatment program, and (5) detoxification compounding. These are the types of registrations required to obtain in pharmacy if it was to perform any of these activities.

A practitioner can have a Federal DEA and IL registration selective for C-II, or C-III through C-V. The registration can be limited to drug class, narcotic versus non-narcotic. An application for controlled substance registration is divided into the following categories:
1. Schedule II narcotic
2. Schedule II non-narcotic
3. Schedule III narcotic
4. Schedule III non-narcotic
5. Schedules IV
6. Schedule V

NON-NARCOTIC SCHEDULES
Under the IL Controlled Substances Act, narcotic and non-narcotic schedules are combined and the 'N' designation is not needed for non-narcotic drugs. The Controlled Substances Registration application and printed licenses will not specifically include the 'N' designation.

Notes:
- Controlled substances belong in a closed system of distribution that is tracked through registration and scheduling. Therefore, access to controlled substances is restricted through registration and scheduling.
- Once a scheduled drug leaves the closed system of distribution, it cannot re-enter.

Tip to know: Dispenser registration is issued to a physician or mid-level practitioner who prescribes a controlled substance.

ILLINOIS REGISTRATION/LICENSURE REQUIREMENT
Illinois requires a separate state controlled substance registration. If an applicant is registered under the Federal law, he or she can complete and file an application for licensure and paid all fees to be registered in IL for controlled substances. The DFPR will notify the applicant **within 30 days** after completing the application in IL if his or her application has been granted. Once granted, he or she

will be licensed in IL to the same extent as his or her Federal registration. The requirement includes proof of federal registration and payment for required fee.

Note: Although, only the DEA registration number of the practitioner needs to be on the prescription, the DEA number and state controlled substances license from both the practitioner and pharmacy are required to have.

(720 ILCS 570/303)

WHO IS ELIGIBLE TO BE APPLICANT?

Both Federal and IL law do not require the applicant of the controlled substances registration to be a pharmacist, but the applicant must be the owner (i.e. sole proprietor, active partner, and corporation). When an entity applies, the registration form should be signed by the owner. If the entity is partnership, any partner who's the owner can complete the form and sign. If it's corporation, any officer or director of the corporation can complete and sign.

POWER OF ATTORNEY

Once registered, the owner becomes a registrant. The registrant may exercise power of attorney by delegating responsibility to another person at the store level, in which, the registrant can authorize one or more persons to issue order for C-I and C-II controlled substances on behalf of the registrant. And this person doesn't have to be located at the registered location. The registrant may revoke the power of attorney at any time using a notice of revocation.

Tip to know:
- In IL, PIC has the responsibilities to order, secure, and dispense controlled substances regardless of whether or not the PIC is the registrant and has the power of attorney.
- Both Federal and IL laws allow the power of attorney to be delegated to anybody, including non-pharmacist owner, unlicensed person, pharmacy technician, and pharmacy interns.

The following persons do not need to register and may legally possess controlled substances:
1. An agent or employee of any registered entity.
2. A common or contract carrier or warehouseman.
3. An ultimate user or a person with a legal prescription.
4. Officers and employees of IL or of the U.S. while performing official duties that require possession of controlled substances.
5. A registered pharmacist who acts in the usual course of his or her employment.
6. A holder of temporary license issues under Section 17 of the Medical Practice Act of 1987.

MULTIPLE REGISTRATION REQUIREMENTS

A separate registration is required for each of the following:
1. Location
    - Each place of business or professional practice with different street address is required to have a separate registration (for example, Walgreens, CVS or other chain pharmacies have thousands of pharmacies that are shared by the same owner).
    - Every location at which a controlled substance is prescribed is not required to have a separate registration.

2. Activity

A pharmacy is required to have multiple registrations (DEA numbers) depending on the activities.

(720 ILCS 570/301 & 302)

SEPARATE REGISTRATION FOR INDEPENDENT ACTIVITIES
Every person who engages in more than one group of independent activities must obtain a separate license for each group of activities. The following groups of activities are considered as independent of each other and required to have a separate registration:
1. Manufacturing controlled substances
   - Purchasing of controlled drugs for the purpose of repackaging for sale within the pharmacy without a prescription or to other registrant registered as a manufacturer.
   - Compounding for office use.
2. Distributing controlled substances
   - This include purchasing activities and location where drugs are stored and shipped to other pharmacies; or
   - Annual distribution of controlled drugs to other pharmacies or practitioners exceeds 5% of the total number of dosage units dispensed.
3. Dispensing C-II through C-V controlled substances (**Note:** Only a dispenser registration is required if a controlled drug is compounded by prescription, manufacturer registration is not required).
4. Engaging in "Detox Compounding"
   - Compounding a controlled drug for sale or distributing to a narcotic treatment program for treating addiction (Remember that narcotic treatment program must be registered with the Federal DEA).
5. Conducting instructional activities with C-II through C-V controlled substances.
6. Conducting instructional activities with C-I controlled substances.
7. Conducting chemical analysis with any controlled substances.

(77 IL ADC Section 3100.50)

EXEMPTIONS FROM REGISTRATION
LOCATIONS
An office used by a licensee where sales of controlled substances are made, but does not contain controlled substances and does not serve as a distribution point.

(77 IL ADC Section 3100.60)

AGENTS AND EMPLOYEES: AFFILIATED PRACTITIONERS
The requirement of licensure is waived for any employee of a person who is licensed to engage in any group of independent activities if the employee is acting in the usual course of his or her employment.

1. An individual practitioner who is an employee of another practitioner licensed to dispense controlled substances may administer and dispense (other than prescribing) controlled substances under the license of the employer (for example, an employee pharmacist who works at Walgreens).
2. Employee practitioners, nurses, and pharmacists have the authority to possess, administer, prescribe, and dispense controlled substances under the DEA registration number of the hospital.

(77 IL ADC Section 3100.80)

COINCIDENT ACTIVITIES

The following activities are considered as coincident activities, in which, a person does not have to obtain a separate registration to engage in those coincident activities:
1. A person licensed to manufacture any controlled substance is authorized to distribute that substance but not other substances that he or she is not licensed to manufacture.
2. A person licensed to manufacture any C-II through C-V controlled substance is authorized to conduct chemical analysis and pre-clinical research (including quality control analysis) with narcotic and non-narcotic Schedule II-V controlled substances.
3. A person authorized by the State of Illinois and the federal government agencies to conduct research with a controlled substance is authorized to manufacture, and distribute that substance to other persons authorized to conduct research with that substance or to conduct chemical analysis.
4. A person licensed to conduct chemical analysis with controlled substances is authorized:
    a. To manufacture and import those substances for analytical purposes, and distribute those substances to persons licensed or authorized to conduct chemical analysis, instructional activities or research with those substances or persons who are exempted from licensure; and
    b. To export those substances to persons in other countries performing chemical analysis or enforcing laws relating to controlled substances or drugs in those countries.
5. A person authorized by the State of Illinois or the federal government agencies to conduct research with C-II through C-V controlled substances is authorized to conduct chemical analysis, to manufacture, and to distribute those substances to other persons licensed or authorized to conduct chemical analysis or research with those substances and to persons exempted from licensure.
6. A person licensed to dispense C-II through C-V controlled substances is authorized to conduct instructional activities with those substances.

A single license to engage in any group of independent activities may include one, or more controlled substances listed in the Schedules authorized in that group of independent activities.

(77 IL ADC Section 3100.50)

The DFPR may deny issuance of a license to an applicant who applied for a registration to manufacture, distribute, or dispense Schedules I or II controlled substances, if it would be inconsistent to the public interest. Practitioners who are licensed to dispense controlled substances in Schedules II-V are authorized to conduct instructional activities with these controlled substances under IL law.

ADDING SCHEDULE II TO PHARMACY CONTROLLED SUBSTANCES LICENSE
Pharmacies, that want to add Schedule II to an IL Pharmacy Controlled Substances license following the DEA rescheduling of Hydrocodone Combination Products, should meet the security requirements as the inspection will be required. The pharmacy's PIC that meet these requirements may mail a request to the IL Department to add Schedule II. If pharmacies are located outside of IL, they must include a copy of a DEA registration at the same address showing Schedule II, and include the original IL Controlled Substances license. A photocopy of the pharmacy license may be posted until the new license is printed. The original license must be returned.

RENEWAL PERIODS
REGISTRATION/LICENSURE TO DISPENSE
Every certificate of registration or license to dispense Schedules II through V controlled substances expires on the date the certificate holder's professional license expires. The holder of a certificate of registration may renew the certificate during the month preceding the expiration date and must pay the required fee.
OTHER CONTROLLED SUBSTANCES REGISTRATIONS
Every certificate of registration to conduct instructional activities, to conduct chemical analyses, and as a manufacturer or wholesale distributor, expires on December 31 of each even numbered year.

The registrant must notify the Department if there's a change of address within 30 days after the change. Failure to receive a renewal form is not an excuse for failure to pay the renewal fee.

FEES

	Registration/Licensure:	Fee	Renewal Fee
1	Registration To Dispense C-II through C-V	$5	$5/year
2	Licensure for Mid-Level Practitioner Controlled Substances	$5	$5/year
3	Registration To Conduct Instructional Activities	$5	$5/year
4	Registration To Conduct Chemical Analyses	$50	$50/year
5	§Registration As Manufacturer or Wholesale Distributor	$50	$50/year

Table 1: *Registration/Licensure Fees and Renewal Fees.* §Fee for Certificate of Registration as Manufacturer or Wholesale Distributor of controlled substances that may be dispensed without a prescription is $15; the renewal fee is $15/year.

Government institutions that manufacture, distribute or dispense controlled substances, or engage in chemical analyses or instructional activities, are waived from these fees.

(77 IL ADC Section 3100.30)

MID-LEVEL PRACTITIONER REGISTRATION
The DFPR shall register licensed physician assistants (PAs), licensed advanced practice nurses (APNs), and prescribing psychologists to prescribe and dispense controlled substances. This also includes

euthanasia agencies to purchase, store, or administer animal euthanasia drugs if they have completed appropriate application for prescribing or dispensing controlled substances, and pay all required fees and under the following conditions described below.

I. **WITH RESPECT TO PA & APN:**
   If there's a delegated authority that allows-
   - PA to prescribe any Schedule III-V controlled substances by a physician, or to prescribe or dispense any Schedule II controlled substances by a supervising physician through written delegation of authority.
   - APN to prescribe any Schedule III-V controlled substances by a collaborating physician, or to prescribe or dispense any Schedule II controlled substances by a supervising physician.
   - A PA and APN can prescribe or dispense C-II drugs under the following conditions:
     1. Specific C-II controlled substances in oral, topical or transdermal route of administration can be performed. The schedule II drug must be identified by either brand or generic name. If the C-II drug has to be injected or in other route of administration, they are _NOT_ allowed to perform on the patient.
     2. They must discuss the condition of any patient monthly with the physician.
     3. All prescriptions are limited to **30-day supply or less**. Only after an approval of the physician, they can issue more prescriptions.
     4. They must provide evidence of **45 contact hours or 3 academic semester hours** in pharmacology. For the PA, this provides by the Accreditation Review Commission on Education for the Physician Assistant (ARC-PA).
     5. They must complete at least **5 hours of CE** in pharmacology annually.

NEW CONTROLLED SUBSTANCE APPLICATION
A PA or APN that does not currently hold an IL controlled substance license should submit an application, Notice of Delegated Prescriptive Authority for Controlled Substances form, and the application fee. PAs must also submit the Notice of Employment or Supervisory Control. Evidence of completion of at least 45 contract hours, or 3 academic semester hours in pharmacology as stated on the above must be submitted.

ADDING SCHEDULE II PRESCRIPTIVE AUTHORITY
To add C-II prescriptive authority to an existing controlled substances license, an update Notice of Prescriptive Authority form, and official transcript or letter from the school verifying completion of 45 graduate contact hours or 3 semester hours in pharmacology must be submitted if the original controlled substances license was issued after July 1, 2011. No fee is required for adding Schedule II. The license doesn't need to be reprinted, and the original license doesn't have to be returned as no schedule is printed on the license. The written collaborative or supervision agreement must reflect C-II delegation.

II. **WITH RESPECT TO APNs CERTIFIED AS A NURSE PRACTITIONER, NURSE MIDWIFE, OR CLINICAL NURSE SPECIALIST IN A HOSPITAL AFFILIATE**
   This health care provider can prescribe any C-II through V controlled substances by the hospital affiliate upon a physician's recommendation. In order to prescribe any C-II drugs,

the health care provider must meet the conditions similar to those followed by the PA and APN, as listed in the above numbers (1) to (5).

III. WITH RESPECT TO ANIMAL EUTHANASIA AGENCIES
The euthanasia agency needs to obtain a license from the DFPR, and obtain a registration number from the Department.

IV. WITH RESPECT TO PRESCRIBING PSYCHOLOGISTS
Prescribing psychologists must have been delegated authority to prescribe any non-narcotic C-III through V controlled substances by a collaborating physician, and complete the appropriate application forms and required fees.

(720 ILCS 570/303.05 & 307)

APPLICATION FOR MID-LEVEL PRACTITIONER CONTROLLED SUBSTANCES LICENSE
An applicant for a mid-level practitioner controlled substances license must file an application provided by the Department. The application must include the following:
1. The license number of the PA or APN; the license must be active and in good standing.
2. The license number and controlled substances license number of the delegating or collaborating physician.
3. A delegation of C-II through C-V controlled substances must be electronically input. A printout of the inputted delegation can serve as written notice of delegation of prescriptive authority if it is signed by the physician. A separate notice of prescriptive authority should be submitted by each supervising or collaborating physician; and
4. The required fee.

Applicants for PA or APN controlled substance licenses that authorize the prescribing and dispensing of C-II controlled substances, must meet education requirements. This applies to licenses that were issued on or after August 11, 2011. The Department will impose a maximum fine of $50 per prescription if any PA or APN writes a controlled substance prescription without having valid prescriptive authority.

A euthanasia agency applicant for a mid-level practitioner controlled substances license must file an application on forms provided by the Department. The application must include (1) the euthanasia agency license number with an active and good standing license, and (2) the required fee.

(77 IL ADC Section 3100.85)

The mid-level practitioner is only licensed to prescribe the schedules of controlled substances a physician has given the authority to prescribe. A PA and APN can only prescribe medications and controlled substances stated in the written delegation of authority. An animal euthanasia agency does not have any authority to prescribe controlled substances. A physician may delegate prescriptive authority to a PA and APN. After completing all registration requirements, a PA, APN, and animal euthanasia agencies may be issued a mid-level practitioner controlled substances license for IL. Schedule I and II controlled substances can only be distributed between registrants in accordance to a written order.

MODIFICATION IN LICENSURE

Any licensee who wants to modify his or her license to authorize the handling of additional controlled substances can submit a letter of request including the substances and/or Schedules to be added to his or her registration to the Director.

(77 IL ADC Section 3100.280)

TERMINATION OF REGISTRATION

The license of any person terminates if the person (1) dies, (2) ceases legal existence, (3) discontinues business or professional practice, (4) has his or her primary professional license in any status other than active, or (5) changes his or her name or address as shown on the license. If there's any such change as listed in (2), (3) and (5), the licensee should notify the Division **within 10 days.**

The pharmacist cannot fill a prescription issued by a PA or APN if the delegated authority terminates. Transferring of license or any authority to prescribe controlled drug is not permissible.

(77 IL ADC Section 3100.290 & 3100.300)

RECORD AND INVENTORY REQUIREMENTS GENERALLY

An annual inventory should be conducted with an actual count of the inventory on hand for all C-II controlled substances, and an approximated inventory for all C-III, C-IV and C-V controlled substances. The inventory must be maintained for **at least 5 years.**

WHAT HAPPENS WHEN THERE'S A LOSS OR THEFT OF CONTROLLED SUBSTANCES?
The licensee must conduct an approximate count inventory with a start date of the last inventory for the controlled substance that was either lost or stolen. The licensee is required to file with the DEA a Report of Theft or Loss of Controlled Substances (Form 106), a copy with the printed name of the person who signed the form must be sent to the Division within one business day after submission to the DEA. Failure to do so will result in discipline of the licensee. Schedule V controlled substance PSE is an exception that does not required to be reported to the DEA if there's theft or loss of PSE, because although PSE is a C-V in IL, it is not scheduled under federal law.

(77 IL ADC Section 3100.360)

RECORDKEEPING

Every practitioner who is required to be registered to manufacture, distribute or dispense controlled substances, or purchase, store, or administer euthanasia drugs must keep records, and maintain inventories to comply with the recordkeeping and inventory requirements in the U.S.

Note: Federal law requires that all records concerning controlled substances must be maintained for at least 2 years for inspection by the DEA, but IL has stricter law that requires all records of controlled substances to be maintained for **at least 5 years.**

(720 ILCS 570/306)

WHAT IS THE RECORDKEEPING PERIOD FOR A WRITTEN CONTROLLED SUBSTANCE PRESCRIPTION?
If it's a written prescription, the practitioner who filled the prescription or the pharmacy that dispensed the prescription, must retain the file for a period of **5 years**. This file must be readily accessible for inspection by an officer or employee engaged in the enforcement of this Act. If the specific prescription is computer generated and printed at the prescriber's office, the date does not need to be handwritten. Facsimile or oral controlled substance prescriptions are also maintained for 5 years.

All records of purchases and sales of controlled substances must be maintained for **at least 2 years**.

(720 ILCS 570/312)

ISSUANCE OF A PRESCRIPTION

WHO ARE ENTITLED TO ISSUE PRESCRIPTIONS?
A prescription for controlled substance can be issued only by an individual practitioner who (1) holds an active professional license as an individual practitioner in IL, and (2) holds an active controlled substances license or is exempted from licensure.

An employee or agent of the individual practitioner may communicate a prescription issued by the individual practitioner in order of that practitioner.

(77 IL ADC Section 3100.370)

WHAT HAPPENS IF A PHARMACIST SUSPECT A PRESCRIPTION'S PURPOSE IS TO HELP THE PATIENT CONTINUING HIS OR HER DEPENDENCE ON THE PRESCRIBED CONTROLLED SUBSTANCE?
A pharmacist should only fill a prescription of a controlled substance issued for a legitimate medical purpose. If the prescription is for a narcotic drug dependent person with purpose of helping him or her to continue the dependence of the drug, the pharmacist must not fill the prescription. It is the responsibility of the prescriber for the proper prescribing and dispensing (for example, administering) of controlled substances, but a corresponding responsibility rests with the pharmacist who fills the prescription. The person who knowingly fills an invalid controlled substance prescription, as well as the person issuing it, will be subject for penalties relating to controlled substances.

CAN A PRACTITIONER (I.E. PHYSICIAN, PHYSICIAN ASSISTANT, ETC.) SELF-PRESCRIBE OR SELF-DISPENSE CONTROLLED SUBSTANCES?
A practitioner cannot self-prescribe or self-dispense (for example, self-administer) controlled substances. A practitioner may not prescribe controlled substances to an immediate family member unless there is a bona fide practitioner-patient relationship, and appropriate record are maintained for all treatment of the family member.

(77 IL ADC Section 3100.380)

A practitioner may sign a paper prescription in the same manner as he or she would sign a check or legal document (for example, J.H. Smith or John H. Smith). A computer-generated prescription is printed out by the practitioner, and must be manually signed.

The secretary or agent of a practitioner may prepare a prescription for a signature. A pharmacist, who fills a prescription, is required to recognize if the prescription is prepared appropriately. Neither a pharmacist nor a pharmacy technician may act as an agent for a practitioner.

(77 IL ADC Section 3100.390)

SCHEDULE II CONTROLLED SUBSTANCE EMERGENCY PRESCRIPTIONS

A C-II controlled substance must be issued as a written prescription order for the prescription to be valid. In the case of an emergency, where failure to issue such prescription might result in death or intense suffering, the prescriber may issue an oral prescription which includes a statement explaining the reason for the emergency.

WHAT MUST A PHYSICIAN DO WHEN IT COMES TO A C-II EMERGENCY PRESCRIPTION?
Within 7 days after issuance of the emergency prescription, the prescriber must provide the dispensing pharmacist a written prescription for the emergency quantity prescribed. The date of the emergency prescription and "Authorization for Emergency Dispensing" should be written on the face of the prescription. The prescriber can deliver the written prescription in person or by mail. If delivering by mail, the prescriber must make sure it's postmarked within the 7-day period.

WHAT MUST A PHARMCIST DO FOR A C-II EMERGENCY PRESCRIPTION?
After receiving the written prescription, the dispensing pharmacist is required to attach it to the emergency oral prescription received earlier that was written down. If the prescriber fails to deliver the written prescription for the emergency prescription that was dispensed, the dispensing pharmacist must notify the DFPR. All prescriptions for Schedule II drugs should include both a written, and numerical notation of quantity on the face of the prescription. A Schedule II drug cannot be refilled.

(720 ILCS 570/309)

CAN A PHARMACIST ACCEPT AN ELECTRONIC PRESCRIPTION FOR A CONTROLLED SUBSTANCE?
A pharmacist may accept an electronic prescription for Schedule II, III, IV, and V controlled substances issued by an authorized prescriber if done in accordance with the federal rules for electronic prescriptions for controlled substances.

(720 ILCS 570/311.5)

REQUIREMENTS FOR DISPENSING CONTROLLED SUBSTANCES

A pharmacist may dispense a Schedule II-V controlled substance to any person with a written, or electronic prescription of any prescriber. The prescription must contain the following:

1. The date of when the prescription is issue.
2. Signature of the person prescribing or electronically validated on the day when it's issued.
3. The name and address of the patient.
4. The full name, address and registry number related to controlled substances of the prescriber (DEA number), if he or she is required to be registered.
5. The drug name, strength, dosage and form; and
6. Quantity of the drug dispensed in both written and numeric forms.

Notes:
- If a prescription is written, it must be in ink with a pen, typewriter, computer printer, or with an indelible pencil.
- If a prescription is electronically transmitted, the prescriber's electronic or handwritten signature, initial, thumb print or other electronic identification, must be affixed to face of the prescription.
- More than one prescription is allowed per prescription blank for Schedule III, IV or V drug.
- Only one prescription is allowed per prescription blank for Schedule II drug.

An animal prescription for a controlled substance needs to state the species of the animal or the animal's common name as well as the owner's full name and address on the prescription. Pharmacists who fill the prescription need to write the date of filling and their signature on the face of the prescription. If the prescription is for a non-controlled substance, the owner's last name with the animal's common name is sufficient.

SCHEDULE II DRUG PRESCRIPTIONS
WHEN WILL A SCHEDULE II DRUG PRESCRIPTION BECOME INVALID?
In Illinois, a prescription for schedule II drug is valid for 90 days.

WHAT ARE THE REQUIREMENTS FOR DISPENSING A SCHEDULE II DRUG?
A prescription for a C-II drug is valid only if it's written, or electronically transmitted by the prescriber. A facsimile or oral C-II prescription is not acceptable. There's an exception for oral C-II prescription if it falls under emergency dispensing requested by a physician.

C-II prescription can only be issued for a **30-day supply or less**, and can be valid for **up to 90 days** after the date of issuance, except when a physician issues multiple prescriptions **(sequential 30-day supplies)** for the same C-II drug authorizing up to a 90-day supply. Before authorizing a **90-day supply**, the physician must meet both of the following conditions:
1. Each separate prescription must be issued for a legitimate medical purpose; and
2. The individual physician must provide written instructions on each prescription (other than the first prescription, if the prescribing physician intends for the prescription to be filled immediately) indicating the earliest date on which a pharmacy may fill that prescription.
3. Physician documents in the medical record of a patient the medical necessity for the amount, and duration of the three sequential 30-day prescriptions for Schedule II narcotics.

CAN A PRESCRIPTION FOR C-II DRUG BE REFILLED?
No, the general rule is C-II control substances are not refillable.

WHAT MAY A PHARMACIST NOT CHANGE IN A C-II DRUG PRESCRIPTION?
A pharmacist may not change the following components of a C-II prescription:
1. Date written, or add the date.
2. Name of the patient.
3. Name of the prescriber, or add a signature; and
4. Name of the drug.

Any other components of a prescription for a C-II controlled substance may be changed after consultation with the prescriber.

Tip to know: Federal and IL laws prohibit prescriptions with post-dating. For instance, if the date a prescription received is on 1/1/2017, but it was mistakenly dated as 1/2/2017 by the prescriber. The pharmacy cannot accept this post-dated prescription and cannot hold it until 1/2/2017.

(720 ILCS 570/309), (720 ILCS 570/312) & (77 IL ADC Section 3100.400)

SCHEDULE III-V DRUG PRESCRIPTIONS
WHEN WILL SCHEDULE III, IV, OR V DRUG PRESCRIPTIONS BECOME INVALID?
A prescription for Schedule III, IV or V controlled substance can only be filled **within 6 months** after the issued date, and can only be refilled **5 times or less,** unless the prescription is renewed in writing by the prescriber.

IS A FACSIMILE OR ORAL PRESCRIPTION FOR SCHEDULE III-V DRUG ACCEPTABLE?
Instead of a written prescription, a pharmacist may dispense Schedule III-V to any person either through a facsimile or oral prescription. The oral prescription must be written down on a prescription order by the pharmacist with the following criteria:
1. Date and time of when received by pharmacist.
2. Full name and address of the ultimate user.
3. Full name, address, and registry number of the prescriber.
4. Pharmacist's signature and date on the face of the prescription.

WHAT ARE THE REQUIREMENTS FOR DISPENSING NONPRESCRIPTION SCHEDULE V DRUGS?
Except for any non-prescription targeted methamphetamine precursor, a controlled substance included in Schedule V cannot be distributed or dispensed other than for a medical purpose and only under the following conditions:
1. Only personally by a person registered to dispense a Schedule V or only personally by a pharmacist that can sell (i.e. verify age of purchaser, complete log book, etc.). A pharmacy technician may ring up the order at the end.
2. The patient must be at least 21 years old with 2 positive documents of identification.
3. Dispenser must record the name & address of the purchaser, product name & quantity, date and time of purchase, & dispenser's signature.
4. Under federal and IL laws, a person may obtain up to 4 ounces of a C-V controlled substance.
5. No person can purchase or be dispensed **within 96-hour period more than 120 ml, or more than 120 g*** of any Schedule V drug which contains codeine, dihydrocodeine, or any salts.

*Anything more than 120 g of these products or their combination is considered illegal possession.

A person, who's qualified and registered to dispense controlled substances, is not allowed to maintain or keep in stock **more than 4.5 L** of each Schedule V controlled substance plus any additional quantity of controlled substance necessary to fill the largest number of prescription orders filled in any one week of the previous year.

(720 ILCS 570/312)

WHAT ARE THE REQUIREMENTS FOR REFILLING SCHEDULE III-V CONTROLLED SUBSTANCES?
Each refilling of a prescription of a Schedules III, IV or V controlled substance should be entered on the back of the prescription, or in the electronic prescription record and indicate the following:
1. Date, quantity and name or initials of the dispensing pharmacist for each prescription.
2. Date of dispensing indicated by the pharmacist; and
3. The amount dispensed.

If the pharmacist only signs or initials, and dates the back of the prescription, he or she is considered to have dispensed a refill for the full-face amount of the prescription.

CAN A PHARMACIST CONTACT THE PRESCRIBER TO REFILL A PRESCRIPTION FOR SCHEDULES III-V?
If a patient requests or has an agreement to utilize a pharmacy auto-fill program, medication adherence plan, or long term care, a pharmacist may contact the prescriber to refill a Schedule III, IV or V controlled substance.

(77 IL ADC Section 3100.410)

Table 2 shows a side-by-side of Illinois Law vs. Federal Law for C-V controlled substances:

	Requirements	Illinois Law	Federal Law
1	Age of the patient for purchase	At least 21 years old	At least 18 years old
2	Identification (ID)	Two positive IDs	One valid ID
3	Number of refill	5 refills or 6 months (whichever comes first)	No limits
4	Time limit on purchase	At least 96 hours	At least 48 hours
5	Recordkeeping	At least 2 years	At least 2 years
6	Report to DPRF	Send copy of the sale to DFPR the following month by the 15th	

Table 2: *IL Law vs. Federal Law for C-V Controlled Substances*

THE CONTAINER LABEL FOR CONTROLLED SUBSTANCES

Whenever a pharmacist dispenses any controlled substances, except a non-prescription Schedule V product or non-prescription methamphetamine precursor, he or she must affix to the container (1) a label indicating date of initial fill, (2) pharmacist's name and address, (3) patient name, (4) prescriber name, (5) directions for use, cautionary statements, dosage and quantity, and (6) drug name.

RESPONSIBILITIES OF A PHARMACIST AND PRESCRIBER IN A CONTROLLED SUBSTANCE TRANSACTION

The prescriber has the responsibility for the proper prescribing, or dispensing of controlled substances. The prescriber's dispensing does not include the actual filling, but includes the administration of the controlled substances. The pharmacist on the other hand has the responsibility for proper filling of a prescription for controlled substances.

PRE-PRINTED PRESCRIPTIONS

A pre-printed prescription is a written prescription of a drug indicated before the time of issuance, including a pre-inked stamp applied to a prescription blank. This is not a written prescription generated by a computer in the prescriber's office.

IS A PRE-PRINTED PRESCRIPTION FOR A CONTROLLED SUBSTANCE ACCEPTABLE?

A prescriber cannot pre-print a prescription for any controlled substance nor can any practitioner issue, or fill a pre-printed prescription for any controlled substance. A prescriber may use a machine or electronic device to individually generate a printed prescription, and the prescriber is required to affix his or her manual signature.

MAILING OF CONTROLLED SUBSTANCES

A controlled substance may be mailed only if all of the following conditions are met:
1. The controlled substances are not dangerous or likely to cause injury to a person's health.
2. The inner container of a parcel containing the controlled substance must be marked with seals, and be placed in a secure outer container.
3. If the controlled substances consist of prescription medicines, the inner containers must be labeled with the name and address of the pharmacy dispensing the prescription.
4. The outside wrapper or container must be free of markings that indicate the nature of the contents.

(720 ILCS 570/312)

Section 312 does not apply if the controlled substances are administered in the following:
1. Hospitals or institution. However, the prescription for the controlled substance must be in writing on the patient's record, signed by the prescriber, and dated. It should also state the name and quantity ordered and the quantity actually administered.
2. Long-term care facility for residents under 22 years old.
3. Drug abused treatment programs.

The recordkeeping for the above entities listed in (1) and (2) above is **2 years**.

FAXING OF SCHEDULE II CONTROLLED SUBSTANCES

A prescription for a Schedule II drug to be compounded for direct administration to a patient in a long-term care facility, or hospice program may be transmitted by facsimile by the prescriber to the pharmacy providing home infusion services. This facsimile serves as the original prescription.

(720 ILCS 570/313)

PARTIAL FILLING OF PRESCRIPTIONS
Partial fills are not considered as full refills. The total quantity dispense in all partial fillings must not exceed the total quantity prescribed.

SCHEDULE III-V CONTROLLED SUBSTANCE PRESCRIPTIONS
The partial filling of a prescription for a C-III, IV or V is allowed **within 6 months** after the date of issuance. Each partial filling should be recorded similar to a refill, but is not considered as a refill.

SCHEDULE II CONTROLLED SUBSTANCE PRESCRIPTIONS
IL law states the remaining portions of the partially filled prescription for a C-II controlled substance must be filled **within 72 hours**. C-II controlled substance prescriptions are not refillable. A pharmacist may partially fill the prescription, and dispense the remaining quantity at a later date, only under the following circumstances:

1. If the pharmacist is unable to supply the full quantity at the time the prescription is presented.
    - If the remaining cannot be filled within 72 hours, the pharmacist must notify the prescriber. No further quantity may be supply beyond the 72-hour period without a new prescription.

2. If a patient is in a long-term care facility (LTCF) or is terminally ill.
    - The pharmacist must write "terminally ill" or "long-term care facility patient" on the prescription.
    - For each partial fill, (1) the date, (2) quantity dispensed, (3) quantity remaining, and (4) identification of the pharmacist, should be recorded on the back of the prescription (or on another appropriate record, uniformly maintained, and readily retrievable).
    - The prescription for "terminally ill" or "LTCF patient" is valid for **60 days** from the issued date.

(77 IL ADC Section 3100.420)

CAN A PHARMACIST IN IL FILL A PRESCRIPTION FOR A CONTROLLED SUBSTANCE ISSUED BY A PRESCRIBER LOCATED OUTSIDE OF IL?
An IL pharmacist may fill a controlled substance prescription issued by a prescriber from another State who holds an active DEA registration.

(77 IL ADC Section 3100.430)

ORDERING C-II CONTROLLED SUBSTANCES
The pharmacist must complete DEA form 222 to order C-II drugs. The original DEA form 222 should be maintained for **2 years** by the selling or transferring licensee. The copy of DEA form 222 should also be maintained for **2 years** by the ordering licensee.

(77 IL ADC Section 3100.500)

MEDICATION SHOPPING AND PHARMACY SHOPPING
Medication shopping is when a person fraudulently or intentionally obtains any controlled substance, or prescription for a controlled substance from a prescriber or pharmacy while being supplied a controlled substance by another prescriber or pharmacy without disclosing the fact of the existing controlled substance to the prescriber or pharmacy. Pharmacy shopping is similar to medication shopping; it occurs when the person fraudulently or intentionally obtains from a pharmacy while being supplied by another pharmacy. Medication/pharmacy shopping is illegal.

The Prescription Monitoring Program (PMP) will inform the prescribers, dispensers, and their designated personnel of potential medication shopping. The program can identify a person, within 30-day period, of having 3 or more prescribers or 3 or more pharmacies, or both, that do not share a common electronic file for controlled substances. For example, think of when a patient tries to have his or her controlled substance filled within a 30-day period, at three different pharmacies, CVS, Walgreens and Jewel Osco pharmacy, but they do not utilize a common electronic file. This should be a red flag to investigate further.

A prescriber or pharmacist is not required by the IL law to request any patient medication disclosure, report any patient activity, or prescribe or refuse to prescribe or dispense any medications.

(720 ILCS 570/314.5)

PRESCRIPTION MONITORING PROGRAM (PMP)
The Department requires pharmacies to report their dispensing of Schedule II, III, IV and V controlled substances. Each time a Schedule II-V drug is dispensed, the dispenser must report the dispensing activity to the IL PMP, including the following information:
1. Patient's name and address.
2. Patient's date of birth and gender.
3. National drug code (NDC) number of the controlled substance dispensed.
4. Date of dispensing.
5. Quantity dispensed and days supply.
6. Dispenser's Drug Enforcement Administration (DEA) registration number.
7. Prescriber's DEA number.
8. Dates the controlled substance is filled.
9. Payment type used to purchase (i.e. Medicaid, cash, third-party insurance).
10. Patient's location code (i.e. home, nursing home, outpatient, etc.) for the controlled substance other than those filled at a retail pharmacy.

For long-term care pharmacies, the dispensing of controlled substance is not required to be reported, but patient medication profiles must be transmitted to the PMP monthly or more frequently if established by administrative rule.

WHAT IS THE DEADLINE FOR REPORTING DISPENSING OF A CONTROLLED SUBSTANCE?
The information must be transmitted every day using (1) an electronic device compatible with the receiving device of the central repository, (2) a computer diskette, (3) a magnetic tape, or (4) a

pharmacy universe claim form or Pharmacy Inventory Control form. The information should be transmitted no later than the end of the next business day after the date of dispensing the controlled substance.

WHAT HAPPENS IF YOU DON'T REPORT A CONTROLLED SUBSTANCE TO THE PMP?
Failure to report will result in a civil fine of $100 per day from the time the report was required. If there's no dispensing of a controlled substance, the pharmacy does not have to report.

EXEMPTIONS FROM REPORTING CONTROLLED SUBSTANCE DISPENSING TO THE PMP
Exemptions include the following:
1. Inpatient drug orders (i.e. hospital, long-term care facility).
2. Medications dispensed from a hospital emergency room or for discharging (if the quantity of the discharging medication is more than 72-hour supply, reporting is required).
3. Controlled substances administered in narcotic treatment program.
4. Controlled substances administered via infusion at home, in hospital or long-term care.

Information collected by the PMP will be kept confidential. Although reporting to PMP is required, PMP does not need to review each report.

(720 ILCS 570/316 & 318)

ADVISORY COMMITTEE
The advisory committee of the PMP is composed of prescribers and dispensers, including 4 physicians, 1 advanced practice nurse, 1 PA, 1 optometrist, 1 dentist, 1 podiatrist, and 3 pharmacists. They advise the Department on the professional performance of prescribers and dispensers.

(720 ILCS 570/320)

CENTRAL REPOSITORY FOR COLLECTION OF INFORMATION FROM THE PHARMACY
The Department has a central repository for the collection of information transmitted from the pharmacies that report their dispensing activities of controlled substances. The central repository must have the capability for receiving all the information (listed under numbers (1) to (10) under PMP) transmitted from the pharmacies.

(720 ILCS 570/317)

MANUFACTURE, DELIVERY, OR POSSESION OF A CONTROLLED SUBSTANCE
It is illegal to manufacture, deliver, or possess a controlled substance other than methamphetamine. Anyone who violates this is guilty of a Class X felony and sentences to a term of imprisonment for at least 6 years depending on the amount and the type of the controlled substance.

(720 ILCS 570/401)

UNAUTHORIZED POSSESSION OF A PRESCRIPTION FORM
Anyone who commits the offense of an unauthorized possession of a prescription form when they knowingly do the following:
1. Change a properly issued prescription form.
2. Possesses a blank prescription form without authorization or possesses a counterfeit prescription form; or
3. Possesses a prescription form that is not issued by a licensed prescriber.

The sentence for this violation is a Class 4 felony and fine of $100,000 or less. The fine for each subsequent offense is $200,000 or less.

(720 ILCS 570/406.2)

SECURITY REQUIREMENTS
All applicants and licensees must provide effective controls, and procedures to guard against theft and diversion of controlled substances. The Division uses the security requirements as standards for the physical security controls and operating procedures necessary to prevent diversion.
- The degree of physical security controls should be based on the Schedules, quantity, and type and form of controlled substances (e.g., bulk liquids or dosage units, usable powders or non-usable powders.
- Any additional security evidence, including video surveillance, computer access logs or records, or falsified prescription/medical documentation that captures diversion or other illicit activity involving controlled substances must be available to the Division upon request, along with a copy of any DEA Form 106 filed.
- Personal bags of any kind, including purses, handbags and backpacks, are prohibited in any area where controlled substances are handled and/or stored.
- A basic alarm system that detects unauthorized entry into the pharmacy area. This does not apply to 24-hour pharmacies that never close.
- All pharmacies are required to maintain a key to the licensed pharmacy area held by an employee of the pharmacy who is a pharmacist or a pharmacy technician.

(77 IL ADC Section 3100.310)

PHYSICAL SECURITY CONTROLS FOR PRACTITIONERS
C-1 and C-II controlled substances must be stored in a securely locked, substantially constructed cabinet.

C-III, C-IV and C-V controlled substances must be stored in a locked, substantially constructed cabinet. Pharmacies may disperse those substances throughout the stock of non-controlled substances in a manner so as to obstruct the theft or diversion of controlled substances.

(77 IL ADC Section 3100.340)

FACTORS TO EVALUATE PHYSICAL SECURITY SYSTEMS

The Division considers the following to evaluate the security system of a licensee or applicant to maintain effective controls against theft or controlled substances diversion:
1. Type of activity conducted.
2. Type and form of controlled substances handled.
3. Quantity of controlled substances handled.
4. Location of the pharmacy stores and the relationship those locations bear on security needs.
5. Type of building construction and the general characteristics of the building.
6. Type of closures on vaults, safes and secure enclosures, and their availabilities.
7. Adequacy of key control systems and/or combination lock control systems.
8. Adequacy of electric detection and alarm systems.
9. Extent of unsupervised public access to the facility, including the presence and characteristics of perimeter fencing, if any.
10. Adequacy of supervision over employees having access to manufacturing and storage areas.
11. Procedures for handling business guests, visitors, maintenance personnel, and non-employee service personnel.
12. Availability of local police protection or of the licensee's or applicant's security personnel.
13. Adequacy of the licensee's or applicant's system for monitoring the receipt, manufacture, distribution and disposition of controlled substances in its operations; <u>and</u>
14. Applicability of the security requirements contained in all federal, State and local laws and regulations governing the management of waste.

(77 IL ADC Section 3100.320)

DEPARTMENT OF FINANCIAL AND PROFESSION REGULATION (DFPR)

The DFPR will inspect, copy, and verify the correctness of records, reports or other documents required to be kept under the Controlled Substances Act. The DFPR will also execute and serve administrative inspection notices, warrants, subpoenas, and summonses.

(720 ILCS 570/501)

AUTHORITY TO MAKE INSPECTIONS

The Division, through its inspectors, is authorized to enter controlled premises and conduct administrative inspections of those premises for the purpose of the following:
1. Inspecting, copying and verifying the correctness of records, reports or other documents required to be kept. Upon the Division's request, the licensee's agent or employee must produce those records.
2. Inspecting within reasonable limits and in a reasonable manner all pertinent equipment, finished and unfinished controlled substances, containers and labeling found at the controlled premises relating to the Act.
3. Making a physical inventory of all controlled substances on hand at the premises.

4. Collecting samples of controlled substances or any other relevant evidence (in the event any samples are collected during an inspection, the inspector will issue a receipt for the samples to the owner, operator or agent in charge of the premises).

A suspension or revocation of registration or denial of licensure may result if the licensee refuses, or the person in charge refuses to allow inspection and fully comply with the inspection.

(77 IL ADC Section 3100.440 & 3100.460)

EMERGENCY MEDICATION KITS

Long-term care facilities may store controlled substances in an emergency medication kit if it has met the Illinois Department of Public Health for the facility's particular level of care ("DPH Standards"). The following requirements must be met when controlled substances are stored in emergency medication kits:

1. Controlled substances for emergency medication kits must be obtained from a DEA registered hospital, pharmacy or practitioner.
2. Emergency medication kits must be safeguarded as provided in DPH Standards.
3. Only nurses on duty, consultant pharmacist or practitioner shall have access to controlled substances stored in emergency medication kits.
4. **No more than 10 different controlled substances** are placed in an emergency medication kit, and no more than **3 single, injectable doses** of each controlled substance.
5. Controlled substances in emergency medication kits may be administered only under the emergency conditions only by nurses or practitioners.
6. A proof-of-use sheet is contained in the emergency medication kit for each separate controlled substance included. Entries should be made on the proof-of-use sheet by the nursing staff or practitioner when any controlled substances from the kit are used. The pharmacist is required to maintain for **2 years** a copy of all completed proof-of-use sheets.
7. Whenever the emergency medication kit is opened, the pharmacist should be notified **within 24 hours**. During any period that the emergency kit is opened, a shift count shall be done on all controlled substances until the kit is closed or locked by the consultant pharmacist. Shift counts are not mandatory when the kit is sealed. Proper forms for shift counts should be placed in the emergency medication kit.
8. The pharmacist is required to check the controlled substances in the emergency medication kit at least monthly and document inside the kit.
9. Failure to comply will result in loss of the privilege of having or placing controlled substances in emergency medication kits.

(77 IL ADC Section 3100.520)

The following table shows five years vs. two years' requirements under IL law

1	All Dispensing records	5 years
2	Controlled substance inventory when there's a change in PIC	5 years
3	All purchase/sale records	2 years
4	DEA form 222	2 years
5	DEA form 106	2 years

Table 3: Five years vs. Two years' requirements

IL Pharmacy Law Practice Exam

Objectives
- This is a 126-question exam that mimics the IL pharmacy portion of the MPJE exam. Use these questions as a supplement to test your self-study learning and go back to review questions missed.
- Ensure to time yourself at 1 hour and 45 minutes to complete the questions in one sitting.
- Answers can be reviewed after the IL pharmacy law exam section.
- If you do not get above a 75% score, it's prudent to review the laws discussed in the previous chapters and review the IL Statutes online for a deeper review.

GOOD LUCK!

1. Which of the following is NOT a requirement to qualify as a member in the IL State Board Pharmacy?
    A. Pharmacist members with at least 5 years of pharmacy practice experience in any state
    B. Pharmacist members who are licensed in IL and in good standing
    C. Non-pharmacist public members are not licensed in IL or in other state
    D. Pharmacist members who hold a BS in Pharmacy
    E. All of the above are true

2. Who can remove members out of the Illinois State Board of Pharmacy?
    A. State Senator
    B. Governor
    C. Secretary
    D. FDA
    E. None of the above

3. Which of the following aspects of "patient counseling" CANNOT be performed by a pharmacy technician?
    A. Proper directions for use
    B. Obtaining medication history
    C. Acquiring patient's allergies and health conditions
    D. Offering counseling by a pharmacist or student pharmacist
    E. Both A and D

4. Which of the following individuals may counsel the patient?
    I. Pharmacist
    II. Student pharmacist
    III. Pharmacy technician

    A. I
    B. II
    C. III
    D. I and II
    E. I, II, and III

5. A pharmacy kept all records of their prescriptions in an electronic record keeping system for 4 years. Is the pharmacy compliant with the Pharmacy Practice Act?
    A. Yes, all prescriptions shall be preserved for no more than 5 years
    B. Yes, all prescriptions shall be preserved for at least 4 years
    C. No, all prescriptions shall be preserved for at least 5 years
    D. No, all prescriptions shall be preserved for more than 5 years
    E. None of the above

6. Which of the following statement is FALSE concerning vaccine administration by a pharmacist?
    A. A pharmacist can administer vaccinations to patients 10 years of age or older
    B. A pharmacist can vaccinate a patient who's 14 years old or older with a valid prescription
    C. A pharmacist can administer the live Influenza vaccine to a 10-year-old boy
    D. A pharmacist can administer the Tdap vaccine in an 8-year-old girl
    E. Both A and D

7. If a pharmacist dispensed a Tdap vaccine on June 1st, 2017. When would be the last date to make an entry of the Tdap vaccine by the pharmacist or designated personnel?
    A. June 29
    B. June 26
    C. June 30
    D. June 28
    E. None of the above

8. Which of the following health care provider(s) is/are permitted to issue prescriptions?
    I. Physician
    II. Physical therapist
    III. Optometrist
    IV. Psychologist

    A. I
    B. I and II
    C. I and III
    D. I and IV
    E. I, II and III

9. What is the civil penalty if a person who practices, offers to practice, attempts to practice, or hold oneself out to practice pharmacy without being licensed?
    A. $5000
    B. > $5000
    C. $10000
    D. $15000
    E. None of the above

10. Which of the following statement(s) regarding "compounding" is accurate?
    A. The pharmacy can dispense compounded products if the prescription is patient specific
    B. Compounding includes the preparation and mixing of components, and the flavorings
    C. Compounding a commercially available product is never permitted
    D. Compounding a product containing combination of ingredients in strengths that are not commercially available is permitted if there's a valid prescription order
    E. None of the above

11. Which of the following activities may be performed by a pharmacy technician in Illinois?
    A. Offer counseling under the direct supervision of a pharmacist
    B. Obtain a verbal prescription transfer from another pharmacy by phone
    C. Perform clinical conflict resolution under the direct supervision of a pharmacist
    D. Fill a prescription without supervision from a pharmacist
    E. Both A and B

12. Which of the following statement(s) regarding "dispense or dispensing" is correct?
    I. Dispense involves interpreting and evaluating a prescription drug order
    II. Preparation and delivery of a drug or device to a patient in suitable container appropriately labeled is considered as part of dispensing
    III. Dispense includes interpreting and evaluating a prescription drug order, including the delivery of a drug to the patient within the pharmacy store while the pharmacist is on duty and the pharmacy is open

    A. I
    B. II
    C. III
    D. I and II
    E. II and III

13. Which of the following accurately describes the duties of a PIC when a pharmacy ceases operation? Select all that apply.
    A. Within 20 days, the PIC must notify the Department of the intended manner of disposition for all prescriptions.
    B. Within 20 days, the PIC must provide the Department with a copy of the closing inventory of controlled substances along with a statement indicating the intended manner of disposition for all prescriptions.
    C. If the PIC dies or is physically incompetent of performing required duties, the owner of the pharmacy must assume the duties of the PIC.
    D. The PIC assumes no duties in notifying the Department when the pharmacy ceases operation since it is the pharmacy owner's responsibility.
    E. Within 30 days, the PIC must notify and send the Department a copy of the closing inventory of controlled substances, along with a statement of how the pharmacy intends to dispose all prescription drugs and files.

14. Which of the following statements regarding continuing education for pharmacists is accurate?
    A. Pharmacists need 30 hours of ACPE accredited CE during 24 months before the expiration of the license
    B. 30 hours of ACEP accredited CE is required during 32 months before the expiration of the license
    C. 20 hours of ACEP accredited CE is required during 24 months before the expiration of the license

D. Pharmacists need 20 hours of ACPE accredited CE during 32 months before the expiration of the license
E. None of the above

15. Which of the following statements concerning pharmacy board examinations is/are true?
    I. The Department allows the examination to be administered more than 3 times per year
    II. If an applicant fails to pass an exam for licensure within 3 years after filing his/her application, the application is denied
    III. After applicants take the exam, within 7 weeks of the exam date, they must call the Department for their results

    A. I
    B. II
    C. II and III
    D. I and III
    E. I and II

16. Which of the following information is *NOT* on the prescription drug label affixed on the drug bottle for dispensing?
    A. The prescription number
    B. The date when the prescription was written
    C. The name of the pharmacy
    D. The direction for use
    E. All of the above are included on the prescription label

17. Remote prescription processing does *NOT* include:
    A. Transferring prescription information
    B. Discussing therapeutic intervention with prescribers
    C. Providing drug information
    D. Mailing the prescription drug to the patient
    E. Providing patient counseling

18. Which of the following statements regarding the practice of tele-pharmacy is/are correct?
    I. When providing tele-pharmacy services, the pharmacist can perform their pharmacy services at the home pharmacy as long as it is connected to the remote pharmacy via live video and audio
    II. The PIC is responsible for the practice of tele-pharmacy at the remote pharmacy, including the oversight of its automated medication system
    III. A registered pharmacist must be present at a remote pharmacy site

    A. I
    B. II
    C. III and II
    D. I and II
    E. I and III

19. A remote automated pharmacy system can be used:
    I. If there is an audio and video linked to a home pharmacy so a pharmacist can counsel the patient each time a medication is dispensed from the system
    II. Only for dispensing refills
    III. If there is an audio and video linked to a home pharmacy so pharmacy personnel can make the offer to counsel the patient before dispensing the medication

    A. I
    B. I and II
    C. II and III
    D. III and I
    E. None of the above

20. When is it appropriate for a pharmacist to substitute a brand name drug with a generic?
    I. If the selected generic drug product has the same dosage form and the active ingredient is less than 2% different from the active ingredient compared to the brand name drug
    II. If the physician indicates the drug may be substituted by signing his or her name on top of the "may substitute" line
    III. If the selected drug product is a generic drug that is determined to be therapeutically equivalent to the substituted drug by the FDA

    A. I
    B. I and II
    C. II and III
    D. I and III
    E. None of the above

21. Which of the following conditions must a pharmacy meet in order to practice tele-pharmacy?
    A. A tele-pharmacy must store all of its data inside a secure, HIPAA-compliant server.
    B. An automated dispensing machine may be used with the practice of tele-pharmacy after inspection and approval by the Department.
    C. There must be a registered pharmacist who can supervise and train certified pharmacy technicians at the remote pharmacies.
    D. Both A and B
    E. Both A and C

22. Which of the following statements regarding electronic image prescription is/are accurate?
    I. An electronic image cannot serve as the original prescription.
    II. An electronic image can serve as the original prescription if the pharmacy's computer system can capture an unalterable electronic image of the prescription order.
    III. The pharmacy's computer system must be able to print and provide all prescription information within 72 hours upon the Department's request.

    A. I

B. I and II
C. II and III
D. I and III
E. I, II, and III

23. Which of the following statements are correct about the pharmacy staff's responsibilities in the practice of tele-pharmacy?
    I. A PIC must ensure the home pharmacy has enough staff on duty.
    II. A pharmacist or student pharmacist may perform patient counseling through telecommunication.
    III. The preparation of prescriptions for dispensing may be performed by a registered pharmacy technician.

    A. I
    B. I and II
    C. II and III
    D. III and I
    E. I, II, and III

24. JD who is the owner of Caremax Pharmacy in Wisconsin, is applying for a license to establish another pharmacy in IL in 2017. In December 2016, Caremax Pharmacy's license in Wisconsin was revoked. Which of the following statements is correct?
    I. The Department may issue JD a license to establish the new pharmacy in IL, if she can provide sufficient evidence indicating rehabilitation of Caremax pharmacy in Wisconsin.
    II. The Department will go after any earlier complaint against her Caremax Pharmacy in Wisconsin and conduct a hearing.
    III. If there's not enough evidence to go against JD's Caremax Pharmacy in Wisconsin, the Department will issue a license to establish the new pharmacy in IL.

    A. I
    B. I and II
    C. II and III
    D. III and I
    E. I, II, and III

25. The Department may refuse, revoke, or suspend a license/registration or take any disciplinary action as needed, including fines for each violations or combination of the violations that should be:
    A. ≤ $15,000
    B. ≥ $10,000
    C. $20,000
    D. ≤ $10,000
    E. None of the above

26. Which of the following statements could cause violations and discipline?
    A. Selling drug samples
    B. Failing to dispense any drug in "good faith"
    C. Overcharging for professional services
    D. Engaging in unprofessional, dishonorable, or unethical conduct that's likely to deceive, defraud, or harm the public
    E. All of the above

27. Which of the following statements regarding revocation and suspension is/are accurate?
    I. The Director of the Department may suspend a licensed or registered person immediately without a hearing if he or she is found to have been convicted of a felony in other state
    II. The Board will have a hearing within 15 days of the suspension
    III. The Director of the Department may suspend a licensed or registered person immediately without a hearing if he or she is found to be posed immediate danger to the public

    A. I
    B. I and II
    C. II and III
    D. III and I
    E. I, II, and III

28. BD practices as a pharmacist without being licensed in IL for the first time. Which of the following is BD's penalties for unlicensed practice?
    A. He is guilty of a Class A misdemeanor
    B. He is guilty of a Class 4 felony
    C. He is guilty of both Class A misdemeanor and Class 4 felony
    D. He is not guilty of anything, because BD has a Canada pharmacy license
    E. None of the above

29. Under which of the following circumstances can a Secretary base its final decision on the attorney's/hearing officer's report? Select all that apply.
    A. If the defendant requests a direct appeal to the Secretary
    B. Within 7 business days after the defendant's request for an appeal to the Secretary, the Secretary fails to issue an order to the Board to present their findings, conclusions, and recommendations on the case
    C. If the Board fails to present their findings, conclusions, and recommendations on the case within 30 calendar days after the Secretary's issue of order to the Board, which was resulted by the defendant's appeal
    D. The Secretary fails to issue an order within 30 calendar days after what happens in (C)
    E. All of the above

30. What is the maximum number of prescription drugs' or medical devices' prices that the pharmacy may disclose upon a patient's request?
    A. 10
    B. 5
    C. 15
    D. 20
    E. None of the above

31. How much does it cost for a pharmacist to renew his or her license?
    A. $75/year
    B. $25/year
    C. $100/year
    D. $50/year
    E. None of the above

32. Which of the following license(s)/certificate(s) can be placed on inactive status?
    I. Pharmacist
    II. Pharmacy
    III. Pharmacy technician

    A. I
    B. I and II
    C. II and III
    D. I and III
    E. I, II, and III

33. Which of the following behavior(s) is NOT considered as unprofessional and unethical conduct by a licensee or registrant?
    A. Failing to establish and maintain effective controls against diversion of prescription drugs
    B. Discriminating in any manner against any person based upon his or her race, creed, color, gender, sexual orientation, age or national origin
    C. Failing to exercise sound professional judgment with respect to the accuracy and authenticity of any prescription drug order dispensed
    D. Substituting a generic drug product with a different manufacturer than the original prescribe generic drug product given that they're both therapeutically equivalent as determined by the FDA
    E. All of the above

34. When must a licensee or registrant inform the Division if he or she is discipline in another state?
    A. Within 30 days
    B. Within 60 days
    C. Within 90 days
    D. Within 10 days
    E. None of the above

35. Which of the following conduct can result in violation(s)? Select all that apply.
    A. Engaging in the practice of pharmacy when the person is not authorized to practice pharmacy
    B. Compounding or selling any drug or chemical recognized in USP/NF for internal or external use, which has same strength, quality, purity, or bioavailability as determined by USP/NF
    C. Purchasing prescriptions drugs from any source that fails to meet the Wholesale Drug Distribution Licensing Act
    D. Compounding or selling any drug or chemical with the strength and purity that are below standards
    E. None of the above

36. AB is a pharmacist that has worked at CVS for over 10 years. However, for the last 6 months, after her husband tragically passed away from a car accident, AB became less talkative and showed signs of depression. Lately, she would show up smelling like alcohol and cigarette about two to three times a week, but she seemed much better (did not appear as depressed), and more like her usual talkative self. She hasn't made any dispensing errors. Will there be a discipline for the conduct imposed on AB?
    A. No, because AB hasn't made any dispensing errors
    B. No, because alcohol helped her cope with the death of her husband better and she seemed to be more like her usual self
    C. Yes, because there is a fact pattern of AB's being under the influence of alcohol while on duty
    D. Yes, but there has to be someone who sees her drinking alcohol at work
    E. None of the above

37. Which of the following statement(s) regarding dispensing errors is/are correct?
    A. Failing to exercise sound professional judgment with respect to the accuracy and authenticity of any prescription drug order dispensed
    B. Failing to dispense the appropriate quantity
    C. Failing to physically deliver the medication to the patient
    D. Both A and B
    E. Both B and C

38. Within how many days, after a pharmacist administers a vaccine to a patient, must they report to the patient's primary doctor regarding the vaccination?
    A. Within 30 days
    B. Within 60 days
    C. Within 5 days
    D. Within 20 days
    E. None of the above

39. Which of following requirement(s) must a pharmacist meet in order to perform a vaccination/immunization is/are accurate?
    A. Successfully completed a training course accredited by the ACPE or similar professional body approved by the Division

B. Maintaining a current Basic Life Support Certification for Healthcare Providers issued by the American Heart Association, the American Red Cross
   C. Only the pharmacy is required to have a current copy or electronic version of the CDC reference "Epidemiology and Prevention of Vaccine—Preventable Diseases" available at the location where vaccinations are given
   D. A and B
   E. A, B, and C

40. How long must all vaccination records be kept?
    A. 3 years
    B. 4 years
    C. 5 years
    D. 10 years
    E. None of the above

41. Which of the following information should be included on vaccination records? Select all that apply.
    A. The name, address and patient's date of birth
    B. Date of vaccination
    C. Name, dose, manufacturer, lot number, and beyond use date of the vaccine
    D. Name and address of the patient's primary health care provider
    E. Vaccine information statement that was provided to the patient

42. Under the Ryan Haight Online Pharmacy Consumer Protection Act of 2008, a valid prescription is valid only if: Select all that apply.
    A. It's issued for a legitimate medical purpose
    B. The patient has a face-to-face interaction with the pharmacist
    C. At least one physician face-to-face evaluation with the patient
    D. At least two physician face-to-face evaluations with the patient
    E. None of the above

43. Which of the following statements regarding the renewal of license/certificate is/are NOT accurate? Select all that apply.
    A. Every pharmacist license issued expires on March 31 of each even-numbered year
    B. Every pharmacy license issued expires on March 31 of each odd-numbered year
    C. The holder of the license or certificate of registration can pay the required fee to renew it during the 30 days before the expiration date
    D. Certificate of registration as a pharmacy technician that expires annually on March 31
    E. Every pharmacy technician certificate issued expires on March 31 annually

44. Which of the following about continuing education for pharmacists is/are true?
    A. CE is not required if it is the first renewal of an original licensure
    B. Completion of 30 hours of CE during the 24 months before the expiration date of the license
    C. CE is required in the first renewal of an original licensure

D. Both A and B
  E. Both B and C

45. Which of the following is <u>NOT</u> considered as pre-printed prescription(s)? (Select all that apply)
    A. A written prescription in which the name of the drug has been indicated prior to the time of issuance
    B. A written prescription with pre-inked stamp of the drug name that applies to a prescription blank
    C. A prescription that is printed in advance and manually signed by the prescriber
    D. A computer generated prescription that is printed, manually signed and faxed by the prescriber
    E. Both C and D

46. If a non-controlled substance prescription was written in 1/1/2017, which of the following dates will be the last date the patient can fill or refill his or her prescription?
    A. 1/1/2018
    B. 12/31/2017
    C. 7/1/2017
    D. 4/1/2017
    E. None of the above

47. Amy called in on 2/1/2017 for a refill of her PRN digoxin prescription. Her original digoxin prescription was issued in 2/1/2016. Can this prescription be refilled?
    A. Yes, because Amy's doctor indicated on the original prescription that it's an as needed refill
    B. No, because no non-controlled substance prescription can be refilled (1) year after the original issuance date
    C. Yes, because her prescription has not expired yet
    D. No, because her prescription has expired six months ago
    E. None of the above

48. Which of the following statements about refilling a C-III, C-IV, or C-V controlled-substance prescription is accurate?
    A. The pharmacist has the authority to combine or consolidate refills without calling the patient's prescriber
    B. The pharmacist has the authority to combine or consolidate refills without calling the patient's prescriber, but he or she has to use his or her professional judgment to call the doctor before combining when the patient is in immediate need of the medication
    C. The pharmacist is allowed to combine or consolidate refills without calling the patient's prescriber, but he or she has to use his or her professional judgment to call the doctor before combining, because the patient has shown pattern of addiction to the prescribed drug
    D. The pharmacist cannot combine or consolidate refills without the prescriber's permission

E. None of the above

49. Under which of the following circumstances are pharmacies not required to dispense prescribed drugs to the patient? Select all that apply.
    A. If based on the pharmacist's professional judgment, she or he determines the drug should not be dispensed due to a drug-drug interaction
    B. The medication is out of stock
    C. The medication is not available, because it's in shortage according to the Nation guidelines
    D. The medication is not available, because it's in shortage according to the Board of Pharmacy
    E. The drug prescription is not valid

50. What alternatives should a pharmacy provide the patient when the prescribed drug cannot be filled? Select all that apply.
    I. Contact the patient's prescriber to address the clinical concerns identified, which is the main reason why the drug cannot be filled
    II. Contact the patient and let him or her know the prescribed drug is out of stock and cancel the prescription
    III. Return the unfilled prescription to the patient as the patient has requested

    A. I
    B. I and II
    C. II and III
    D. III and I
    E. I, II, and III

51. Which of the following statements regarding rules and regulations for internet and mail-order pharmacies dispensing prescription drugs to IL residents is/are accurate? Select all that apply.
    A. The mail-order pharmacy may be licensed as a non-resident pharmacy if it has an active license in the state where the dispensing facility is located, and the drugs are dispensed from in order to operate as a mail-order pharmacy in IL
    B. The pharmacy has to maintain its record of drugs dispensed to IL residents
    C. The pharmacy is compliant with all directions and requests by the law for information from the Board of Pharmacy of each state where the pharmacy is licensed. The pharmacy must respond directly to all communications from the Board or Department concerning any circumstances arising from the dispensing of drugs to IL residents
    D. The pharmacy can have its regular hours of operation as 5 days a week as long as it meets the minimum of 40 hours a week
    E. The pharmacy can have its regular hours of operation as 6 days a week as long as it meets the minimum of 32 hours a week

52. A pharmacy operates as a tele-pharmacy at a remote site in IL but has a home pharmacy in Michigan. Which of the following individuals or entities must have a license in IL in order to practice tele-pharmacy in IL? (Select all that apply)
    A. The tele-pharmacy in IL
    B. The home pharmacy in Michigan
    C. The PIC who oversees the tele-pharmacy in IL
    D. A and C
    E. A, B and C

53. Which of the following tele-pharmacy sites may receive written prescription orders?
    I. Remote dispensing site
    II. Remote consultation site
    III. Remote automated pharmacy system (RAPS)

    A. I
    B. I and II
    C. II and III
    D. I, II, and III
    E. III and I

54. How long does a remote tele-pharmacy have to deliver the written prescription orders to its home pharmacy?
    A. 24 hours
    B. 36 hours
    C. 48 hours
    D. 72 hours
    E. None of the above

55. How long must a pharmacy keep its record of each transaction with the automated pharmacy system?
    A. 1 year
    B. 2 years
    C. 3 years
    D. 4 years
    E. 5 years

56. Which of the following information must be included on a label of parenteral solutions with added drug? Select all that apply.
    A. Brand and/or generic name of the drug
    B. Beyond use date & date of admixture
    C. Name & strength of drugs added
    D. Name, concentration & volume of the base parenteral solution
    E. Expiration date of the drug added

57. A parental solution was repackaged on January 31, 2017; the BUD on its manufacturer's container is March 1, 2018. Which of the following statements concerning the beyond use date of parenteral solutions with drug added for future use is/are accurate?
    I. If the individual monograph specifies a beyond use date of 6 months, then the pharmacist should use this as the beyond use date for this medication.
    II. The beyond use date of the medication should be the beyond use date that's listed on the manufacturer's container.
    III. Unless specified in the individual monograph, the beyond used date must not be later than the beyond use date on the manufacturer's container or one year from the date the drugs is repackaged, whichever is earlier.

    A. I
    B. I and II
    C. II and III
    D. III and I
    E. I, II, and III

58. Which of the following information are labeling requirements for immediate use medications via unit dose for a specific patient? Select all that apply.
    A. Name of the resident
    B. Resident's room and bed number
    C. Dispensing date
    D. Quantity dispense
    E. Prescriber's name

59. Which of the following regarding hospital automated dispensing systems is/are correct?
    I. Automated dispensing systems can be accessed when the pharmacy is open
    II. Automated dispensing systems can be used as an after-hour cabinet and emergency kit
    III. Automated dispensing systems can be used in nuclear pharmacy

    A. I
    B. I and II
    C. II and III
    D. III and I
    E. I, II and III

60. Which of the following is/are required to be documented on a log from someone who removes a drug from an after-hour cabinet?
    A. The authorized person's signature
    B. The quantity removed
    C. The time of removal
    D. The name of the medication removed
    E. All of the above

61. Which of the following statements regarding emergency kits is/are correct?
    I. The beyond use date of the emergency kit is based on the earliest beyond use date of any drug in the kit
    II. After an emergency kit has been used, the seal has been broken, or the kit is expired, it must be secured and returned to the pharmacy to be checked and restocked
    III. If an emergency kit expired and is returned to the pharmacy but the pharmacy is closed, the authorized person can leave the emergency kit outside of the pharmacy where the pharmacist can easily see

    A. I
    B. I and II
    C. II and III
    D. III and I
    E. I, II, III

62. Which of the following must be included on the label of an investigational new drug? Select all that apply.
    A. Name of drug, strength and dose
    B. Beyond use date
    C. Name and location of the patient
    D. Reference code to identify source and lot number
    E. All of the above

63. What is/are the requirement(s) of pharmacies preparing sterile products (i.e. parenteral products)?
    I. The area of the pharmacy should be designed to minimize outside traffic and airflow disturbances from activity within the facility
    II. It must have a sufficient size to accommodate a laminar airflow hood, barrier isolation chamber, and to provide proper storage of drugs and supplies under appropriate conditions of temperature, light, moisture, sanitation, ventilation and security
    III. It must be ventilated in a way so that it doesn't interfere with the proper operation of the sterile product preparation apparatus

    A. I
    B. I and II
    C. II and III
    D. I, II, and III
    E. None of the above

64. Which of the following statements regarding patient counseling is/are correct?
    I. If a patient refuses to accept counseling, the pharmacist must document it
    II. If the pharmacist does not document that counseling is refused by the patient, then it's considered that the offer to counsel was accepted and counseling was provided
    III. The pharmacist must notify the PIC if the patient refuses to accept counseling

    A. I
    B. I and II
    C. II and III
    D. I, II, and III
    E. None of the above

65. Which of the following statements regarding sales of syringes or needles without a prescription is correct?
    A. A person 18 years or older may purchase up to 30 sterile hypodermic syringes daily without a prescription from a pharmacist in a pharmacy
    B. Syringes or needles sold must be stored at a pharmacy that limits access to the syringes or needles to authorized personnel at the pharmacy
    C. The pharmacy must maintain recordkeeping of the sale transaction for 5 years
    D. The Board of Pharmacy must provide materials for proper disposal of needles and syringes to the pharmacies that choose to sell them
    E. None of the above

66. Which of the following medications is/are classified as Schedule II controlled substances under IL law? Select all that apply.
    A. Lisdexamfetamine
    B. Strattera
    C. Meprobamate
    D. Dexmethylphenidate
    E. Nembutal

67. If a new cough syrup contains 15 mg of codeine phosphate and 150 mg of guaifenesin in each 10 mL dose, this product would likely be classified as:
    A. Schedule II
    B. Schedule III
    C. Schedule IV
    D. Schedule V
    E. Non-controlled substance

68. If a medication contains 320.5 mg acetaminophen, 30 mg of caffeine, and 16 mg of dihydrocodeine, this product would be classified as:
    A. Schedule II
    B. Schedule III
    C. Schedule IV
    D. Schedule V
    E. Non-controlled substance

69. A physician or practitioner who prescribes controlled substances requires which of the following types of registration under the IL Controlled Substances Act to prescribe Schedule II-V medications?
    A. Prescriber
    B. Dispenser
    C. Manufacturer
    D. Distributor
    E. All of the above

70. When receiving an oral Schedule III-V prescription, a pharmacist must write down what on a prescription order? Select all that apply.
    A. Physician's DEA number
    B. Date and time of when received the oral prescription
    C. Name and address of the ultimate user
    D. Pharmacist's DEA number
    E. Pharmacist's signature and date on the face of the prescription

71. A patient's doctor issues two prescriptions of Vyvanse, each with a 30-day supply. The patient requests to have a 60-day supply instead, because he has to be out of town for six weeks. As a pharmacist, what is the most appropriate action you should take? Assuming today's date is 1/1/2017; based on the doctor's written instruction, the earliest dates to be filled for the first and second prescriptions are 1/1/2017 and 1/31/2017, respectively.
    A. Call the prescribed physician first to get permission before dispensing 60 tablets
    B. Dispense 30 tablets and advise the patient only 30 tablets can be dispensed at a time, the next 30 tablets can be filled on 1/31/2017 as written by the prescriber on the prescription
    C. Fill the prescription as requested by the patient
    D. Ask the patient to request another prescription issued on 1/1/2017 from his doctor
    E. Advise the patient 30 tablets can be supplied now and the remaining 30 tablets will be filled in 72 hours

72. This organization has the authority to reschedule, add, or delete all controlled substances in the Schedules:
    A. Board of Pharmacy
    B. FDA
    C. Department of Financial and Professional Regulation
    D. Department of Human Health and Services
    E. None of the above

73. A patient presents a prescription for Xanax to your pharmacy. The prescription is for 0.25 mg tablet with a quantity of 30 and five refills. He requests the pharmacist to fill 60 tablets because he has to be out of town for two months. What will you do?
    A. Call the prescribed physician first to get permission before dispensing 60 tablets
    B. Tell the patient only 30 tablets can be dispensed
    C. Dispense 30 tablets now and the remaining be dispensed at another pharmacy

D. Dispense 60 tablets without calling the doctor, because based on your professional judgment this is appropriate and under the IL law it is permitted
E. None of the above

74. Which of the following regarding a Xanax prescription is/are true? Select all that apply.
    A. The prescription can only be filled within 12 months
    B. The maximum number of refills is 5 times
    C. The prescription has to be renewed by the prescriber after it expires
    D. Both A and B
    E. Both B and C

75. Which of the following prescription drug products can only be refilled 5 times in a 6-month period? Select all that apply.
    A. Ambien tablet
    B. Hydrocodone capsule
    C. Ritalin tablet
    D. Nembutal suppository
    E. Pregabalin capsule

76. Which of the following statements is accurate in regards to the dispensing of a Schedule II controlled substance in emergency cases with an oral prescription?
    A. The date of the emergency prescription and "Authorization for Emergency Dispensing" should be written on the face of the prescription.
    B. Within 7 days after the dispensing of the oral prescription, the physician must provide the written prescription.
    C. The pharmacist must contact the physician regarding the written prescription for the emergency prescription if he or she hasn't received it in 7 days after the dispensing of the emergency prescription.
    D. Both A and B
    E. Both B and C

77. What of the following must be kept for at least 5 years? Select all that apply.
    A. Written controlled substance prescription
    B. Facsimile or oral controlled substance prescription
    C. Records of purchases and sales of controlled substances
    D. Dispensing records of non-controlled substances
    E. DEA form 222 records

78. Which of the following requirements for dispensing Schedule V drugs is/are accurate?
    A. Only a pharmacist and a person registered can dispense Schedule V drugs
    B. The patient must be at least 21 years of age with a positive ID
    C. The dispensing cannot occur, if within 96 hours, more than 120 g of codeine or dihydrocodeine had already dispensed to the same patient
    D. Both A and B
    E. Both A and C

79. Which of the following statements regarding prescription requirements is/are true?
    I. The prescription must be signed and dated by the prescriber on the date of issuance if it's written in pen
    II. An oral prescription for a controlled substance must be reduced to writing by a pharmacist
    III. A prescription can be printed in advance but must be manually signed by the prescriber

    A. I
    B. I and II
    C. II and III
    D. III and I
    E. I, II and III

80. A faxed prescription for compounded C-II controlled substance from a prescriber to a pharmacy is permitted:
    I. If the patient is a resident of a long-term care facility
    II. If the patient is a hospice patient
    III. As long as the prescriber provides a written prescription after the drug is dispensed within 7 days

    A. I
    B. I and II
    C. II and III
    D. III and I
    E. I, II and III

81. Which of the following statements is correct regarding the registration required for manufacturing, distribution, and dispensing?
    I. A community pharmacy is required to file a separate manufacturer registration in order to compound drug products for office use
    II. A separate registration is required when a new community pharmacy is open at a different location than its parent pharmacy owned by the same owner
    III. A community pharmacy is required to apply for a manufacturer registration in order to compound a medication in accordance with a prescription

    A. I
    B. II
    C. III
    D. I and II
    E. II and III

82. Which of the following Schedules can be dispensed without a prescription?
    A. Schedule III
    B. Schedule IV
    C. Schedule V "exempt narcotics"

    D. Schedule IV and V
    E. None of the above may be dispensed without a prescription

83. Which of the following medications may be dispensed without a prescription?
    A. Carisoprodol
    B. Equanil
    C. Restoril
    D. Immodium
    E. None of the above

84. Which of the following statements regarding IL law on Schedule V controlled substances is/are true? Select all that apply.
    A. Only 4.5 L or less per drug product plus the amount of product needed for dispensing during the busiest week can be dispensed per week
    B. Purchases and sales records must be maintained for 2 years
    C. A patient must be 18 years of age or older
    D. No purchases can be made within 96 hours after the first purchase
    E. Purchases and sales records must be maintained for 5 years

85. Which of the following statements regarding medication shopping is/are true?
    I. A potential for medication shopping occurs when a person has 3 or more prescribers that prescribed the controlled substances within a 30-day period.
    II. A potential for medication shopping occurs when a person has 3 or more pharmacies that share a common electronic file for controlled substances within 30-day period.
    III. The pharmacist is required by IL law to refuse to dispense the controlled substance if there's a suspicion of a potential medication shopping.

    A. I
    B. I and II
    C. I and III
    D. II and III
    E. II

86. What must be included on the report of the controlled substance dispensing activity that is to be sent to the Prescription Monitoring Program? (Select all that apply)
    A. Patient's name and address
    B. Patient's gender
    C. Dosage form of drug
    D. NDC number of the controlled substance dispensed
    E. Number of refills

87. Under which of the following circumstances is it not required to report to the Prescription Monitoring Program a controlled substance being dispensed? (Select all that apply)
    A. A long-term care facility makes an inpatient controlled substance order
    B. Controlled substance administered via infusion at home

    C. Medication dispensed for discharging if the quantity of the drug is less than 30 days
    D. Medication dispensed from an emergency room
    E. Medication dispensed in a community pharmacy

88. What is sentence for an authorized possession of prescription form?
    A. Class X felony and fine of $200,000 or less
    B. Class 4 felony and fine of $200,000 or less
    C. Class 4 felony and fine of $100,000 or less
    D. Class X felony and fine of $100,000 or less
    E. None of the above

89. Which of the following would determine if a person committed an offense of an unauthorized possession of a prescription form?
    A. If a person knowingly alters a properly issued prescription form
    B. If a person knowingly possesses a blank prescription form that's authorized by a physician
    C. If a person knowingly possesses a prescription form that's issued by a licensed podiatrist
    D. If a person knowingly possesses a prescription form that's issued by a physical therapist
    E. Both A and D

90. If the patient no longer needs the dispensed controlled substance, can it be returned to the pharmacy?
    A. No, but the patient is required to bring the medication to an authorized collector
    B. No, the controlled substance cannot re-enter a closed system of distribution
    C. Yes, the patient returns the medication within the same day of dispensing
    D. Yes, because the controlled substance needs to be returned for proper disposal
    E. None of the above

91. Which of the following individuals may not prescribe C-II controlled substances?
    A. Hospital resident
    B. Physician assistant
    C. Prescribing psychologist
    D. Nurse practitioner
    E. All of the above

92. Under the IL law, which of the following circumstances is <u>NOT</u> acceptable for dispensing of a controlled substance?
    I. A physician who issues a prescription of Vyvanse for himself, given that he has appropriate record of the diagnosis for his back pain
    II. A physician who issues a prescription of Vyvanse for his spouse, given that there are appropriate records of all treatments he provided to his spouse
    III. A physician who issues a prescription of Vyvanse for his sister, given that there are appropriate records of all treatments he provided to his sister

A. I
B. I and II
C. II and III
D. I, II and III
E. None of the above

93. In which of the following Schedules is a controlled substance not refillable?
    A. Schedule II
    B. Schedule III
    C. Schedule IV
    D. Schedule V
    E. All of the above are refillable

94. How many days is a C-II prescription valid for after the date of issuance?
    A. 7 days
    B. 30 days
    C. 60 days
    D. 90 days
    E. None of the above

95. A patient comes into your pharmacy with a written Vicodin prescription on 7/25/2017 and requests for a fill. You notice the prescription is post dated, meaning the date of issuance is on 7/26/2017. Which of the following is the most appropriate response?
    A. Do not fill the prescription, because you have wait until 7/26/2017 to fill
    B. Do not fill the prescription, because prescription is not acceptable until you call the patient's doctor to verify that the prescription is issued on 7/25/2017
    C. Yes, fill the prescription as the doctor accidentally put down the wrong date
    D. Yes, fill the prescription, but tell the patient to drop off the prescription today and come back tomorrow to pick it up
    E. None of the above

96. What is the maximum number of days supply a Schedule II drug be prescribed and dispensed?
    A. 30 days
    B. 60 days
    C. 90 days
    D. 15 days
    E. There's no limitation in day supply

97. Which of the following conditions can a physician assistant (PA) or advance practice nurse (APN) prescribe or administer C-II control substances? Select all that apply.
    A. Administration of C-II controlled substances in oral, topical, transdermal or injection route
    B. Prescriptions are limited to 90-day supply or less
    C. The PA and APN must provide 45 contact hours in pharmacology
    D. The PA and APN must complete at least 5 hours of CE

E. The prescriptions are limited to 60-day supply

98. What changes may a pharmacist not make to a C-II prescription? Select all that apply.
    A. Patient's name
    B. Add a date on the prescription
    C. Quantity dispensed
    D. Change the name of the prescriber on the prescription
    E. Substitute a brand name drug with a generic drug

99. Which of the following drug products can be refilled 5 times in a 6-month period?
    A. Hydrocortisone
    B. Fluticasone
    C. Nandrolone
    D. A and B
    E. A and C

100. Which of the following is required in order for a hospital physician resident, who is not yet registered with the Federal DEA, to prescribe Dilaudid in the hospital?
    I. The resident must pass a federal controlled substances examination.
    II. The resident may prescribe as permitted by state law, and he or she is acting within the scope of his or her employment under the hospital DEA number.
    III. The resident must be working under the supervision of a physician in order to use the physician's DEA registration number.

    A. I
    B. II
    C. II and III
    D. I and II
    E. The resident cannot legally prescribe Dilaudid

101. TJ comes into your pharmacy store and asks for a refill of his prescription for lisinopril. You check and find out TJ's doctor has passed away three days ago. Can you fill TJ's prescription? Choose the most appropriate reponse.
    A. Yes, refill the prescription; TJ's prescription is still valid until the refill runs out.
    B. Yes, refill the prescription this time, but counsel the patient that he must seek a new physician as soon as possible.
    C. No, the prescription is not valid after the doctor dies.
    D. Yes, refill no more than 30 days.
    E. Yes, refill until TJ finds a new physician.

102. AB is employed as a pharmacist at PharmacyRx. She has a "dispenser" DEA registration. PharmacyRx is now providing a new compounding service at the pharmacy. Will AB need to obtain a separate DEA registration in order for her to do compounding for a controlled substance prescription?
    A. No, only a dispenser registration is required for compounding of a controlled substance that is in accordance to a valid prescription.

B. No, AB is working under the compounding DEA registration of PharmacyRx.
C. Yes, compounding controlled substances is considered as independent activity and requires a separate DEA registration.
D. Yes, compounding controlled substances is considered as manufacturing activity that requires a separate registration.
E. None of the above

103. Which of the following activities will require a separate DEA registration, assuming that Walnut Community Pharmacy has registered with the Federal DEA and IL for dispenser of C-II through C-V controlled substances?
   I. Purchasing of controlled drugs to repackage them for sale without a prescription
   II. Mixing, preparing and packaging of C-II through C-V narcotic for detoxification
   III. Compounding of controlled substances in accordance to a prescription

   A. I
   B. I and II
   C. II and III
   D. III and I
   E. I, II, and III

104. NV, the pharmacist, found fives boxes of Sudafed missing behind the pharmacy counter. What DEA form she must use to file theft or loss of Sudafed?
   A. DEA form 222
   B. DEA form 106
   C. DEA form 223
   D. DEA form 224
   E. Reporting of theft or loss is not required for Sudafed

105. Which of the following medication can be ordered using a DEA form 222?
   I. Demerol tablet
   II. Phenobarbital tablet
   III. Secobarbital capsule

   A. I
   B. I and II
   C. II and III
   D. III and I
   E. I, II and III

106. RxPharmacy does not share a real-time online computerized system with CVS. Which of the following prescriptions may RxPharmacy transfer to CVS only one time for the purpose of refill dispensing?
   I. Modafinil tablet
   II. Pentobarbital solution
   III. Acetaminophen w/Hydrocodone tablet

A. I
B. I and II
C. II and III
D. III and I
E. I, II and III

107. Which of the following prescriptions can be transferred to another pharmacy for original fill dispensing?
    I. Levothroid
    II. Klonopin
    III. Augmentin

    A. I
    B. I and II
    C. II and III
    D. III and I
    E. I, II and III

108. Which of the following statements is/are true regarding dispensing a codeine-containing product?
    I. A product contains 200 mg or less of codeine per 100 mL or per 100 mg is a C-V drug and can be purchase without a prescription
    II. The patient has to be at least 18 years old
    III. The patient must have one positive ID when making a purchase

    A. I
    B. II
    C. III
    D. II and III
    E. I and II

109. Which of following information should be included on a veterinary prescription for ketamine? (Select all that apply)
    A. The full name of the owner
    B. The species or common name of the animal being treated
    C. DEA of the prescriber
    D. The address of the pharmacy
    E. DEA of the pharmacy

110. Which one of the following medication is not a controlled substance?
    A. Empirin with codeine
    B. Dilaudid
    C. Clonopin
    D. Esterified estrogen and methyltestosterone
    E. Empirin

111. TJ comes into your pharmacy and asks to have his prescription fill for Prozac 20 mg. It's written for a quantity of 30 with 2 refills. TJ asks for a quantity of 90 instead. You look at his personal record and see he has a history of suicidal behaviors. What would you do?
    A. Fill the prescription for quantity of 90
    B. Fill the prescription for quantity of 30 because the patient has a history of suicidal behaviors
    C. Tell the patient you cannot fill a quantity of 90 as you will need a prescription for a quantity of 90 to fill
    D. Call TJ's doctor and ask if it is ok to fill a quantity of 90
    E. None of the above

112. After-hour cabinet contains an adequate supply of which of the following:
    I. Medications used in emergency
    II. Non-controlled substances
    III. Most frequently used medications

    A. I
    B. II
    C. III
    D. I and II
    E. I and III

113. Which of the following medications can be stocked in an automated dispensing machine?
    I. A bottle of vancomycin PO syrup for multiple doses
    II. Unit dose package of Ritalin tablets
    III. Chlorhexidine Gluconate Oral Rinse 240 mL bottle for single patient use

    A. I
    B. II
    C. III
    D. I and II
    E. II and III

114. For every prescription order dispensed, the prescription record must contain: Selected all that apply.
    A. Name or initial of the pharmacist
    B. Name of the prescriber
    C. Name or initial of the pharmacy technician that filled or refilled the prescription
    D. The date of dispensing
    E. The prescription number

115. Who can access the dispensing area when a pharmacy is closed?
    I. A registered pharmacy technician
    II. The owner of the pharmacy
    III. A licensed pharmacist

A. I
B. II
C. II and III
D. I and II
E. I and III

116. Under which of the following circumstances, can a pharmacist who has been previously convicted of forcible felony file for a review to apply for a license?
    A. The conviction has been more than 10 years ago
    B. The person has been convicted with armed robbery with no other forcible felony
    C. The person was registered in the list of sex offenders
    D. A and B
    E. All of the above

117. Which of the following should be red flag(s) for potential drug diversion/abuse? Select all that apply.
    A. A patient who comes in with multiple prescription orders that consist of oxycodone, lisinopril and carisoprolol
    B. A patient who has multiple prescribers who specialize in neurology, dermatology, and podiatry
    C. A patient and his or her prescriber are located in unusual distance from your pharmacy
    D. Patients who come in group with prescriptions for the same controlled substance
    E. A patient who comes in with two prescriptions for two different controlled substances, one for Vicodin and the other one for Ativan

118. Brook is a pharmacist at an independent pharmacy. This morning she didn't have time to get breakfast, because the pharmacy was short of one pharmacy technician and busier than usual. It is now noon and Brook wants to walk away from the pharmacy for ten minutes to get a quick lunch. May Brook leave the pharmacy unattended?
    A. No, Brook has to wait until another pharmacist is present to take over.
    B. Yes, as long as a pharmacy technician is present in the pharmacy to deliver medications to the patients in case when they come for pick up.
    C. Yes, as long as Brook displays a sign to notify customers that a pharmacist is not available to provide pharmacy services.
    D. No, a pharmacist must be present in the pharmacy all the time no matter what.
    E. None of the above

119. You receive an oral prescription from a podiatrist over the phone. The podiatrist wants to issue a prescription order for carvedilol for his wife, who has high blood pressure but is experiencing edema in her leg due to amlodipine she is taking. Is this a valid prescription? Which of the following answer choices is accurate? Assume that the podiatrist and his wife have already established a practitioner/patient relationship.
    A. Yes, because a podiatrist can prescribe prescription medications.

B. Yes, in the record, the podiatrist's wife has a diagnosis of high blood pressure; as a result, the prescription does have a legitimate medical purpose.
C. No, the podiatrist cannot issue a prescription order for his immediate family members, including his wife.
D. No, the prescription for carvedilol is not within the ordinary course of the podiatrist's professional practice.
E. None of the above

120. Assuming that you work in a community pharmacy. One of the prescription orders you got is for Androderm transdermal patches. Which of the following information must be included on the prescription order's label of the container?
   A. Pharmacist's name and address
   B. Patient's name
   C. Cautionary statements
   D. A and B
   E. A, B and C

121. Which of the following statements regarding a controlled substance prescription order is/are correct?
   I. If the prescription order is written, the physician must sign in ink with a pen, typewriter or computer printer or with an indelible pen.
   II. If the prescription order is electronically transmitted, the physician must sign with electronic or handwritten signature, initial or thumb print.
   III. If the prescription order is issued orally, it must be reduced in writing.

   A. I
   B. I and II
   C. II and III
   D. I and III
   E. I, II and III

122. Dan is a pharmacist in IL. He missed the renewal date of his license by a few days. Can Dan practice pharmacy during this time while waiting for his license to be reinstated?
   I. No, Dan's license has expired, he is considered unlicensed and cannot practice.
   II. Yes, Dan has paid all the required fees, his license should be active again for him to practice.
   III. No, he has to file an application, proof of 30 hours of continuing education and pay all required fees before he can practice.

   A. I
   B. II
   C. III
   D. I and III
   E. None of the above

123. A patient comes to your pharmacy with a prescription for acetaminophen 300 mg with 60 mg codeine issued by a prescriber who specializes in pain management. The prescription is dated July 31, 2017. Today's date is December 1, 2017. Assuming that the patient has a legitimate medical purpose for this prescription, can you fill this prescription?
    A. Yes, this prescription is issued for a Schedule V controlled substance; in IL, it may be filled up to 6 months from the date of issuance.
    B. No, this prescription is issued for a Schedule II controlled substance; in IL, it may only be filled within 90 days from the date of issuance.
    C. Yes, this prescription is issued for a Schedule III controlled substance; in IL, it may be filled up to 6 months from the date of issuance.
    D. No, this prescription is issued for a Schedule II controlled substance; in IL, it may only be filled within 30 days from the date of issuance.
    E. None of the above

124. Mandy receives a prescription that requires compounding of acetaminophen and codeine. The prescription is as followed:
    Codeine 2 grams/APAP 10 grams
    Cherry syrup 200 mL
    Give 2 teaspoon Q 4 hours PRN HA

    Can this prescription be refilled?
    A. Yes, a prescription for C-III drug has a maximum of 5 times or up to 6 months of refill
    B. Yes, a prescription for C-V drug has a maximum of 5 times or up to 6 months of refill
    C. No, a prescription for C-II drug is not refillable
    D. No, this prescription cannot be compounded under the IL law
    E. None of the above

125. Megan graduated pharmacy school in 2017 and got her license in July 2017. Her license is going to expire on March 31, 2018. How many credits of continuing education must Megan complete prior to her license renewal?
    A. 30 hours of CE
    B. 40 hours of CE
    C. 60 hours of CE
    D. None, the CE requirement is waived for the first renewal period
    E. None of the above

126. You receive a controlled substance prescription for an animal. Is it sufficient to write "Bebe Johnson" assuming that all other required information has been included on the prescription? Bebe is the name of the pet and Johnson is the last name of the pet's owner.
    A. Yes, common name of the pet is sufficient.
    B. Yes, common name of the pet has replaced the species of the pet, so it should be sufficient.
    C. No, the full name of the owner is required.
    D. No, the species of the pet must be included.
    E. None of the above.

Answers to IL Pharmacy Law Practice Exam Questions

1. **A.** Pharmacist members with at least 5 years of pharmacy practice experience in any state

    EXPLANATION:
    Review "Illinois State Board of Pharmacy" under Section 6.
    Answers B, C and D are all correct, except A, because the pharmacist members must have at least 5 years of pharmacy practice experience in IL state not in any state.
    Qualification of IL State Board of Pharmacy members:
    - Pharmacist members must be licensed and in good standing, a graduate of an accredited college of pharmacy or hold a BS in Pharmacy, with at least 5 years of post-licensure experience in the state of Illinois.
    - Non-pharmacist public members are voting members and are not licensed pharmacists in Illinois or any other state.

    (225 ILCS 85/10: Section scheduled to be repealed on January 1, 2018)

2. **B.** Governor

    EXPLANATION:
    Review "Illinois State Board of Pharmacy" under Section 6.
    Governor can remove any Board member for misconduct, incapacity, or neglect of duty.

    (225 ILCS 85/10: Section scheduled to be repealed on January 1, 2018)

3. **A.** Proper directions for use

    EXPLANATION:
    Review "Patient Counseling" under Definitions.
    Out of all other activities in patient counseling, proper directions for use is the job function that a pharmacy technician cannot perform.
    Table 1 gives you a list of activities in patient counseling that pharmacy technician can and cannot perform:

	Patient counseling may include without limitation:	Pharmacist & Student Pharmacist	Pharmacy Technician
1	Obtaining medication history	Yes	Yes
2	Acquiring patient's allergies and health conditions	Yes	Yes
3	Facilitation of patient's understanding of the intended use of the medication	Yes	No
4	Proper directions for use	Yes	No
5	Significant potential adverse events	Yes	No
6	Potential food-drug interactions	Yes	No
7	The need to be compliant with the medication	Yes	No

    Table 1: Patient counseling activities performed by the pharmacist, student pharmacist & pharmacy technician

    (225 ILCS 85/3: Section scheduled to be repealed on January 1, 2018)

4. **D.** I and II

    EXPLANATION:
    Review "Patient Counseling" under Definitions.
    You can refer to **table 1** on the above (answer #3), only pharmacist and student pharmacist can perform patient counseling.

5. **C.** No, all prescriptions shall be preserved for at least 5 years

    EXPLANATION:
    Review "Record Retention" under Section 10: General Provision.
    Every pharmacy must keep all records of prescription in a suitable book, file, or electronic record keeping system for at least 5 years to be available for inspection if asked by the Department.

    (225 ILCS 85/18: Section scheduled to be repealed on January 1, 2018) & (68 IL ADC Section 1330.10)

6. **E.** Both A and D
    A: A pharmacist can administer vaccination to patients who are 10 years of age or older
    D: A pharmacist can administer Tdap vaccine in an 8-year-old girl

    EXPLANATION:
    Review "Vaccinations/Immunizations" under Section 10: General Provision.
    A pharmacist or student pharmacist under the supervision of a pharmacist may administer vaccinations with a valid prescription or standing order by a physician to the following patients:
    - Patients ≥14 years old, or in accordance with hospital pharmacy and therapeutics committee policies and procedures
    - Patients ages 10 and older, limited to live and inactivated Influenza and Tdap (tetanus, diphtheria, acellular pertussis) vaccines

    (68 IL ADC Section 1330.50)

7. **C.** June 30

    EXPLANATION:
    Review "Vaccinations/Immunizations" under Section 10: General Provision.
    A pharmacist who administers any vaccine must report to the patient's primary doctor within 30 days after vaccination.

    (68 IL ADC Section 1330.50)

8. **C.** I and III
    I: Physician

III: Optometrist

EXPLANATION:
Review "Prescribers" under Definitions.
A prescriber is someone who's authorized to issue a prescription, including physician, dentist, optometrist, podiatrist, veterinarian, prescribing psychologist, who issues a prescription, or a physician assistant, advance practice nurse, who issues a prescription for a controlled substance in accordance with a written delegation and collaborative agreement.

Tip to know: Who do you see that are not on this list? These are physical therapist, psychologist, chiropractor, occupational therapist, registered nurse, etc.

Note: A psychologist may only prescribe if he or she has a written delegation and collaborative agreement with a physician to prescribe C-III through C-V controlled substances. Therefore, answer choice "IV. Psychologist" would have been chosen if it is "prescribing psychologist" instead.

(720 ILCS 570/102)

9. **A.** $5000

EXPLANATION:
Review "Unlicensed Practice; Violation; Civil Penalty" under Section 10: General Provision. Any person who practices, attempts to practice, or appears to practice pharmacy without being licensed, must pay a civil penalty to the Department in an amount ≤ $5,000 for each offense.

(225 ILCS 85/5.5: *Section scheduled to be repealed on January 1, 2018*)

10. **D.** Compounding of a product containing combination of ingredients in strengths that are not commercially available is permitted if there's a valid prescription order.

EXPLANATION:
Review "Compounding" under Definitions.
A. The pharmacy can dispense compounded products if the prescription is patient specific. (There's nothing specifically said under "compounding" that the prescription has to be patient specific)
B. Compounding includes the preparation and mixing of components, and the flavorings. (Flavorings are not considered part of compounding)
C. Compounding a commercially available product is never permitted. (Compounding a commercially available product is permitted if there's a valid prescription or in shortage)

(225 ILCS 85/3: *Section scheduled to be repealed on January 1, 2018*)

11. **B.** Obtain a verbal prescription transfer from another pharmacy by phone

EXPLANATION:
Review "Pharmacy Technician Job Functions" under Section 9: Pharmacy Technician.
A. Offer counseling under the direct supervision of a pharmacist. (Only a pharmacist or student pharmacist under the supervision of a pharmacist can perform this job function)
C. Perform clinical conflict resolution under the direct supervision of a pharmacist. (Only a pharmacist or student pharmacist under the supervision of a pharmacist can perform this job function)
D. Fill a prescription without supervision from a pharmacist. (A pharmacy technician cannot perform any pharmacy function within their scope of practice without the present of a pharmacist)

(225 ILCS 85/9: Section scheduled to be repealed on January 1, 2018)

12. **D. I and II**
I: Dispense involves interpreting and evaluating a prescription drug order
II: Preparation and delivery of a drug or device to a patient in suitable container appropriately labeled is considered as part of dispensing

EXPLANATION:
Review "Dispense or Dispensing" under Definitions.
Dispense or dispensing involves interpreting and evaluating a prescription drug order in addition to filling, compounding, packaging, and labeling necessary for delivery the prescription drug order. Recommending, advising, and counseling on the drug contents, therapeutic value, uses, and precaution are also parts of the dispensing process. It does _NOT_ include physical delivery of a drug or device to a patient or patient's representative in a home, institution, or within a pharmacy store while the pharmacist is on duty and the pharmacy is open.

(225 ILCS 85/3: Section scheduled to be repealed on January 1, 2018)

13. **C and E.**
C: In the event when the PIC dies or is physically incompetent of performing required duties, the owner of the pharmacy must assume the duties of the PIC
E: Within 30 days, the PIC must notify and send the Department a copy of the closing inventory of controlled substances, along with a statement of how the pharmacy intends to dispose all prescription drugs and files

EXPLANATION:
Review "Closing a Pharmacy" and "Disposition of Legend Drugs..." under Section 7: Pharmacy
A. Within 20 days, the PIC must notify the Department of the intended manner of disposition for all prescriptions. (Within 30 days not 20 days)
B. Within 20 days, the PIC must provide the Department with a copy of the closing inventory of controlled substances along with a statement indicating the intended manner of disposition for all prescriptions. (Within 30 days not 20 days)

D. The PIC assumes no duties when the pharmacy ceases operation since it is the pharmacy owner's responsibility. (It is the responsibility of the PIC, unless he or she is physically incompetent or deceases)

(225 ILCS 85/17: Section scheduled to be repealed on January 1, 2018)

14. **A.** Pharmacists need 30 hours of ACPE accredited CE during 24 months before the expiration of the license

EXPLANATION:
Review "Continuing Education" under Section 8: Pharmacist.

(68 IL ADC Section 1330.100)

15. **E.** I and II
I: The Department authorizes examination 3 or more times per year
II: If an applicant fails to pass an exam for licensure within 3 years after filing his/her application, the application is denied

EXPLANATION:
Review "NAPLEX/MPJE Examination" under Section 8: Pharmacist.
The Department allows examinations to be given at least 3 times a year to allow students to sit in the exam. The number of attempts to pass the NAPLE or MPJE is five. If an applicant fails or refuses to take an exam, or fails to pass an exam for licensure within 3 years after filing his/her application, the application is denied. After applicants take the exam, the Department will notify applicants of their results within 7 weeks of the NAPLEX/MPJE exam date.

(225 ILCS 85/6: Section scheduled to be repealed on January 1, 2018)

16. **B.** The date when the prescription was written

EXPLANATION:
Review "Prescription Label" under Section 11: Prescription Order.
The following information must be included on the prescription label:
1. Name and address of the pharmacy
2. Name or initials of the person who filled the medication
3. Date medication was filled
4. Name of patient
5. Rx number of prescription
6. Last name of prescriber
7. Directions for use
8. Name of drug, dosage and quantity

(225 ILCS 85/22: Section scheduled to be repealed on January 1, 2018)

17. **D.** Mailing the prescription drug to the patient

    EXPLANATION:
    Review "Remote Prescription Processing" under Section 11: Prescription Order.
    These activities include anything from receiving, evaluating and transferring prescription, to obtaining refills, performing patient counseling and drug regimen review. However, remote prescription processing does not include the dispensing of a prescription drug (i.e. giving or mailing the medication to the patient).

    (225 ILCS 85/25.10: *Section scheduled to be repealed on January 1, 2018*)

18. **D.** I and II
    I: When providing tele-pharmacy service, the pharmacist that provides the pharmacist care can manage it at the home pharmacy as long as it is connected to the remote pharmacy via live video and audio
    II: The PIC is responsible for the practice of tele-pharmacy at the remote pharmacy, including the oversight of its automated medication system

    EXPLANATION:
    Review "Tele-pharmacy" under Section 13: Types of Pharmacies.
    Any type of tele-pharmacy, including remote dispensing, remote consultation, and remote automated pharmacy, must have a video/audio link to make possible the interaction between a patient and a pharmacist for a patient counseling. The PIC is responsible for the practice of tele-pharmacy at a remote pharmacy, including supervision of any automated system.

    (225 ILCS 85/25.15: *Section scheduled to be repealed on January 1, 2018*) & (68 IL ADC Section1330.510)

19. **A.** I: If there is an audio and video linked to a home pharmacy, to allow a pharmacist to counsel the patient each time a medication is dispensed from the system

    EXPLANATION:
    Review "Tele-pharmacy" under Section 13: Types of Pharmacies.
    As mentioned in the explanation for question #18, any type of tele-pharmacy, including remote dispensing and remote consultation, must have a video/audio link to make possible the interaction between a patient and a pharmacist for a patient counseling.

    (225 ILCS 85/25.15: *Section scheduled to be repealed on January 1, 2018*) & (68 IL ADC Section1330.510)

20. **C.** II and III
    II: If the physician indicates that the drug may be substituted by signing his or her name on top of the "may substitute" line

III: If the selected drug product is a generic drug that is determined to be therapeutically equivalent to the substituted drug by the FDA

EXPLANATION:
Review "Biological Products" under Section 10: General Provision.
A pharmacist may substitute a bio-similar product for a prescribed biological product only if all of the following conditions are met:
- The substituted product has been determined by the FDA to be interchangeable with the prescribed biological product;
- The prescribing physician doesn't state in writing, verbally, or electronically that substitution is prohibited or indicate that prescription drug may be substituted; <u>and</u>
- The pharmacy informs the patient about the substitution.

(225 ILCS 85/19.5: *Section scheduled to be repealed on January 1, 2018*)

21. **D.** Both A and B
    A: Tele-pharmacy must store all data inside of secure, HIPAA-compliant servers
    B: An automated dispensing machine may be used in conjunction with the practice of tele-pharmacy after inspection and approval by the Department

    EXPLANATION:
    Review "Tele-pharmacy" under Section 13: Types of Pharmacies.
    A pharmacy must meet the following conditions to practice tele-pharmacy:
    - All contents of an automated pharmacy system must be stored in a secure location and may be recorded electronically.
    - The Department must inspect and approve before an automated pharmacy system may be used together with the practice of tele-pharmacy.
    - The PIC, not the registered pharmacist, is responsible for overseeing the practice of tele-pharmacy, train, and supervise the certified pharmacy technicians at the remote site.

    (225 ILCS 85/25.15: *Section scheduled to be repealed on January 1, 2018*)

22. **C.** II and III
    II: An electronic image can serve as the original prescription if the pharmacy's computer system can capture an unalterable electronic image of the prescription order
    III: The pharmacy's computer system must be able to print and provide all prescription information within 72 hours upon the Department's request

    EXPLANATION:
    Review "Electronic Visual Image Prescription" under Section 11: Prescription Order.
    The electronic image can serve as the original prescription without the need of a hard copy if the pharmacy's computer system can capture an electronic visual image of the prescription order that cannot be altered. The computer system must be able to maintain,

print and provide all of the prescription information **within 72 hours** of the Department's request.

(225 ILCS 85/25.20: Section scheduled to be repealed on January 1, 2018)

23. **B.** I and II
    I: A PIC must ensure that the home pharmacy has enough staff on duty
    II: A pharmacist or student pharmacist may perform patient counseling through telecommunication

    EXPLANATION:
    Review "Tele-pharmacy" under Section 13: Types of Pharmacies.
    To review for the difference between a registered pharmacy technician and a certified pharmacy technician, see section 9.
    It is the certified pharmacy technician at the remote pharmacy that may prepare prescriptions for dispensing not a registered pharmacy technician.

    (225 ILCS 85/25.15: Section scheduled to be repealed on January 1, 2018)

24. **B.** I and II
    I: The Department may issue JD a license to establish the new pharmacy in IL, if she can provide sufficient evidence indicating rehabilitation of Caremax pharmacy in Wisconsin
    II: The Department will go after any earlier complaint against her Caremax Pharmacy in Wisconsin and conduct a hearing

    EXPLANATION:
    Review "Prior Revocation; Hearing" under Section 12: Refusal, Revocation, or Suspension. The Department will go after any earlier complaint filed against the pharmacy and conduct a hearing, regardless if the new pharmacy has been licensed. The Department will not issue the license for the new pharmacy unless the owner presents sufficient evidence indicating rehabilitation.

    (225 ILCS 85/31: Section scheduled to be repealed on January 1, 2018)

25. **D.** ≤ $10,000

    EXPLANATION:
    Review Section 12: Refusal, Revocation, or Suspension.

    (225 ILCS 85/30: Section scheduled to be repealed on January 1, 2018)

    E. All of the above. EXPLANATION:
    Review Section 12: Refusal, Revocation, or Suspension.
    All of these activities can result in violation of Pharmacy Practice Act:
    - Selling drug samples

- Failing to dispense any drug in "good faith"
- Overcharging for professional services
- Engaging in unprofessional, dishonorable, or unethical conduct that's likely to deceive, defraud, or harm the public

(225 ILCS 85/30: *Section scheduled to be repealed on January 1, 2018*)

26. **C.** II and III
II: The Board will have a hearing within 15 days of the suspension
III: The Director of the Department may suspend a licensed or registered person immediately without a hearing if he or she is found to be posed immediate danger to the public

EXPLANATION:
Review "Suspension Without Hearing" under Section 12: Refusal, Revocation, or Suspension. If the licensed or registered person is found to pose an immediate danger to the public, the Director of the Department may immediately suspend his or her license without a hearing. The Board will have a hearing within 15 days of the suspension.

(225 ILCS 85/33: *Section scheduled to be repealed on January 1, 2018*)

27. **A.** He is guilty of a Class A misdemeanor

EXPLANATION:
Review "Enforcement; Penalties" under Section 10: General Provision.

(68 IL ADC Section1330.720)

28. **D.** A, C, and D
A: The defendant can request a direct appeal to the Secretary
C: If the Board fails to present their findings, conclusions, and recommendations on the case within 30 calendar days after the Secretary's issue of order to the Board, which was resulted by the defendant's appeal
D: The Secretary fails to issue an order within 30 calendar days after what happens in (C)

EXPLANATION:
Review "Attorney as Hearing Officer" under Section 12: Refusal, Revocation, or Suspension.

(225 ILCS 85/35.7: *Section scheduled to be repealed on January 1, 2018*)

29. **A.** 10

EXPLANATION:
Review "Current Usual and Customary Retail Price Disclosure" under Section 10: General Provision.
(225 ILCS 85/41: *Section scheduled to be repealed on January 1, 2018*)

30. **A.** $75/year

    EXPLANATION:
    Review "Fees" under Section 10: General Provision.

    (68 IL ADC Section 1330.20)

31. **D.** I and III
    I: Pharmacist
    III: Pharmacy technician

    EXPLANATION:
    Review "Inactive Status" under Section 10: General Provision.
    A pharmacist or pharmacy technician may place his or her license on inactive status, but a pharmacy license cannot be placed on inactive status.

    (225 ILCS 85/13: Section scheduled to be repealed on January 1, 2018)

32. **D.** Substituting a generic drug product with a different manufacturer than the original prescribe generic drug product given that they're both therapeutically equivalent as determined by the FDA

    EXPLANATION:
    Review "Drug Product Substitution under Section 11: Prescription Order.
    Any generic drug that is determined to be therapeutically equivalent by the FDA is available for substitution. A pharmacist can substitute a brand or alternative generic drug if the selected drug product has the same dosage form and active ingredients with no more than 1% difference from the active ingredient to the substituted drug.

    (225 ILCS 85/25: Section scheduled to be repealed on January 1, 2018)

33. **B.** Within 60 days

    EXPLANATION:
    Review Section 12: Refusal, Revocation, or Suspension.

    (225 ILCS 85/30: Section scheduled to be repealed on January 1, 2018)

34. **A, C, and D**
    A: Engaging in the practice of pharmacy when the person is not authorized to practice pharmacy
    C: Purchasing prescriptions drugs from any source that fails to meet the Wholesale Drug Distribution Licensing Act.

D: Compounding or selling any drug or chemical with the strength and purity that are below standards.

EXPLANATION:
Review "Violations" under Section 12: Refusal, Revocation, or Suspension.
B is not correct, because compounding or selling any drug or chemical recognized in USP/NF for internal or external use, which has different *NOT* the same strength, quality, purity, or bioavailability as determined by USP/NF.

(68 IL ADC Section 1330.40)

35. **C.** Yes, because there is a fact pattern of AB's being under the influence of alcohol while on duty

    EXPLANATION:
    Review "Violations" under section 12: Refusal, Revocation, or Suspension.
    If there's a fact pattern, a discipline for the conduct will be likely imposed.

36. **D.** Both A and B
    A: Failing to exercise sound professional judgment with respect to the accuracy and authenticity of any prescription drug order dispensed
    B: Failing to dispense the appropriate quantity

    EXPLANATION:
    Review "Dispense or Dispensing" under Definitions and Section 12: Refusal, Revocation and Suspension.
    Think of what activities are parts of the dispensing of a prescription medication (i.e. interpreting, evaluating, filling, packaging, and labeling of the prescription drug order). Physical delivery of a prescription drug is not part of the dispensing.

    (225 ILCS 85/3: *Section scheduled to be repealed on January 1, 2018*) & (225 ILCS 85/30: *Section scheduled to be repealed on January 1, 2018*)

37. **A.** Within 30 days

    EXPLANATION:
    Review "Vaccinations/Immunizations" under Section 10: General Provision.

    (68 IL ADC Section 1330.50)

38. **A and B**
    A: Successfully completed a training course accredited by the ACPE or similar professional body approved by the Division
    B: a current Basic Life Support Certification for Healthcare Providers issued by the American Heart Association, the American Red Cross

    EXPLANATION:

Review "Vaccinations/Immunizations" under Section 10: General Provision.
C is not accurate, because although the pharmacy is required to have a current copy or electronic version of the CDC reference "Epidemiology and Prevention of Vaccine—Preventable Diseases" available at the location where vaccinations are given, if the pharmacist works outside of a pharmacy, he or she must have this CDC reference at the location where the vaccine is given.

(68 IL ADC Section 1330.50)

39. **C.** 5 years

EXPLANATION:
Review "Vaccinations/Immunizations – Recordkeeping and Reporting" under Section 10: General Provision.

(68 IL ADC Section 1330.50)

40. **A, B, C, D and E**

A: The name, address and patient's date of birth
B: Date of vaccination
C: Name, dose, manufacturer, lot number, and beyond use date of the vaccine
D: Name and address of the patient's primary health care provider
E: Vaccine information statement (VIS) that was provided to the patient

EXPLANATION:
Review "Vaccinations/Immunizations" under Section 10: General Provision.
These vaccination records include the following:
1. The name, address and patient's date of birth
2. Date of vaccination
3. Name, dose, manufacturer, lot number, and beyond use date of the vaccine
4. Name and address of the patient's primary health care provider
5. The name or unique identifier of the administering pharmacist
6. VIS that was provided to the patient

(68 IL ADC Section 1330.50)

41. **A and C**

A: It's issued for a legitimate medical purpose
C: At least one physician's face-to-face evaluation with the patient

EXPLANATION:
Review "Internet Pharmacies" under Section 11: Prescription Order.
A prescription is valid only if (1) it's issued for a legitimate medical purpose, and (2) after at least one physician's face-to-face evaluation with the patient.

(68 IL ADC Section 1330.60)

42. **B and C**
    B: Every pharmacy license issued expires on March 31 of each odd-numbered year
    C: The holder of the license or certificate of registration can pay the required fee to renew it during the 30 days before the expiration date

    EXPLANATION:
    Review "Expiration of License/Certificate" under Section 10: General Provision.
    B is not accurate, because every pharmacy license issued expires on March 31 of each even-numbered year not odd-numbered year. C is not accurate, because the holder of the license or certificate of registration can pay the renewal fee 60 days not 30 days before the expiration date.

    (68 IL ADC Section 1330.80)

43. **Both A and B**
    A: CE is not required if it is the first renewal of an original licensure
    B: Completion of 30 hours of CE during the 24 months before the expiration date of the license

    EXPLANATION:
    Review "Continuing Education" under Section 8: Pharmacist.
    C is not true, because CE is not required if it is the first renewal of an original licensure.

    (68 IL ADC Section 1330.100)

44. **E.** Both C and D
    C: A prescription that is printed in advance and manually signed by the prescriber
    D: A computer generated prescription that is printed, manually signed, and faxed by the prescriber

    EXPLANATION:
    Review "Pre-printed Prescriptions" under Section 17: Illinois Controlled Substances Act & Rules.
    Any prescription is considered pre-printed prescription if the drug name has been indicated on it prior to the time of issuance, including pre-inked stamped that would be applied to a prescription blank. If the prescription is computer generated at the prescriber's office, printed and manually signed by the prescriber, then it is not considered pre-printed prescription.

    (720 ILCS 570/312)

45. **B.** 12/31/2017

    EXPLANATION:

Review Section 13: Types of Pharmacies.
Non-controlled substance prescriptions expire 1 year from the date it was originally issued, regardless of the number of refills remaining or as needed (PRN) refill.

46. **B.** No, because no non-controlled substance prescription can be refiled (1) year after the original issuance date.

EXPLANATION:
Review Section 13: Types of Pharmacies.
Digoxin is a non-controlled drug. Non-controlled substance prescriptions expire 1 year from the date it was originally issued. Therefore, this prescription is invalid and cannot be filled.

47. **C.** The pharmacist is allowed to combine or consolidate refills without calling the patient's prescriber, but he or she has to use his or her professional judgment to call the doctor before combining, because the patient has shown pattern of addiction to the prescribed drug.

EXPLANATION:
Review "Community Pharmacy Services – Tip to know" under Section 13: Types of Pharmacies.
The Pharmacy Practice Act permits a pharmacist to exercise profession judgment and combine refills without calling the doctor. If a patient has shown pattern of addiction to the prescribed drug, you should call the doctor before combining the prescription.

48. **A, B, C and E**
A: When based on the pharmacist's professional judgment, she or he determines that the drug should not be dispensed due to drug-drug interaction.
B: The medication is out of stock.
C: The medication is not available, because it's in shortage according to the Nation guidelines.
E: The prescription of the drug is not valid.

EXPLANATION:
Review "Community Pharmacy Services" under Section 13: Types of Pharmacies.
Under the following circumstances, the pharmacies are not required to delivered prescribed medications:
- When based on the pharmacist's professional judgment, she or he determines if the drug should be dispensed due clinical reasons;
- National or State emergencies or guidelines affecting availability, usage or supplies of drugs;
- Lack of specialized equipment or expertise needed to safely produce, store or dispense drugs, such as certain drug compounding or storage for nuclear medicine;
- Potentially fraudulent prescriptions;
- Unavailability of drug; <u>or</u>
- The drug is not typically carried in similar practice settings in IL.

(68 IL ADC Section1330.500)

49. **D.** III and I
   I: Contact the patient's prescriber to address the clinical concerns
   III: Return the unfilled prescription to the patient as the patient has requested.

   EXPLANATION:
   Review "Community Pharmacy Services" under Section 13: Types of Pharmacies.
   These alternatives include the following:
   - Contact the prescriber to address clinical concerns identified, such as drug-disease contraindication, drug-drug interaction, etc.;
   - Return unfilled prescriptions to the patient if patient requested; or
   - Communicate the original prescription information to a pharmacy of the patient's choice to fill the prescription in a timely manner.

   (68 IL ADC Section1330.500)

50. **A, B and C**
   A: The mail-order pharmacy may be licensed as a nonresident pharmacy if it has an active license in the state where the dispensing facility is located and the drugs are dispensed from in order to operate as a mail-order pharmacy in IL.
   B: pharmacy has to maintain its record of drugs dispensed to IL residents.
   C: pharmacy is compliant with all directions and requests by the law for information from the Board of Pharmacy of each state where the pharmacy is licensed. The pharmacy must respond directly to all communications from the Board or Department concerning any circumstances arising from the dispensing of drugs to IL residents.

   EXPLANATION:
   Review "Rules and Regulations for Internet & Mail-Order Pharmacies" under Section 13: Types of Pharmacies.
   D and E are not accurate, because it should be during the pharmacy's regular hours of operation of not less than 6 days per week and for a minimum of 40 hours per week.

   (225 ILCS 85/16a: Section scheduled to be repealed on January 1, 2018)

51. **E.** A, B and C
   A: The tele-pharmacy in IL
   B: The home pharmacy in Michigan
   C: The PIC who oversees the tele-pharmacy in IL

   EXPLANATION:
   Review "Tele-pharmacy" under Section 13: Types of Pharmacies.
   Each site where tele-pharmacies occur must have a separate pharmacy license. Home pharmacies that are located outside of IL must be licensed in IL as a nonresident pharmacy. The PIC of the remote site must be licensed in IL. The dispensing pharmacist employed by

the nonresident (home) pharmacy is not required to be licensed in IL but must have an active pharmacist license in the state where the nonresident pharmacy is located.

(225 ILCS 85/25.15: *Section scheduled to be repealed on January 1, 2018*)

52. **D.** I, II and III
    I: Remote dispensing site
    II: Remote consultation site
    III: Remote automated pharmacy system (RAPS)

    EXPLANATION:
    Review "Tele-pharmacy" under Section 13: Types of Pharmacies.

    (225 ILCS 85/22b: *Section scheduled to be repealed on January 1, 2018*) & (68 IL ADC Section1330.510)

53. **D.** 72 hours

    EXPLANATION:
    Review "Tele-pharmacy" under Section 13: Types of Pharmacies.
    Written prescriptions must be delivered to the home pharmacy **within 72 hours.**

    (225 ILCS 85/22b: *Section scheduled to be repealed on January 1, 2018*)

54. **E.** 5 years

    EXPLANATION:
    Review "Remote Automated Pharmacy System" under Section 13: Types of Pharmacies.
    A record of each transaction with the automated pharmacy system must be maintained for 5 years.

    (225 ILCS 85/22b: *Section scheduled to be repealed on January 1, 2018*)

55. **B, C and D**
    B: Beyond use date & date admixture
    C: Name & strength of drugs added
    D: Name, concentration & volume of the base parenteral solution

    EXPLANATION:
    Review "Offsite Institutional Pharmacy Services – Labeling Requirements" under Section 13: Types of Pharmacies.

	Labeling Requirements of Medication for Future Use	Parenteral Solutions	Non-Parenteral Repackaged
1	Name, Concentration & Volume of the Base Parenteral Solution	✔	-
2	Name & Strength of Drugs Added	✔	-
3	§Beyond Use Date & Date of Admixture	✔	✔
4	§Reference Code to Identify Source & Lot Number	✔	✔
5	Brand and/or Generic Name	-	✔
6	Strength	-	✔

Table 2: Labeling Requirements of Medications for Future Use (Parenteral Solutions & Non-Parenteral Repackaged).

(68 IL ADC Section1330.520)

56. **D. III and I**
    I: If specified in the individual monograph that beyond use date of the medication is 6 months, then the pharmacist should use this as the beyond use date for this medication.
    III: Unless specified in the individual monograph, the beyond used date must not be later than the beyond use date on the manufacturer's container or one year from the date the drugs is repackaged, whichever is earlier.

    <u>EXPLANATION:</u>
    Review "Offsite Institutional Pharmacy Services – Labeling Requirements" under Section 13: Types of Pharmacies.

    (68 IL ADC Section1330.520)

57. **A, B and E**
    A: Name of the resident
    B: Resident's room and bed number
    E: Prescriber's name

    <u>EXPLANATION:</u>
    Review "Offsite Institutional Pharmacy Services – Labeling Requirements" under Section 13: Types of Pharmacies.

	Labeling Requirements of Medication Prepared for Immediate Use	Specific Resident or Patient	Specific Resident or Patient via Unit Dose
1	Name of the resident	✔	✔
2	Resident's room and bed number	✔	✔
3	Dispensing date	✔	-
4	Date of order	-	✔
5	Name, strength and dosage form of drug <u>or</u> description of the medical device ordered	✔	✔
6	Quantity dispensed	✔	-
7	Directions for use	✔	✔
8	Prescriber's name	✔	✔
9	Beyond use date if less than 60 days from date of dispensing	✔	-

Table 3: Labeling Requirements of Medication Prepared for Immediate Use.

(68 IL ADC Section1330.520)

58. **B.** I and II
    I: Automated dispensing system can be accessed when the pharmacy is open.
    II: Automated dispensing system can be used as after-hour cabinet and emergency kit.

    EXPLANATION:
    Review "Automated Dispensing and Storage Systems – Policies and Procedures" under Section 14: Pharmacy Standards.
    Automated dispensing and storage systems are not to be used in nuclear pharmacies.

    (68 IL ADC Section1330.680)

59. **E.** All of the above
    A: The authorized person's signature
    B: The quantity removed
    C: The time of removal
    D: The name of the medication removed

    EXPLANATION:
    Review "After-Hour Cabinets" under Section 13: Types of Pharmacies.
    A log must be maintained within the cabinet and the person who removes medication must indicate on the log (1) his or her signature, (2) the name of the medication removed, (3) the strength (if applicable), (4) the quantity removed and (5) the time of removal.

    (68 IL ADC Section1330.520)

60. **B.** I and II
    I: The beyond use date of the emergency kit is based on the earliest beyond use date of any drug in the kit.
    II: After an emergency kit has been used or the seal has been broken or the kit is expired, it must be secured and returned to the pharmacy to be checked and restocked.

    EXPLANATION:
    Review "Emergency Kits" under Section 13: Types of Pharmacies.
    A label is affixed to the outside of the emergency kit indicating the beyond use date of the emergency kit. The beyond use date of the emergency kit is based on the earliest beyond use date of any drug in the kit. After an emergency kit has been used or the seal has been broken or the kit is expired, it must be secured and returned to the pharmacy to be checked and restocked by the last authorized user only when the pharmacy opens.

    (68 IL ADC Section1330.520)

61. **B, C and D**
    B: Beyond use date
    C: Name and location of the patient

D: Reference code to identify source and lot number

EXPLANATION:
Review "Onsite Institutional Pharmacy Services – Labels on Investigational New Drugs" under Section 13: Types of Pharmacies.

(68 IL ADC Section1330.530)

62. **D.** I, II and III
I: The area of the pharmacy should be designed to minimize outside traffic and airflow disturbances from activity within the facility.
II: It must have sufficient size to accommodate a laminar airflow hood, barrier isolation chamber, and to provide for the proper storage of drugs and supplies under appropriate conditions of temperature, light, moisture, sanitation, ventilation and security.
III: It must be ventilated in a way so that it doesn't interfere with the proper operation of the sterile products preparation apparatus.

EXPLANATION:
Review "Physical Requirements of Pharmacies Preparing Sterile Products" under Section 14: Pharmacy Standards.
The area should be designed to minimize outside traffic and airflow disturbances from activity within the facility. It must have sufficient size to accommodate a laminar airflow hood (LAF), barrier isolation chamber (BSC), and to provide for the proper storage of drugs and supplies under appropriate conditions of temperature, light, moisture, sanitation, ventilation and security. It must be ventilated in a way so that it doesn't interfere with the proper operation of the sterile products preparation apparatus.

(68 IL ADC Section1330.670)

63. **B.** I and II
I: If a patient refuses to accept counseling, the pharmacist must document it.
II: If the pharmacist does not document that counseling is refused by the patient, then the offer of counseling is considered to be accepted by the patient and that counseling provided.

EXPLANATION:
Review "Patient Counseling" under Section 15: Pharmacy Operations.
If a patient refuses to accept patient counseling, PIC does not need to be notified, but the refusal should be documented. The absence of any record of a refusal to accept the offer to counsel is considered that the offer was accepted and that counseling was provided.

(68 IL ADC Section1330.700)

64. **B.** Syringes or needles sold must be stored at a pharmacy in a manner that limits access to the syringes or needles to pharmacists at the pharmacy or persons designated by the

pharmacists.

EXPLANATION:
Review "Sale of Hypodermic Syringes and Needles" under Section 16: Hypodermic Syringes and Needles Act.
- A. A person 18 years or older may purchase up to 30 sterile hypodermic syringes daily without a prescription from a pharmacist in a pharmacy. (A person 18 years or older may purchase up to 20 sterile hypodermic syringes daily without a prescription not 30)
- C. The pharmacy must maintain recordkeeping of the sale transaction for 5 years. (There are no recordkeeping requirements)
- D. The Board of Pharmacy must provide materials for proper disposal of needles and syringes to the pharmacies that choose to sell them. (It is the IL Department of Public Health not the Board of Pharmacy that provides materials for proper disposal of needles and syringes)

(720 ILCS 635/2 & 2.5)

65. **A, D and E**
    A: Lisdexamfetamine
    D: Dexmethylphenidate
    E: Nembutal

    EXPLANATION:
    Review "Findings Required for Inclusion in Schedule II" under Section 17: IL Controlled Substances Act.
    Make sure you are familiar with brand and generic names for controlled substances. A comprehensive list of all Scheduled drugs is at:
    http://www.deadiversion.usdoj.gov/schedules/

66. **D.** Schedule V

    EXPLANATION:
    Review "Findings Required for Inclusion in Schedule V" under Section 17: IL Controlled Substances Act.
    Schedule V controlled substances have 200 mg or less of codeine or any of its salts, per 100 mL or per 100 g. If 15 mg of codeine per 10 mL dose, how much will be in 100 mL?

    $$15 \text{ mg} / 10 \text{ mL} = x / 100 \text{ mL}$$
    $$1.5 \text{ mg} / 1 \text{ mL} = x / 100 \text{ mL}$$
    $$x = 150 \text{ mg}$$

    There are 150 mg of codeine per 100 mL; therefore it is a Schedule V controlled substance.

    (720 ILCS 570/211 & 212)

67. **B.** Schedule III
    EXPLANATION

Review "Findings Required for Inclusion in Schedule III & V" under Section 17: IL Controlled Substances Act.
- There are more than 10 mg of dihydrocodeine (16 mg) per dose. Therefore, this can't be a C-V controlled substance.
- Schedule III controlled substances have 1.8 g or less of dihydrocodeine per 100 mL <u>or</u> 90 mg or less per dosage unit, with one or more active, non-narcotic ingredients in recognized therapeutic amounts. This medication contains dihydrocodeine with non-narcotic ingredients with recognizable therapeutic amounts (APAP 320.5 mg and caffeine 30 mg).
- The medication is a Schedule III controlled substance.

(720 ILCS 570/207 & 208)

68. **B.** Dispenser

   EXPLANATION:
   Review "Registration Required for Manufacturing, Distribution & Dispensing" under Section 17: IL Controlled Substance Act.
   Dispenser registration is issued to a physician or mid-level practitioner who prescribes a controlled substance. There's no such thing as prescriber registration.

   (720 ILCS 570/301 & 302)

69. **A, B, C, and E**
   A: Physician's DEA number
   B: Date and time of when received the oral prescription
   C: name and address of the ultimate user
   E: Pharmacist's signature and ate on the face of the prescription

   EXPLANATION:
   Review "Schedule III-V Drug Prescriptions" under Section 17: IL Controlled Substances Act. The oral prescription must be written down on a prescription order by the pharmacist with the following criteria:
   1. Date and time of when received by pharmacist.
   2. Full name and address of the ultimate user.
   3. Full name, address, and registry number of the prescriber.
   4. Pharmacist's signature and date on the face of the prescription.

   (720 ILCS 570/312)

70. **B.** Dispense 30 tablets and advise the patient only 30 tablets can be dispensed at a time, the next 30 tablets can be filled on 1/31/2017 as written by the prescriber on the prescription

   EXPLANATION:
   Review "Schedule II Drug Prescriptions" under Section 17: IL Controlled Substances Act.

A practitioner may provide individual patients with up to three (3) 30-day supply prescriptions for the same schedule II controlled substance, written all on the same day, to be filled sequentially over the course of 90 days. A pharmacist should only dispense the medication on the earliest date that he or she can fill the prescription as written by the prescriber on the prescription.

(77 IL ADC Section 3100.400)

71. **C.** Department of Financial and Professional Regulation

    EXPLANATION:
    Review "Department Duties Related to Schedules" under Section 17: IL Controlled Substances Act.
    The Department of Financial and Professional Regulation in IL (DFPR) is also known as the Department has the authority to reschedule, add, or delete all controlled substances in the Schedules.

    (720 ILCS 570/201)

72. **D.** Dispense 60 tablets without calling the doctor, because based on your professional judgment this is appropriate and under the IL law it is permitted to do so

    EXPLANATION:
    Review "Community Pharmacy Services" under Section 13: Types of Pharmacies.
    A pharmacist is allowed to combine or consolidate refills without calling the physician in order to provide the patients greater quantity, up to the total quantity authorized on the original prescription, plus any refills.

73. **Both B and C**
    B: The maximum number of refill is 5 times
    C: The prescription has to be renewed by the prescriber after it expires

    EXPLANATION:
    Review "Schedule III-V Drug Prescription" under Section 17: IL Controlled Substances Act.
    Alprazolam (Xanax®) is a C-IV drug; therefore, it only can be refilled 5 times or less or 6 months or less, whichever comes first. Once it expires, the prescription has to be renewed by a prescriber in order to be filled again.

    (720 ILCS 570/312)

74. **A, D and E**
    A: Ambien tablet
    D: Nembutal suppository
    E: Pregabalin capsule

EXPLANATION:
Review Section 17: IL Controlled Substances Act
Schedule III-V controlled substance prescriptions can be refilled 5 times in a 6-month period.
- A. Ambien tablet (C-IV)
- B. Hydrocodone capsule (C-II)
- C. Ritalin tablet (C-II)
- D. Nembutal suppository (C-III)
- E. Pregabalin capsule (C-V)

(720 ILCS 570/205 & 206), (720 ILCS 570/207 & 208), (720 ILCS 570/209 & 210), (720 ILCS 570/211 & 212) & (720 ILCS 570/312)

75. **Both A and B**
A: The date of the emergency prescription and "Authorization for Emergency Dispensing" should be written on the face of the prescription.
B: Within 7 days after the dispensing of the oral prescription, the physician must provide the written prescription.

EXPLANATION:
Review "Schedule II Controlled Substance Emergency Prescriptions" under Section 17: IL Controlled Substances Act.
C is not accurate, because if the prescriber fails to deliver the written prescription for the emergency prescription that was dispensed, the dispensing pharmacist must notify the DFPR not contacting the prescriber.

(720 ILCS 570/309)

76. **A, B and D**
A: Written controlled substance prescription
B: Facsimile of controlled substance prescription
D: Dispensing records of non-controlled substances

EXPLANATION:
Review "Table 3" under Section 17: IL Controlled Substances Act

(720 ILCS 570/312), (225 ILCS 85/18: *Section scheduled to be repealed on January 1, 2018*) & (68 IL ADC Section 1330.10)

77. **E.** Both A and C
A: Only a pharmacist and a person registered to dispense Schedule V drugs, can dispense
C: The dispensing cannot occur if within 96 hours, more than 120 g of codeine or dihydrocodeine had already dispensed to the same patient

EXPLANATION:
Review "Schedule III-V Drug Prescription" under Section 17: IL Controlled Substances.
B is not accurate, because the patient must be at least 21 years of age with two positive IDs.

(720 ILCS 570/312)

78. **E.** I, II and III
    I: The prescription must be signed and dated by the prescriber on the date of issuance if it's written in pen.
    II: An oral prescription for a controlled substance must be reduced to writing by a pharmacist.
    III: A prescription can be printed in advance but must be manually signed by the prescriber.

    EXPLANATION:
    Review "Prescriptions" under Definitions and "Schedule III-V Drug Prescriptions; Pre-Printed Prescriptions" under Section 17: IL Controlled Substances Act.

    (225 ILCS 85/3: *Section scheduled to be repealed on January 1, 2018*) & (720 ILCS 570/312)

79. **B.** I and II
    I: the patient is a resident of a long-term care facility.
    II: If the patient is a hospice patient.

    EXPLANATION:
    Review "Faxing of Schedule II Controlled Substances" under Section 17: IL Controlled Substances Act.
    A prescription for a Schedule II drug to be compounded for direct administration to a patient in a long-term care facility, or hospice program may be transmitted by facsimile by the prescriber to the pharmacy providing home infusion services.

    (720 ILCS 570/313)

80. **D.** I and II
    I: A community pharmacy is required to file a separate manufacturer registration in order to compound drug products for office use
    II: A separate registration is required when a new community pharmacy is open at a different location than its parent pharmacy owned by the same owner.

    EXPLANATION:
    Review "Multiple Registration Requirements" under Section 17: IL Controlled Substances Act. A community pharmacy is not required to apply for a manufacturer registration in order to compound a medication if it is in accordance with a prescription. A dispenser registration is all it needs. Each place of business or professional practice with different street address is required to have a separate registration (for example, Walgreens, CVS or other chain pharmacies have thousands of pharmacies that are shared by the same owner). Manufacturer registration is required if the pharmacy has to perform compounding for office use.

    (720 ILCS 570/301 & 302) & (77 IL ADC Section 3100.50)

81. **C.** Schedule V "exempt narcotics"

    EXPLANATION:
    Review "Finding Required for Inclusion in Schedule V" under Section 17: IL Controlled Substances Act.
    C-V controlled substances that are exempt narcotics are permitted to be sold without a prescription by both Illinois and Federal laws.

    (720 ILCS 570/211 & 212)

82. **D.** Immodium

    EXPLANATION:
    See https://www.deadiversion.usdoj.gov/schedules/ for a comprehensive list of controlled substances
    Immodium is an anti-diarrheal agent that is available OTC.

83. **B and D**
    B: Purchases and sales records should be maintained for 2 years
    D: No purchases can be made within 96 hours after the first purchase

    EXPLANATION:
    Review "Schedule III-V Drug Prescriptions" under Section 17: IL Controlled Substances Act.
    A. Only 4.5 L or less per drug product plus the amount of product needed for dispensing during the busiest week can be dispensed per week. (No **more than 4.5 L** is allowed to be maintained or kept in stock of each Schedule V controlled substance plus any additional quantity of controlled substance necessary to fill the largest number of prescription orders filled in any one week of the previous year)
    E. A patient must be 18 years of age or older. (A patient must be at least 21 years old)
    E. Purchases and sales records must be maintained for 5 years (These records must be kept for 2 years not 5 years)

    (720 ILCS 570/312)

84. **I.** A potential medication shopping occurs when a person has 3 or more prescribers that prescribed the controlled substances within a 30-day period.

    EXPLANATION:
    Review "Medication Shopping and Pharmacy Shopping" under Section 17: IL Controlled Substances Act.
    A potential for medication shopping occurs when a person has 3 or more pharmacies that do not share a common electronic file for controlled substances within 30-day period. The pharmacist is not required by IL law to refuse to dispense the controlled substance if there's a suspicion of a potential medication shopping.

(720 ILCS 570/314.5)

85. **A, B and D**
A: Patient's name and address
B: Patient's gender
D: NDC number of the controlled substance dispensed

EXPLANATION:

Review "Prescription Monitoring Program" under Section 17: IL Controlled Substances Act. The following information must be included in the report to the IL Prescription Monitoring Program:
1. Patient's name and address.
2. Patient's date of birth and gender.
3. National drug code (NDC) number of the controlled substance dispensed.
4. Date of dispensing.
5. Quantity dispensed and days supply.
6. Dispenser's Drug Enforcement Administration (DEA) registration number.
7. Prescriber's DEA number.
8. Dates the controlled substance is filled.
9. Payment type used to purchase (i.e. Medicaid, cash, third-party insurance).
10. Patient's location code (i.e. home, nursing home, outpatient, etc.) for the controlled substance other than those filled at a retail pharmacy.

(720 ILCS 570/316 & 318)

86. **A, B and D**
A: A long-term care facility makes an inpatient controlled substance order
B: Controlled substance administered via infusion at home
D: Medication dispensed from an emergency room

EXPLANATION:

Review "Prescription Monitoring Program" under Section 17: IL Controlled Substances Act. The following are exemptions from reporting controlled substance dispensing to the PMP:
- Inpatient drug orders (i.e. hospital, long-term care facility).
- Medications dispensed from a hospital emergency room or for discharging (if the quantity of the discharging medication is more than 72-hour supply, reporting is required).
- Controlled substances administered in narcotic treatment program.
- Controlled substances administered via infusion at home, in hospital or long-term care.

(720 ILCS 570/316 & 318)

87. **C.** Class 4 felony and fine of $100,000 or less

EXPLANATION:

Review "Unauthorized Possession of a Prescription Form" under Section 17: IL Controlled Substances Act.

The sentence for unauthorized possession of a prescription form is a Class 4 felony and fine of $100,000 or less.

(720 ILCS 570/406.2)

88. **E.** Both A and D
    A: If a person knowingly alters a properly issued prescription form
    D: If a person knowingly possesses a prescription form that's issued by a physical therapist

    EXPLANATION:
    Review "Unauthorized Possession of a Prescription Form" under Section 17: IL Controlled Substances Act.
    Anyone who commits the offense of an unauthorized possession of a prescription form when they knowingly do the following:
    1. Change a properly issued prescription form.
    2. Possesses a blank prescription form without authorization or possesses a counterfeit prescription form; or
    3. Possesses a prescription form that is not issued by a licensed prescriber.
    In answer D, physical therapist is not a prescriber; therefore, he or she does not have tha authority to issue prescription.

    (720 ILCS 570/406.2)

89. **B.** No, because the controlled substance cannot re-enter a closed system of distribution

    EXPLANATION:
    Review "Registration Required for Manufacturing, Distribution & Dispensing" under Section 17: IL Controlled Substances Act.
    Controlled substances belong in a closed system of distribution that is tracked through registration and scheduling. Once a scheduled drug leaves the close system, it cannot re-enter the closed system of distribution. If a patient does not need the controlled substance any more, he or she is not required to bring to authorized collector or to law enforcement for destruction. The person is permitted to destroy it his or herself.

90. **C.** Prescribing psychologist

    EXPLANATION:
    Review "Prescribers" under Definitions, "With Respect to Prescribing Psychologists" and "Agents and Employees: Affiliated Practitioners" under Section 17: IL Controlled Substances Act.
    A prescribing psychologist may have delegated authority to prescribe non-narcotic C-III through V controlled substances by a collaborating physician, but not C-II. Prescribers with

dispenser license for controlled substances and prescribers, who practice in a health care entity that's licensed as institutional practitioner, may prescribe C-II controlled substances.

(720 ILCS 570/102), (77 IL ADC Section 3100.80) & (77 IL ADC Section 3100.85)

91. **A.** A physician who issues a prescription of Vyvanse for himself, given that he has appropriate record of the diagnosis for his back pain

    EXPLANATION:
    Review "Issuance of a Prescription" under Section 17: IL Controlled Substances Act.
    A practitioner cannot self-prescribe or self-dispense (for example, self-administer) controlled substances. A practitioner may not prescribe controlled substances to an immediate family member unless there is a bona fide practitioner-patient relationship, and appropriate record are maintained for all treatment of the family member.

    (77 IL ADC Section 3100.380)

92. **A.** Schedule II

    EXPLANATION:
    Review "Schedule II Drug Prescriptions" under Section 17: IL Controlled Substances Act.
    General rule is that C-II prescriptions are not refillable.
    (720 ILCS 570/309)

93. **D.** 90 days

    EXPLANATION:
    Review "Schedule II Drug Prescriptions" under Section 17: IL Controlled Substances Act.
    Under the new IL law, a prescription for C-II is valid up to 90 days. The old IL law was 7 days.

    (720 ILCS 570/312)

94. **A.** Do not fill the prescription, because for the prescription to be valid, it needs to be dated as of and signed on the day it's issued.

    EXPLANATION:
    Review "Schedule II Drug Prescriptions" under Section 17: IL Controlled Substances Act.
    Federal law and IL law prohibit prescriptions with post-dating. A pharmacy cannot accept this prescription.

95. **A.** 30 days

    EXPLANATION:
    Review "Schedule II Drug Prescriptions" under Section 17: IL Controlled Substances Act.

C-II prescription can only be issued for a 30-day supply or less, and can be valid for up to 90 days after the date of issuance, except when a physician issues multiple prescriptions (sequential 30-day supplies). For instance, if a prescription has a total of 3 sequential 30-day supplies, the pharmacist may dispense a maximum of 90-day-supply if based on his or her professional judgment, it is appropriate to do so.

(720 ILCS 570/312)

96. **C and D**
    C: The PA and APN must provide 45 contact hours in pharmacology
    D: The PA and APN must complete at least 5 hours of CE

    EXPLANATION:
    Review "With Respect to PA & APN" under Section 17: IL Controlled Substances Act.
    A. Administration of C-II controlled substances in oral, topical, transdermal or injection route. (Administration of C-II controlled substances in oral, topical, or transdermal)
    B. Prescriptions are limited to 90-day supply or less. (30-day supply or less)
    E. Prescriptions are limited to 60-day supply (30-day supply or less)

    (720 ILCS 570/303.05)

97. **A, B and D**
    A: Patient's name
    B: Add a date on the prescription
    D. Change the name

    EXPLANATION:
    Review "Schedule II Drug Prescriptions" under Section 17: IL Controlled Substances Act.
    A pharmacist may not change the following components of a C-II prescription:
    1. Date written, or add the date.
    2. Name of the patient.
    3. Name of the prescriber, or add a signature; <u>and</u>
    4. Name of the drug.
    (77 IL ADC Section 3100.400)

98. **C. Nandrolone**

    EXPLANATION:
    Nandrolone is the only controlled substance that is Scheduled III. Fluticasone and hydrocortisone are both steroid agents and are not controlled substances. See https://www.deadiversion.usdoj.gov/schedules/ for a comprehensive list of controlled substances.

99. **B. II**

II: The resident may prescribe as permitted by state law, and he or she is acting within the scope of his or her employment under the hospital DEA number.

EXPLANATION:
Review "Agents and Employees: Affiliated Practitioners" under Section 17: IL Controlled Substances Act.
Employee practitioners (i.e. physician resident), nurses, and pharmacists have the authority to possess, administer, prescribe, and dispense controlled substances under the DEA registration number of the hospital.

(77 IL ADC Section 3100.80)

100. **B.** Yes, refill the prescription this time, but counsel the patient that he must seek a new physician as soon as possible.

EXPLANATION:
If a prescriber has deceased, the prescription is no longer valid. According to the DFPR, when a pharmacist becomes aware that a physician is no long treating the patient, he or she should counsel and inform the patient of the need to seek a new doctor as soon as possible. The pharmacist may use his or her professional judgment to provide a sufficient amount of maintenance medications until the patient finds a new doctor. Answer E may be appropriate, but answer B is the most appropriate choice.

101. **A.** No, only a dispenser registration is required for compounding of a controlled substance that is in accordance to a valid prescription.

EXPLANATION:
Review "Separate Registration for Independent Activities" under Section 17: IL Controlled Substances Act.
Only a dispenser registration is required if a controlled drug is compounded by prescription. A separate manufacturer registration is required if compounding is not in accordance to a written prescription order and is for office use only.

(77 IL ADC Section 3100.50)

102. **B.** I and II
I: Purchasing of controlled drugs for the purpose of repackaging for sale without a prescription
II: Mixing, preparing and packaging of C-II through C-V narcotic for detoxification

EXPLANATION:
Review "Separate Registration for Independent Activities" under Section 17: IL Controlled Substances Act.
Purchasing of controlled drugs to repackage them for sale without a prescription and compounding controlled substances for use in narcotic treatment program are considered independent activities, and therefore they will require separate registrations. With a

dispenser registration, Walnut pharmacy may compound controlled substances with prescriptions; manufacturer registration is not required.

(77 IL ADC Section 3100.50)

103. **E.** Reporting of theft or loss is not required for Sudafed

EXPLANATION:
Review "Record and Inventory Requirements Generally" under Section 17: IL Controlled Substances Act.
Even though Illinois classifies pseudoephedrine as a controlled substance, it is not classified as such on the federal level. Thus, filling out a DEA form 106 is not required.

(77 IL ADC Section 3100.360)

104. **D.** III and I
　　I: Demerol tablet
　　III: Secobarbital capsule

EXPLANATION:
Review "Findings Required for Inclusion in Schedule II" and "Findings Required for Inclusion in Schedule IV" under Section 17: IL Controlled Substances Act. See https://www.deadiversion.usdoj.gov/schedules/ for a comprehensive list of controlled substances.
Both Demerol tablet and Secobarbital capsule are C-II controlled substances. Phenobarbital tablet is a C-IV drug.

(720 ILCS 570/205 & 206) & (720 ILCS 570/209 & 210)

105. **A.** I
　　I: Modafinil tablet

EXPLANATION:
Review "Procedures for Transferor Pharmacy" under Section 10: General Provision.
A prescription for Schedule III, IV and V drugs may be transferred only from the original pharmacy and only one time if RxPharmacy does not share a real-time online computerized system with CVS. Modafinil is C-IV whereas pentobarbital and acetaminophen w/hydrocodone are C-II controlled substances. If two or more pharmacies share a real-time online computerized system (i.e. CVS pharmacy stores), then it is not considered a transfer and therefore, there would be no limit to the number of transaction.

(68 IL ADC Section 1330.720)

106. **E.** I, II and III
　　I: Levothroid

II: Klonopin
III: Augmentin

EXPLANATION:
Review "Procedures for Transferor Pharmacy" under Section 10: General Provision.
Per federal law, it is okay to transfer for a refill dispensing only (thus NO original or first time fill can be done), but the federal specifies to go with the state laws if they will allow the transfer - https://www.deadiversion.usdoj.gov/21cfr/cfr/1306/1306_25.htm. IL law permits transferring for an original fill or refill dispensing of controlled substances, "a prescription for Schedule III, IV and V drugs may be transferred only from the original pharmacy and only one time for the purpose of original fill or refill dispensing and may not be transferred further."

(68 IL ADC Section 1330.720)

107. **A.** I
I: A product that contains 200 mg or less of codeine per 100 mL or per 100 mg is a C-V drug and can be purchase without a prescription

EXPLANATION:
Review "Findings Required for Inclusion in Schedule V" and "Schedule III-V Drug Prescriptions" under Section 17: IL Controlled Substances Act.
The patient must be older than 21 years old with 2 positive documents of identification.

(720 ILCS 570/212) & (720 ILCS 570/312)

108. **A, B and C**
A: The full name of the owner
B: The species or common name of the animal being treated
C. DEA of the prescriber
EXPLANATION:
Review "Requirements for Dispensing Controlled Substances" under Section 17: IL Controlled Substances Act.
Ketamine is a C-III controlled substance. An animal prescription for a controlled substance needs to state the species of the animal or the animal's common name as well as the owner's full name and address on the prescription. Pharmacists who fill the prescription need to write the date of filling and their signature on the face of the prescription.

720 ILCS 570/312

109. **E.** Empirin

EXPLANATION:
Review "Findings Required for Inclusion in Schedule III" under Section 17: IL Controlled Substances Act. See https://www.deadiversion.usdoj.gov/schedules/ for a comprehensive list of controlled substances.

Empirin is the brand name of aspirin and is not a controlled substance. Do not mistaken Empirin with Empirin #3® and Empirin #4®, which are C-III controlled substances that contain aspirin with codeine.

110. **D.** Call TJ's doctor and ask if it is ok to fill quantity of 90

    EXPLANATION:
    Review "Refusal, Revocation, or Suspension" under Section 17: IL Controlled Substances Act. As a pharmacist, you must exercise sound professional judgment when dispensing a prescription drug order. In this case, you learned that TJ has a history of suicidal behaviors. And fluoxetine has a black box warning for increasing risk of suicidal thinking and behavior in children, adolescents, and young adults. Although, there's no law that prohibits combining this prescription order, when he requested for a higher quantity of refill, you must call his prescriber and ask if's ok to fill a quantity of 90.

    (68 IL ADC Section 1330.30)

111. **C.** III

    III: Most frequently used medications

    EXPLANATION:
    Review "After-hour cabinets" under Section 13: Types of Pharmacies.
    After-hour cabinet is a locked cabinet located outside of the pharmacy area containing a minimal supply of the most frequently required medication.
    (68 IL ADC Section1330.520)

112. **B.** II

    II: Unit dose package of Ritalin tablets

    EXPLANATION:
    Review "Stocking or Restocking Medications" under Section 14: Pharmacy Standards.
    All medications stored in the systems must be packaged as a unit of use for single patient (e.g., unit dose tab/cap, tube of ointment, inhaler, etc.) and labeled properly as indicated in the labeling requirements for sterile solutions with/without added drug or diluent, and non-parenterals repackaged for future use.

    (68 IL ADC Section1330.680)

113. **A and C**

    A: Name or initial of the pharmacist
    C: Name or initial of the pharmacy technician that filled or refilled the prescription

    EXPLANATION:
    Review "Community Pharmacy Services – Recordkeeping Requirements for Dispensing Prescriptions Drugs" under Section 13: Types of Pharmacies.

For every prescription dispensed, the prescription record must contain the (1) name, (2) initials or (3) other unique identifier of the pharmacist who dispenses the prescription drugs. If the pharmacy technician dispenses the prescription, then the name, initial or the unique identifier of both the pharmacist and the pharmacy technician must be included on the prescription record.

(68 IL ADC Section1330.500)

114. **E.** I and III
    I: A registered pharmacy technician
    III: A licensed pharmacist

    EXPLANATION:
    Whether it's a community pharmacy, or onsite or offsite institutional pharmacy, when the pharmacy is closed, the public and any employees who are not registered, are not allowed to have access to the filling and dispensing area.

115. **D.** A and B
    A: The conviction has been more than 10 years ago
    B: The person has been convicted with armed robbery with no other forcible felonies

    EXPLANATION:
    Review "Pharmacist license for Previously Convicted First-Time Applicant or License Permanently Revoke or Denied" under Section 8: Pharmacist.
    A pharmacist or other healthcare worker who was permanently revoked or denied due to a forcible felony (i.e. first or second degree murder, robbery, kidnapping a child, armed violence, etc.) may file a Petition for Review that's available on the Department's website if the conviction date has been more than 5 years ago.

116. **C and D**
    C: patient and his or her prescriber are located in unusual distance from your pharmacy
    D: Patients who come in groups with prescriptions for the same controlled substance

    EXPLANATION:
    Review "What is the Pharmacist's Role in Drug Diversion or Abuse Prevention?" under Section 13: Types of Pharmacies.
    A. A patient who comes in with multiple prescription orders that consist of oxycodone, lisinopril and carisoprolol (Drug cocktail consists of hydrocodone, alprazolam and carisoprodol, or hydrocodone is replaced by oxycodone in this group of medications)
    B. A patient who has multiple prescribers who specialize in neurology, dermatology, and podiatry. (Multiple prescribers for the same medication, possible doctor or medication shopping)

117. **C.** Yes, as long as Brook displays a sign to notify customers that a pharmacist is not available to provide pharmacy services.

EXPLANATION:
Review "Community Pharmacy Services – Staffing of the Pharmacy" under Section 13: Types of Pharmacies.
A sign must be conspicuously displayed of (1) the pharmacy's schedule of services whenever the hours of the pharmacy are different from those of the establishment where the pharmacy is located, <u>and</u> (2) message regarding the unavailability of a pharmacist to provide pharmacy services when the pharmacy is open.

(68 IL ADC Section1330.500)

118. **D.** No, the prescription for carvedilol is not within the ordinary course of the podiatrist's professional practice.

EXPLANATION:
A podiatrist specializes in diagnosing and treating conditions of the foot, ankle, and related structures of the leg. Carvedilol is used for the treatment of high blood pressure in this case, and therefore is not within the ordinary course of the podiatrist's professional practices.

119. **E.** A, B and C
    A: Pharmacist's name and address
    B: Patient's name
    C: Cautionary statements

EXPLANATION:
Review "The Container Label for Controlled Substances" under Section 17: IL Controlled Substances Act. See https://www.deadiversion.usdoj.gov/schedules/ for a comprehensive list of controlled substances.
Androderm is a C-III controlled substance. Whenever a pharmacist dispenses any controlled substances, except a non-prescription Schedule V product or non-prescription methamphetamine precursor, he or she must affix to the container (1) a label indicating date of initial fill, (2) pharmacist's name and address, (3) patient name, (4) prescriber name, (5) directions for use, cautionary statements, dosage and quantity, <u>and</u> (6) drug name.

(720 ILCS 570/312)

120. **E.** I, II and III
    I: If the prescription order is written, the physician must sign in ink with a pen, typewriter or computer printer or with an indelible pen.
    II: If the prescription order is electronically transmitted, the physician must sign with electronic or handwritten signature, initial or thumb print.
    III: If the prescription order is issued orally, it must be reduced in writing.

EXPLANATION:

Review "Requirements for Dispensing Controlled Substances" under Section 17: IL Controlled Substances Act.

(720 ILCS 570/312) & (77 IL ADC Section 3100.400)

121. **A.** No, Dan's license has expired, he is considered unlicensed and cannot practice.

    EXPLANATION:
    Review "Expiration of License/Certificate" under Section 10: General Provision.
    The registrant is responsible to notify the Division of any change of address, because failure to receive a renewal form is not considered as an excuse for failure to pay the renewal fee. If the person practices on an expired license or certificate, he or she has committed unlicensed practice and is subject to discipline.

    (68 IL ADC Section 1330.80)

122. **C.** Yes, this prescription is issued for a Schedule III controlled substance; in IL, it may be filled up to 6 months from the date of issuance.

    EXPLANATION:
    Review "Schedule III-V Drug Prescriptions" under Section 17: IL Controlled Substances Act. Acetaminophen 300 mg with 60 mg codeine is a C-III controlled substance. A prescription for Schedule III, IV or V controlled substance can only be filled within 6 months after the issued date, and can only be refilled 5 times or less.

    (720 ILCS 570/312)

123. **C.** No, a prescription for C-II drug is not refillable

    EXPLANATION:
    Calculation:
    a) Determine the amount of codeine in 100 mL of cherry syrup:
        2 g codeine ÷ 200 mL cherry syrup = 1 g in 100 mL of cherry syrup
    b) Determine the amount of codeine per dose
        1 tsp = 5 mL; 2 tsp = 10 mL; 1 dose = 2 tsp
        1 g = 1000 mg in 100 mL
        1000 mg/100 mL = x/10 mL
        x = 100 mg in 10 mL or 2 tsp
    Because there are 100 mg of codeine per dose, this is a C-II drug. C-II is not refillable.

124. **D.** None, the CE requirement is waived for the first renewal period

    EXPLANATION:
    Review "Continuing Education" under Section 8: Pharmacist.

    (68 IL ADC Section 1330.100)

125. **C.** No, the full name of the owner is required.

EXPLANATION:
Review "Requirements for Dispensing Controlled Substances" under Section 17: IL Controlled Substances Act.
An animal prescription for a controlled substance needs to state the species of the animal or the animal's common name as well as the owner's full name and address on the prescription. Pharmacists who fill the prescription need to write the date of filling and their signature on the face of the prescription.

IL Pharmacy Law Bonus Questions

Objectives
- This is a 30-question bonus question exam that mimics the IL pharmacy portion of the MPJE exam. Use these questions as a supplement to test your self-study learning and go back to review questions missed.
- You will notice these questions are random and may not be found in the IL law statutes. This has been done to give an actual feel for the IL MPJE examination.
- Answers can be reviewed after the IL pharmacy law bonus question section.

1. Which drug does not require a prescription? Select all that apply.
    A. Zegerid
    B. Zantac 150
    C. Nexium 24HR
    D. Prevacid 24HR
    E. R and N Insulin

2. Which drug strength(s) is/are available as OTC?
    A. Omeprazole/sodium bicarbonate 40 mg
    B. Zegerid 20 mg
    C. Humulin R U-500
    D. Both A and B
    E. Both B and C

3. The label of a repackaged OTC product must contain the following information: (Select all that apply)
    A. Adequate directions for safe and effective use
    B. BUD (Beyond Use Date)
    C. Active and inactive ingredients
    D. Name and address of the manufacturer
    E. Instructions for safe storage

4. A prescription for medical oxygen is good for:
    A. 30 days
    B. 90 days
    C. 6 months
    D. 12 months
    E. Lifetime

5. A prescription drug label must contain the following information: (Select all that apply)
    A. Adequate directions for safe and effective use
    B. Adequate directions for use
    C. A "Caution: Federal law prohibits dispensing without a prescription" statement
    D. "Rx Only"
    E. NDC number

6. Responsibilities of the PIC include:
    A. Provide and deliver drugs for in-patient care
    B. Supervise pharmaceutical care
    C. Participate in the Drug Formulary Committee
    D. Both A and B
    E. Both B and C

7. The following does/do not violate HIPAA: (Select all that apply)
    A. A patient sees another patient's name on the sign-in sheet
    B. A customer overheard a pharmacist's counseling a patient at the pharmacy counter
    C. Pharmacist shares information of a patient with another healthcare provider
    D. A pharmacist provides patient's personal information to his or her healthcare provider
    E. None of the above

8. Which of the following is/are example(s) of drug adulteration? Select all that apply.
    A. A community pharmacy that has a fire in its pharmacy, but the fire does not affect the area where all the medications are
    B. A prescription drug is dispensed without a prescription
    C. A compounded drug's dosage strength is shown to be less than its prescribed dosage strength
    D. A tablet of amlodipine is dropped on the floor
    E. A label affixed on the drug bottle that states a lower dose per tablet than the actual dose of a tablet in the bottle

9. A prescription for methadone that is prescribed by a physician who's employed by a narcotic treatment program:
    A. May be filled in most community pharmacies
    B. May be filled in a community pharmacy only if the prescriber is permitted to treat outpatients with addiction providing that he or she has a DEA number that confirms that
    C. May not be filled in a community pharmacy
    D. May only be filled in an outpatient health facility pharmacy
    E. None of the above

10. Which of the following statements regarding narcotics treatment program is true?
    A. A practitioner who is not part of the narcotic treatment program may prescribe narcotic substances to an addicted individual to relieve the acute withdrawal symptoms for a maximum of three days
    B. A practitioner who is not part of the narcotic treatment program may administer narcotic substances to an addicted individual to relieve the acute withdrawal symptoms for a maximum of three days
    C. A practitioner who is not part of the narcotic treatment program may administer one narcotic substance treatment to an addicted individual to relieve the acute withdrawal symptoms for one day at a time.
    D. Both A and B
    E. Both B and C

11. Which of the following statement regarding buprenorphine use in detoxification treatment is correct?
    A. A physician may only administer buprenorphine for "in office use" provided that he/she has a DEA registration for C-III through C-V
    B. A physician may prescribe, dispense or prescribe buprenorphine in office-based settings if he/she has a valid DEA number for C-III through C-V
    C. A physician must obtain a separate DEA registration for opioid treatment program in order to dispense or prescribe buprenorphine
    D. Both B and C
    E. None of the above

12. A prescriber requests to purchase APAP/Codeine for office use. Which of the following statement is true?
    A. The prescriber must complete a DEA form 222 and send it to the pharmacy
    B. The prescriber cannot make this purchase for office use
    C. The prescriber must provide a prescription to the patient and disclose to the patient a right to have the prescription filled elsewhere before dispensing
    D. Both A and C
    E. None of the above

13. When must a new scheduled drug be inventoried?
    A. On the same day the drug's new schedule is effective
    B. No later than 48 hours
    C. No later than 72 hours
    D. Within 6 months
    E. Within 12 months

14. Which of the following statements regarding reverse distributors is/are true?
    A. Reverse distributors are permitted to be authorized collectors of controlled substances
    B. The first letter of DEA number for a reverse distributor is G
    C. A reverse distributor must file DEA form 222 for C-II controlled substances that are taken back from the pharmacy for disposal purposes
    D. Both A and B
    E. Both A and C

15. What types of record can be stored at centralized pharmacy location?
    A. Invoices of all legend drugs
    B. Inventory records
    C. Controlled substances prescription records
    D. Both A and B
    E. A, B, and C

16. Patient package insert for an estrogen drug product must contain which of following information? Select all that apply.
    A. The name and place of business of the manufacturer, pack, or distributor
    B. The name of the drug
    C. A statement regarding the benefits and proper uses of estrogens
    D. The contraindications for use
    E. A description of the most serious risks associated with the use of estrogen

17. A patient comes in your pharmacy with a prescription for hydrocodone/APAP. However, your pharmacy is out of the generic medication. The patient now prefers to have the brand name instead since that's what your pharmacy has in stock? Note that on the prescription, the physician does not indicate whether the medication is or is not substitutable. What should you do?
    A. Dispense the brand name medication
    B. Inform the patient that you cannot fill the prescription until the generic is in stock again
    C. Call the physician to ask if it's ok to dispense the brand name medication
    D. Call the patient's insurance to check if the brand name medication is covered before dispensing
    E. None of the above

18. Who can make a request for non-child resistant packaging?
    I. Pharmacist
    II. Physician
    III. Patient

    A. I
    B. I and II
    C. II and III
    D. III and I
    E. I, II and III

19. Which of the following regarding patient counseling is correct?
    A. Illinois requires that patient counseling on all new and refill prescriptions
    B. If patient counseling is refused, the pharmacist does not need to document that in the pharmacy's records
    C. Mail order prescriptions do not require patient counseling
    D. A pharmacist is not required to counsel when drugs are not dispensed
    E. Both A and D

20. A new Rx drug is delivered to a bed-ridden patient. How can a pharmacist offer patient counseling this situation?
    A. Call the patient to offer patient counseling after the drug is delivered
    B. Ask the delivery person to offer patient counseling to the patient or patient's representative
    C. Write a note to the patient that you may contact him or her for consultation in person at the pharmacy or by toll-free phone number, and put the note in an envelope to have it delivered to the patient with the medication
    D. Have a pharmacy technician call to ask the patient's representative to come to the pharmacy store for patient counseling
    E. None of the above

21. Which of the following individual have authorization to access the emergency kit?
    A. Registered nurse
    B. Advance nurse practitioner
    C. Nurses who's authorized for that purpose
    D. A and B
    E. A, B and C

22. Which of the following statements regarding emergency kit is/are true?
    A. Entries should be made on the proof-of-use sheet by the nursing staff or practitioner when any controlled substances from the kit are used
    B. A proof-of-use sheet must be placed on the emergency medication kit
    C. If the emergency medication kit is opened, the pharmacist should be notified within 24 hours
    D. Both A and B
    E. Both A and C

23. Which of the following statements regarding automated dispensing system in LTCF is correct?
    A. The automated dispensing system is overseen by the PIC
    B. LTCF has the responsibility to oversee the automated dispensing system
    C. Medications in the automated dispensing system belong to the LTCF's inventory
    D. Both A and B
    E. Both A and C

24. Pharmacist receives a discipline under which of the following circumstances? (Select all that apply)
    A. Not reporting to the Department when he or she is relocating to another pharmacy for the summer
    B. Refuse to perform patient counseling to a patient when a new drug is dispensed
    C. Refuse to perform patient counseling to a patient when a refill is dispensed
    D. Refuse to fill a controlled substance prescription he or she thinks is drug abuse
    E. B and C

25. If there's a technical issue with remote automated dispensing system:
    A. The pharmacy technician should manually retrieve prescriptions on file
    B. The pharmacist asks the pharmacy technicians to record everything manually until the problem is fixed
    C. The pharmacist should come to the site and stay there until the problem is fixed
    D. Both B and C
    E. A, B and C

26. How long a pharmacy license is good for how long?
    A. 1 year
    B. 2 years
    C. 4 years
    D. Until the PIC dies or leaves the pharmacy, then it s good for 30 days
    E. None of the above

27. A 16-year-old female patient who comes into the pharmacy to purchase Plan B One Step without a prescription. What should a pharmacist do?
    A. Only sell if the patient has an ID
    B. Inform her that she needs to have her parents here in order for her to buy
    C. Sell the Plan B as requested
    D. Refuse to sell
    E. None of the above

28. A female patient comes to your pharmacy and asks to purchase Plan B One Step, but you are out of stock for Plan B, she asks for a substitution. What will you tell her?
    A. Tell her that Plan B is the only choice she has
    B. Tell her that Plan B does not have a generic medication
    C. Tell her that you can substitute Plan B with Levororgestrel that goes by a different brand name
    D. Both A and B
    E. Both B and C

29. Which of the following statements regarding tamper evident packaging is true?
    A. OTC products must be packaged in tamper-evident package and properly labeled
    B. The retail package must contain a statement that identifies featured prominently placed on the packaged and in a way that it will not be affected if the tamper-evident feature is missing
    C. OTC drug products must have at least two barriers to entry
    D. Both A and B
    E. A, B, and C

30. If a pharmacist works in two different pharmacy locations of the same the owner:
    A. He or she can print a copy of his or her original license and keep the copy at the second location
    B. He or she can carry the wallet copy of the license to the second location, keep the original license at the first location
    C. Apply to the Department for another license to practice at the second location
    D. Both A and C
    E. Both B and C

IL Pharmacy Law Bonus Question Explanations

1. **A, B, C, D, and E.**

   <u>EXPLANATION:</u>
   All of these products are now over the counter medications, you may buy without a prescription. The formulations of the 20 mg OTC capsules (Nexium® 24HR) and the prescription 20mg capsules (NEXIUM®) contain the same active ingredient, esomeprazole, although there are differences in indications and directions for use. The 20 mg NEXIUM® capsule will continue to be available by prescription. Other dosages of NEXIUM® will continue to be available by prescription only. Nexium® 24HR is indicated for adults (18 years and older) with frequent heartburn — when you have heartburn two or more days a week — whereas prescription NEXIUM® is indicated for many acid-related conditions.

   Both While Prevacid®24HR and Prilosec OTC® are both OTC PPIs, they contain different active ingredients. Prevacid®24HR is the only PPI approved for OTC treatment of frequent heartburn that contains the active ingredient lansoprazole. Prilosec OTC®, like some store brand OTC PPIs, contains omeprazole magnesium. Prevacid®24HR is the first and only OTC PPI for the treatment of frequent heartburn approved in its original formulation.

   Both prescription Zegerid® and Zegerid OTC® contain the same active ingredients, omeprazole and sodium bicarbonate. The differences between them are the dosage strengths and indications. Zegerid OTC® is available in 20 mg dosage strength and indicated for frequent heartburn. Prescription Zegerid® is available as both 20 mg and 40 mg dosage strengths and indicated for conditions that require a doctor's diagnosis and treatment.

   Both generic name of Zantac 150® contain the same active ingredient ranitidine. However, both have different indication, OTC Zantac 150 is indicated for GERD whereas prescription Zantac 150 is indicated for antacids.

   For insulin, see table below for a list of Rx and OTC insulin drugs

Insulin	Brand	Rx/OTC
Insulin Aspart	Novolog	Rx
Insulin Aspart Protamine/Insulin Aspart	Novolog Mix 70/30	Rx
Insulin Detemir	Levemir	Rx
Insulin Glargine	Basaglar	Rx
	Lantus	Rx
	Toujeo	Rx
Insulin Glulisine	Apidra	Rx
Insulin Lispro	Humalog	Rx
Insulin Lispro Protamine/Insulin Lispro	Humalog Mix 75/25	Rx
	Humalog Mix 50/50	Rx
Insulin Injection	Humulin R U-100	OTC

Regular (R)	Humulin R U-500	Rx
	Novolin R	OTC
Insulin Isophane Suspension (NPH)/Regular Insulin (R)	Humulin 70/30	OTC
	Novolin 70/30	OTC
Insulin Isophane Suspension (NPH)	Humulin N	OTC
	Novolin N	OTC
Oral Inhalation Insulin	Afrezza	Rx

2. **B.** Zegerid 20 mg

   EXPLANATION:
   A. Omeprazole/sodium bicarbonate 40 mg. (Omeprazole/sodium bicarbonate is available OTC with dosage strength 20 mg not 40 mg)
   B. Zegerid 20 mg. (The generic drug is Omeprazole/sodium bicarbonate 20 mg is available OTC)
   C. Humulin R U-500. (Humulin R U-100 is available OTC not the Humulin R U-500; see insulin table in question 1 answer)

3. **A, B, C, D and E**

   EXPLANATION:
   The label of repackaged OTC products must contain the following information:
   - Name of the product and its drug class
   - BUD (Beyond Use Date)
   - Net contents of the product by weight or numerical count
   - Name of all active ingredients, as well as the quantity of active and certain inactive ingredients
   - Name of any habit-forming drugs in the product
   - Adequate directions for safe and effective use
   - Instructions for safe storage
   - Cautions and warnings statement for consumer protection
   - Name and address of the manufacturer, distributor, or packer

   Note: Hospital repackaged label for use in the hospital is not the same as the repackaged OTC label.

4. **E.** Lifetime

   EXPLANATION:
   In general prescriptions for CPAP and Oxygen therapy are valid for life. Prescriptions can be written by any of the following licensed professionals: MD (medical doctor), PCP (Primary Care Physician), Psychiatrist, Dentist, Doctor of Osteopathy, Physician's Assistant, Nurse Practitioner, or Naturopathic Physician. Prescriptions from Chiropractors, Optometrists, Podiatrists, and Psychologists are not acceptable unless the prescriber is also a licensed MD or DO.

5. **B, C and D**
   B: Adequate directions for use
   C: A "Caution: Federal law prohibits dispensing without a prescription" statement
   D: "Rx Only"

   EXPLANATION:
   Review "Prescription Label" under Section 11: Prescription Order.
   Prescription drugs cannot be made safe by including adequate directions for use; therefore, they may only be obtained lawfully through a prescription. "Adequate directions for safe and effective use" is only applicable to OTC medications since they do not require prescriptions. Only OTC medications required NDC number on their labels. If the question specifically asks about a prescription drug label affixed to the bottle for dispensing, then "Rx Only" phrase is not applicable.

   (225 ILCS 85/22: Section scheduled to be repealed on January 1, 2018)

6. **B.** Supervise pharmaceutical care

   EXPLANATION:
   Review "PIC" under Section 14: Pharmacy Standards.
   - Supervision of all employees' activities related to the practice of pharmacy.
   - Establishment and supervision of the method for storage and safekeeping of pharmaceuticals, including security maintenance used when the pharmacy is closed and
   - Establishment and supervision of the recordkeeping system for the purchase, sale, delivery, possession, storage and safekeeping of drugs.

   (68 IL ADC Section1330.660)

7. **D.** A pharmacist provides patient's personal information to his or her healthcare provide

   EXPLANATION:
   Review "Protected Health Information (PHI)" under Section Definitions: Pharmacy Practice Act 225 ILCS 85/3 and
   https://www.hhs.gov/sites/default/files/ocr/privacy/hipaa/understanding/summary/privacysummary.pdf
   HIPAA requires that PHI be maintained and used by healthcare providers, health plans, and other covered entities, or a person/entity need the information to perform those services, unless patient authorization is obtained for treatment, payment, and healthcare operation purposes.

   (225 ILCS 85/3: Section scheduled to be repealed on January 1, 2018)

8. **A, C, and D**
   A: A community pharmacy that has a fire in its pharmacy, but the fire does not affect the area where all the medications are
   C: A compounded drug's dosage strength is shown to be less than its prescribed dosage strength
   D: A tablet of amlodipine is dropped on the floor

   EXPLANATION:
   Review "Adulterated Drugs" from the following FDA website
   https://www.fda.gov/ICECI/ComplianceManuals/CompliancePolicyGuidanceManual/ucm074367.htm l"
   A. A community pharmacy that has a fire in its pharmacy, but the fire does not affect the area where all the medications are. (Even though the fire hasn't reached the area where all the medications are, but the smoke and heat could have had altered the drugs' chemistry. Remember always stay on the safe side, we must consider all drugs adulterated)
   C. A compounded drug's dosage strength is shown to be less than its prescribed dosage strength. (A drug is considered adulterated if its strength or quality or purity falls below compendium standards)
   D. A tablet of amlodipine is dropped on the floor. (The meaning of adulteration is contamination)

9. **C.** May not be filled a community pharmacy

   EXPLANATION:
   Review "Methadone" under Section 5: Federal Controlled Substances Law.
   Methadone is not valid through the typical retail pharmacy distribution channels for the purposes of detoxification or maintenance therapy for drug addiction.

10. **B.** A practitioner who is not part of the narcotic treatment program may administer narcotic substances to an addicted individual to relieve the acute withdrawal symptoms for a maximum of three days

    EXPLANATION:
    The individual must receive the narcotics at a registered narcotic treatment program. As a result, methadone may be dispensed or administered but not prescribed.

11. **B.** A physician may prescribe, dispense or prescribe buprenorphine in office-based settings if he/she has a valid DEA number for C-III through C-V

    EXPLANATION:
    Review "Subutex and Suboxone Approved to Treat Opiate Dependence" from the following FDA website https://www.fda.gov/Drugs/DrugSafety/ucm191521.htm
    In October, 2002, buprenorphine is approved by the FDA approved two new buprenorphine drug products (Subutex and Suboxone) to treat opiate dependence.

12. **C.** The prescriber must write a prescription for APAP/Codeine and must write "for office use" on the script

EXPLANATION:
In-office dispensing programs are often limited to certain categories of patients based on payer type for reimbursement. Typically, these are workers' compensation or personal injury patients, and exclude federal healthcare payers unless requirements are met.

Unlike with pharmacy licenses, which enable a pharmacy to dispense prescription drugs, most states allow physicians to purchase and dispense drugs under their physicians' licenses. Nevertheless, states will typically require the dispensing physician to satisfy various requirements, such as: providing a prescription to the patient; requiring a disclosure to the patient of the right to have the prescription filled elsewhere; requiring the physician to obtain additional permits; requiring that medications be labeled properly and dispensed or directly supervised by the physician; requiring secure storage of drug inventory; limiting controlled substance dispensing; and satisfying various pharmacy recordkeeping requirements.

Federal regulations set forth specific physical security controls for practitioners:
- Controlled substances shall be stored in a "securely locked, substantially constructed cabinet." The intent is that controlled substances must be adequately safeguarded for the area.
- Criminal background and DEA screening of all potential employees is critical.
- Practitioners are required to notify the DEA of the theft or significant loss of any controlled substances within one business day of discovery of the loss or theft. When determining whether a loss is significant, the practitioner is required to consider certain factors, including the quantity and type of controlled substances lost, and whether they are likely candidates for diversion, considering local trends and other indicators. We advise practitioners to report any loss to the DEA, in case the diverted drugs are traced back to the practitioner's office.
- Practitioners must maintain inventories and readily retrievable records of controlled substances dispensed in their practices, and the records must be maintained and available for inspection for at least two years. Practitioners are not required to keep records of controlled substances they prescribe, although some do. Practitioners also are not required to keep records of controlled substances administered in their practices unless the dispensing or administering of controlled substances is a regular part of their practice and the patient is charged for the drug.

13. **A.** On the same day the drug's new schedule is effective

    EXPLANATION:
    Review "Inventory Requirements" at the following DEA website
    https://www.deadiversion.usdoj.gov/21cfr/cfr/1304/1304_11.htm

14. **E.** Both A and C
    A: Reverse distributors are permitted to be authorized collectors of controlled substances
    C: A reverse distributor must file DEA form 222 for C-II controlled substances that are taken back from the pharmacy for disposal purposes

EXPLANATION:
Review "C-II" under Section 5: Federal Controlled Substances Law
Letter "G" is for Department of Defense Practitioners. P/R are for Manufacturer/Distributor/Researcher/Analytical Lab/Importer/Exporter/Reverse Distributor/Narcotic Treatment Program.

15. **A.** Invoices of all legend drugs

EXPLANATION:
Review "Disposition of Legend Drugs on Cessation of Pharmacy Operation" under Section 7: Pharmacy.
Invoices of all legend drugs and inventory record are required to be kept for 5 years. Invoices can be maintained on site or at a central location where they are readily retrievable. If invoices are on site, they must be kept for at least one year from the date of the invoice.

(225 ILCS 85/17: *Section scheduled to be repealed on January 1, 2018)*

16. **A, B, C, D and E**
    A: The name and place of business of the manufacturer, pack, or distributor
    B: The name of the drug
    C: A statement regarding the benefits and proper uses of estrogens
    D: The contraindications for use
    E: A description of the most serious risks associated with the use of estrogen

EXPLANATION:
Review "Patient package inserts for estrogens" at the following FDA website
https://www.accessdata.fda.gov/scripts/cdrh/cfdocs/cfcfr/CFRSearch.cfm?fr=310.515
The following information should be on the patient package inserts for estrogens:
- The name of the drug.
- The name and place of business of the manufacturer, packer, or distributor.
- A statement regarding the benefits and proper uses of estrogens.
- The contraindications to use, i.e., when estrogens should not be used.
- A description of the most serious risks associated with the use of estrogens.
- A brief summary of other side effects of estrogens.
- Instructions on how a patient may reduce the risks of estrogen use.
- The date, identified as such, of the most recent revision of the patient package insert.

17. **C.** Call the physician to ask if it's ok to dispense the brand name medication

EXPLANATION:
Although the pharmacist may substitute brand name medication to generic medication without having to call the patient's physician, this prescription is for a controlled substance and a generic medication. You must use your professional judgment to make a decision whether to call the patient's doctor. In this case, you should call the doctor to make sure that it's ok to substitute to brand name.

18. **C.** II and III
    II: Physician
    III: Patient

    EXPLANATION:
    A physician may request that a prescribed medication not be dispensed in child-resistant closures, & this request will be honored as long as it is made for each prescription to which it applies (i.e., no "blanket requests"). However, patients may request that all dispensed drugs not be placed in child-resistant containers.
    http://www.cpsc.gov//PageFiles/113945/384.pdf

19. **E.** Both A and D
    A: Illinois requires that patient counseling on all new and refill prescriptions
    D: A pharmacist is not required to counsel when drugs are not dispensed

    EXPLANATION:
    Review "Patient Counseling" at the following website
    http://www.idfpr.com/forms/DPR/FAQPharmPatientCounseling.pdf

20. **C.** Write a note to the patient that you may contact him or her for consultation in person at the pharmacy or by toll-free phone number, and put the note in an envelope to have it delivered to the patient with the medication

    EXPLANATION:
    Review "Patient Counseling" at the following website
    http://www.idfpr.com/forms/DPR/FAQPharmPatientCounseling.pdf

21. **D.** A and B
    A: Registered nurse
    B: Advance nurse practitioner

    EXPLANATION:
    Nursing staff or practitioner are authorized to access emergency medication kits.

22. **E.** Both A and C
    A: should be made on the proof-of-use sheet by the nursing staff or practitioner when any controlled substances from the kit are used
    C: If the emergency medication kit is opened, the pharmacist should be notified within 24 hours

    EXPLANATION:
    Review "Emergency Medication Kit" under Section 17: Illinois Controlled Substance Act. A proof-of-use sheet must be placed inside the emergency medication kit not on it.
    (77 IL ADC Section 3100.520)

23. **A.** The automated dispensing system is overseen by the PIC

    EXPLANATION:
    One of the PIC's responsibilities are to oversee the automated dispensing system at the LTCF.

24. **E.** B and C
    B: Refuse to perform patient counseling to a patient when a new drug is dispensed
    C: Refuse to perform patient counseling to a patient when a refill is dispensed

    EXPLANATION:
    The pharmacist license expires on March 31 of each even-numbered year. If the pharmacist only relocates for 3 months of the summer, he or she should be fine as long as he or she does not practice without a license. A pharmacist has the right to refuse to fill a controlled substance prescription if based on his or her professional judgment that the prescription is not for a legitimate medical reason.

25. **E.** A, B and C

    EXPLANATION:
    This actually happened on September 22, 2015 when a massive outage occurred across 8,200 U.S. Walgreen stores from a computer glitch in their systems. If this occurs, the stores or areas need to manually retrieve prescriptions they have on file, manually fill prescriptions, and even contact other stores to obtain prescription information not available on site.

26. **A.** 1 year

    EXPLANATION:
    Review "Expiration of License/Certificate" under Section 10: General Provision.

27. **C.** Sell the Plan B as requested

    EXPLANATION:
    IL has no age restriction for Plan B purchase.

28. **E.** Both B and C
    B: Tell her that Plan B does not have a generic medication
    C: Tell her that you can substitute Plan B with Levonorgestrel that goes by a different brand name

    EXPLANATION:
    Plan B One Step contains active ingredient levonorgestrel, which is also found in other brand name product, such as Next Choice One Dose, My Way, and Take Action, but for cheaper price.

29. **D.** Both A and B
    A: OTC products must be packaged in tamper-evident package and properly labeled

B: The retail package must contain a statement that identifies featured prominently placed on the packaged and in a way that it will not be affected if the tamper-evident feature is missing

EXPLANATION:
Search and review "Packaging and Labeling Control" from the following FDA website. OTC drug products must have one or more barriers to entry that, if breached or missing from the package, provide consumers with evidence that tampering may have occurred. Packages must contain unique designs or other characteristics that typically cannot be duplicated. Additionally, to alert the consumer to the specific tamper-evident features, the retail package must contain a statement that identifies the feature, is prominently placed on the package, and is placed in a way that it will be unaffected if the tamper-evident feature is missing or breached.

30. **B.** He or she can carry the wallet copy of the license to the second location, keep the original license at the first location

EXPLANATION:
If employed at one or more pharmacies, pharmacists should carry a wallet-sized license issued by board when working at location that does not display a current two-year renewal license. The original full size license information can be kept on display at the pharmacist's main location or home store location where the majority of the time they work.

Like the Guide? Help us help you more!

- Please help positively (5/5) rate this book on Amazon.com if you liked this book, search title "**Illinois Pharmacy Law**", find our book and rate us under customer reviews.

- Access our website for more guides, or to make recommendations/suggestions at: www.rxpharmacist.com.

- Want to share feedback? We would love to hear! Send us a recommendation and any comments/suggestions to: help@rxpharmacist.com.

Made in the USA
Columbia, SC
15 January 2018